D1008573

MARKETING CHAMPIONS

Practical Strategies for Improving Marketing's Power, Influence, and Business Impact

Roy A. Young, Allen M. Weiss, and David W. Stewart

WILEY

John Wiley & Sons, Inc.

Copyright © 2006 by Roy A. Young, Allen M. Weiss, and David W. Stewart.
All rights reserved.

Published by John Wiley & Sons, Inc., Hoboken, New Jersey.
Published simultaneously in Canada.

No part of this publication may be reproduced, stored in a retrieval system, or
transmitted in any form or by any means, electronic, mechanical, photocopy-
ing, recording, scanning, or otherwise, except as permitted under Section 107
or 108 of the 1976 United States Copyright Act, without either the prior written permission of the Publisher, or authorization through payment of the appropriate per-copy fee to the Copyright Clearance Center, Inc., 222 Rosewood
Drive, Danvers, MA 01923, (978) 750-8400, fax (978) 646-8600, or on the
web at www.copyright.com. Requests to the Publisher for permission should
be addressed to the Permissions Department, John Wiley & Sons, Inc., 111
River Street, Hoboken, NJ 07030, (201) 748-6011, fax (201) 748-6008, or
online at http://www.wiley.com/go/permissions.

Limit of Liability/Disclaimer of Warranty: While the publisher and author
have used their best efforts in preparing this book, they make no representa-
tions or warranties with respect to the accuracy or completeness of the contents
of this book and specifically disclaim any implied warranties of merchantability
or fitness for a particular purpose. No warranty may be created or extended by
sales representatives or written sales materials. The advice and strategies con-
tained herein may not be suitable for your situation, and you should consult a
professional where appropriate. Neither the publisher nor author shall be liable
for any loss of profit or any other commercial damages, including but not limited to special, incidental, consequential, or other damages.

For general information on our other products and services please contact our
Customer Care Department within the United States at (800) 762-2974, outside the United States at (317) 572-3993, or fax (317) 572-4002.

Wiley also publishes its books in a variety of electronic formats. Some content
that appears in print may not be available in electronic books. For more information about Wiley products, visit our website at www.wiley.com.

ISBN-13: 978-0-471-74495-5
ISBN-10: 0-471-74495-6

Printed in the United States of America

10 9 8 7 6 5 4 3 2 1

This book is dedicated to our loving families
Sharon, Hava, and Shoshana
Debbie, Katie, and Ryan
Lenora, Sarah, and Rachel

Contents

Preface

Are You a Marketing Champion?

Marketing is the engine of any enterprise. Financial resources may be the fuel that the engine needs to run, but, infused with fuel, the marketing engine propels the organization forward. Management guru Peter Drucker, writing 50 years ago, said, "Any business enterprise has two — and only these two — basic functions: innovation and marketing."[1] Drucker's claim is no less true today.

Yet in many organizations, marketing is underutilized. We find marketing practitioners frustrated at not being able to make the essential contributions to their company's success that they're capable of — and that they're ideally positioned to provide. Peer managers and members of the executive team have difficulty articulating how, precisely, the marketing function can help the organization grow and meet its strategic objectives. Equally troubling, marketers themselves face a challenge in describing the value of their work in terms that other executives understand. Put simply, marketers struggle to master the language of business. We wrote *Marketing Champions* to help marketers surmount these obstacles — so they can deliver their promised value, and so they *and* their companies can reap the benefits.

---

1. Peter F. Drucker, *The Practice of Management*, Harper & Row, 1954.

WHY THIS BOOK?

Marketing Champions is for marketers (and their bosses) who want not only to help their companies thrive but also to shape satisfying, successful careers in this important profession. The single best career move a marketing practitioner can make is to market him- or herself internally — to ensure that others in the organization understand marketing's power and promise. This book shows you how to do just that. When you use the language of business to help top executives and peer managers see what marketing has to offer, you build vital credibility and authority and boost your chances of winning promotions and salary increases. Perhaps most important for your career prospects, you sweeten the odds of gaining a seat at your company's strategy table.

We also believe that marketers have much to contribute to the welfare of society. At their best, marketing professionals generate profits for their firms by providing relevant products and services that meet real needs of human beings. And marketers are uniquely positioned to both anticipate and fulfill those needs.

Clearly, all organizations need marketers to address the most crucial imperatives on top management's agenda to-day — including focusing on the customer, resisting downward pressure on prices, improving customer loyalty, boosting revenues through increased sales, and staying ahead of the competition by adapting to change flexibly and quickly. Accomplished marketers possess both the skills and tools required to address all these challenges and more.

Yet surveys of chief executive officers (CEOs) reveal a lack of confidence in their companies' marketing organizations,[2] and studies of senior marketers have found they face a revolving door in and out of the organization. In the fall of 2004, a survey by executive search firm Spencer Stuart found

---

2. CEO Confidence Index: Optimism Soars to New Levels, *Chief Executive*, June 2004, where the CEO Confidence Index reveals that only 18% of CEOs are "very satisfied" with their marketing organizations.

the average tenure of chief marketing officers (CMOs) to be just 23 months.[3] Why? Three reasons.

For one thing, many top-level executives and nonmarketing managers fail to see the connection between what the marketing function does and how the organization gets paid. These executives have difficulty grasping the notion that marketers manage demand so as to create and harvest cash flow — the raw profits a firm makes after covering the costs of developing and delivering its products and services. At its most fundamental level, marketing's role is to make the company's cash register make that oh-so-satisfying "Cha-ching!" sound while simultaneously dazzling the firm's customers. It's every customer's experiences with the firm — experiences that marketing professionals powerfully mold — that bring him or her back to the cash register again and again. As long as other executives perceive no connection between marketing and hard, cold cash flowing into the company, marketers will find it virtually impossible to exercise their influence and thus deliver value to their organization.

Marketers face an additional hurdle as well: To demonstrate profitability — an imperative deriving primarily from the financial markets — many companies have come under enormous pressure to reduce costs and to meet new standards for financial accountability that require a clear and demonstrable link between marketing activities and financial returns to the firm. In this environment, many executives view marketing as a discretionary expense — among the first line items squeezed to present a better-looking balance sheet and income statement. In organizations where marketing activities do not in fact directly affect short- or long-term financial performance, slashing marketing budgets may in fact be the right thing to do. More often, however, tightening marketing expenditures harms the company. Marketing professionals' work constitutes an investment that generates both short- *and*

3. Spencer Stuart, "CMO Tenure: Slowing Down the Revolving Door," 2004, available at http://www.spencersturat.com/pdflib/CMO_brochureU1.pdf.

long-term financial returns for their enterprise. It is ironic that many marketers, who do a great job explaining a product's or service's value, have had such difficulty explaining their contributions to senior managers and peers.

Finally, in many organizations, the marketing function lacks repeatable and transparent processes — a situation that does not typically describe other professional disciplines (including finance, research and development, and operations). A CFO, for example, can always say, "We ran the numbers following generally accepted accounting practices and financial formulas" and show her conclusions in computer-generated reports. Her colleagues sitting around the conference table accept those conclusions as authoritative. But the marketing profession lacks similar formulas and standards of practice and has few (if any) standards for measurement and accountability. For example, how precisely should a marketing team go about determining prices? Segment markets? Build a brand? Measure performance? Different companies approach these marketing activities in different ways. Thus, many senior executives regard marketers' decisions as unreliable or poorly informed.

Yet this situation doesn't mean that marketing practitioners cannot establish consistent, visible processes to show the line of reasoning behind their proposals and decisions or that marketing has no hope of being viewed as a professional discipline on par with other disciplines. It is in the interests of the firm, consumers, and marketers that marketing's contribution be recognized, nurtured, and supported. And transparent, repeatable processes can help. But the purpose of this book is not to explain precisely how to carry out key marketing activities; there are numerous resources out there that offer to do just that. Rather, we argue that it doesn't matter as much how a marketing group goes about establishing prices, segmenting markets, and handling other marketing activities. What matters more is that the group selects a set of processes, communicates them to others in the organization, and uses them consistently.

This book shows you how to clear all of the above-described

hurdles and, in the process, transform yourself into a marketing champion. Let us be clear about what we mean by a marketing champion. Champions are recognized for their achievements, successes, and contributions; as a result, they enjoy others' respect and they exert power, influence, and authority. We wrote this book to help marketers achieve the respect and influence they are due. However, champions are recognized only because they succeed at something that others perceive as valuable. When we talk about marketing champions, we mean those who excel at making their organizations successful *and* who make others in their organizations successful — in tangible, measurable ways. And we mean marketing professionals to whom others look for advice and opinions on how the company can leverage growth opportunities and fulfill other key strategic objectives.

As you will discover in the chapters that follow, marketing champions anticipate changes in the business climate in which their companies operate. They develop strategies for helping their organizations seize advantage of those changes, and they actively execute those strategies by winning the collaboration and cooperation of their bosses, peers, and employees. They focus their time and energy on what they can change, not what they can't. As a result, their organizations value their contribution and view them as essential leaders in the drive to gain a competitive edge and leave rival firms scrambling. Marketing champions are recognized and appreciated because they make the entire *team* a winner.

THE MARKETING CHAMPION'S IMPERATIVE

To exert your influence, gain credibility, and win support for your ideas, you need to market your value within your organization. Many other books stress the importance for a company to adopt a market or customercentric orientation but leave marketers without a road map for making the changes needed to provide this redirection. The message is always about companywide change initiated at the top. Yet even without a directive from the top, marketers can make positive, fundamental changes that benefit their companies and their standing.

To become a marketing champion — and thereby ensure your company's and your own success — you must master mission-critical competencies. We present these competencies in the following themes that recur throughout this book:

- **Tie marketing to cash flow** by identifying and articulating the causal links between marketing expenditures and activities, intermediate marketing outcomes, cash-flow drivers, and (ultimately) cash flow.
- **Communicate marketing's outcomes,** rather than activities and tactics. Other professional functions are defined and recognized by their outcomes: R&D invents new products. Operations produces and delivers offerings. Sales sells products. Finance finds the capital to fuel the means of production. Marketing's outcomes are new sources of cash and cash itself.
- **Speak the common language of business** that other executives use and appreciate.
- **Develop systematic, transparent, and repeatable processes** that enable you to back up your ideas, defend your assumptions, and win support for your work.
- **Understand and serve internal customers' needs** by using the same marketing tools you employ to address external customers' needs. Identify internal constituencies' pain, tell their story, communicate with messages that generate the behaviors you want, and develop lasting relationships with them by meeting their needs.

By acquiring and honing these competencies, you demonstrate your value and earn a reputation as a marketing champion. Your credibility and influence expand, and you deliver the results your organization needs to excel. Don't assume you have to wait for your company's culture to change before you can become a marketing champion: Even CEOs cannot change their entire organization's culture. But no matter

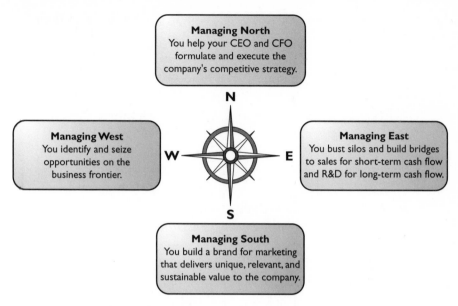

Figure P.1 The marketing compass for internal management.

where you work, there are always steps you can take now to correct misperceptions of marketing's value.

THE MARKETING COMPASS

To help you pinpoint critical leverage points for change, we've developed the notion of the marketing compass as a visual representation of the internal constituencies you must manage in order to become a marketing champion as shown in Figure P.1. We envision these internal constituencies as four points on a compass, with you at the center:

Managing North, you help your CEO and CFO formulate and execute the company's competitive strategy. More junior marketers help their superiors support the strategic objectives of their immediate supervisors.

Managing East, you bust those all-too-common functional silos that prevent your organization from operating in top form. You replace silos with bridges to sales, helping professionals in that function to generate revenues in the short term.

And you build bridges to R&D, so these peer managers and experts can develop new offerings in the longer term that meet customers' needs in ways competitors can't copy.

Managing South, you build a brand for marketing in your organization — a brand that communicates marketing's power to deliver unique, relevant, and sustainable value to the company. Using internal resources (staff) as well as external resources (agencies, vendors, and partners) under your control, you fulfill marketing's brand promise.

Finally, managing West, you identify opportunities on the business frontier for marketing as a group or function in your organization and for your own professional development.

We've organized *Marketing Champions'* 12 chapters to reflect this notion of a compass. Part 1 of the book illuminates the landscape of obstacles that prevent marketers from delivering their promised value to their organizations. The chapters in this section place a special emphasis on marketing's role in generating cash flow and the advantages of translating marketing terminology into the more commonly shared language of business that other executives use. Parts 2, 3, 4, and 5 explain how to manage perceptions of marketing among your North, East, South, and West constituencies, respectively.

Most chapters conclude with a SWOT Analysis exercise that helps you assess marketing's strengths, weaknesses, opportunities, and threats inside your organization. Keyed to the chapter's major themes, these exercises enable you to identify where you should focus your change efforts.

ABOUT OUR RESEARCH

To write this book, we relied on numerous sources. Our web site, MarketingProfs.com, provided a treasure trove of information. This online resource, which has over 180,000 subscribers, contains a library of articles by experts, including academics, consultants, and practitioners. The practices and suggestions in *Marketing Champions* come from our own expertise as well as the best of more than 2,000 articles contributed by over 300 marketing experts. One of us also served as editor of the *Journal of Marketing* and was able to bring the best of the academic world to this book.

Subscribers to MarketingProfs.com also provided valuable information. We surveyed readers to learn about the obstacles facing marketing professionals inside their organizations and to garner strategies and solutions from those who have successfully surmounted those obstacles. We received responses to several surveys from more than 3,000 subscribers who practice marketing in a wide range of organizations. From these responses, we conducted in-depth follow-up interviews with more than 60 marketing practitioners.

In addition, we interviewed senior mangers in all types of organizations — many in marketing, but others in finance, R&D, operations, accounting, sales, and general management. These professionals included executives from *Fortune* 1000 companies (Visa, Bristol Myers Squibb, and Pitney Bowes) who serve in both business-to-consumer (B-to-C) and business-to-business (B-to-B) organizations and who manage large marketing budgets. Interview subjects also included individuals from small start-up organizations with only a strategic plan and investors (Iona Technologies and InternetViz). Moreover, we interviewed marketers from non-profit organizations that use marketing primarily in their fund-raising efforts (March of Dimes) as well as officials from local government agencies that use marketing to serve the public (The City of New York).

To further ensure that a rich array of organizations had representation in our book, we drew on the perspectives of such diverse sources as academics (Columbia University, the University of Southern California, and the University of California at Los Angeles), consultants (Enterprise Marketing Management, Gartner Group, Trout & Partners, and Prophet), advertising agencies (Burson Marsteller), and executive search professionals (Korn/Ferry and Spencer Stuart). All of these sources have worked extensively with marketing executives and their organizations.

The three of us bring to this book roughly 100 years' collective experience in marketing. Roy Young, a graduate of the

Stern School of New York University, worked for 10 years in the magazine division of Time, Inc. in line and staff positions. He then served in several consulting and marketing research firms, including Yankelovich & Partners. He has experience as an executive search consultant with a specialization in marketing. Currently, he is the director of strategy and development at MarketingProfs.com. and serves as a consultant and coach to marketing executives.

Allen Weiss is the founding publisher of MarketingProfs .com, a weekly online newsletter that provides practical tools and know-how in many forms, including online seminars, workshops, benchmark reports, buyer's guides, and thought-leader panel discussions. He is Professor of Marketing at the Marshall School of Business at the University of Southern California.

David Stewart is the Robert E. Brooker Professor of Marketing at the Marshall School of Business, a former editor of the *Journal of Marketing,* and the current editor of the *Journal of the Academy of Marketing Science.* He is well recognized among industry professionals and marketing academics for his work on measurement and marketing research, marketing communication, branding, and marketing strategy.

By opening this book, you've taken a major step toward becoming a marketing champion. As you read the chapters that follow and begin putting into practice the ideas and tools found within, we invite you to contact us with your thoughts and feedback. Let us know which concepts and approaches prove most useful to you and which could benefit from refining. Share with us additional ideas that you glean as you sharpen your influence within your organization and begin generating new kinds of results. Tell us what you find most challenging about Managing North, East, South, and West — and how you address those challenges. Our greatest source of support and information is each other, and we hope you'll contribute to the marketing profession's store of practical knowledge and wisdom by contacting us with your ideas. Meanwhile, we wish you success as you embark on your journey toward becoming a marketing champion!

PART ONE

Understand the Landscape

1

Defy Marketing Myths

In most organizations, top executives and nonmarketing managers don't clearly see how the marketing function contributes value to the enterprise. If you are at all like the marketing executives we've surveyed and interviewed, this is not news to you. What you're experiencing has stemmed in large part from myths about marketing's purpose and value that pervade the business arena. As one interviewee at Advanced Micro Devices told us, "Marketing is vastly misunderstood at AMD and every company that I've worked at, including Dell. Strategic marketing and marketing communications tend to be done at the business-unit level, and brand development or advertising is typically a corporate-level function. The most difficult activity is identifying a strategy: What products should we make? What markets should we go after? What should our messaging be? How do we price our products or services? These are the least measurable activities and the least attended to by executives."

A director of brand development at a furniture manufacturer cited an additional reason that senior managers don't understand marketing: "It encompasses so many different activities. It's not like accounting, where every company does about the same thing and there are specific guidelines on what to do. Different companies use marketing in different ways."

Indeed, the misunderstanding of marketing's value and purpose is widespread. In a survey we conducted of nearly 2,000 marketing executives, 68 percent of the respondents said that compared to other professional functions in their organization, marketing is "much less" or "less" understood. And 48 percent maintained that marketing is "much less" or "less" valued. The findings vary little across company size and industry.

Companies pay a high price for this underestimation of marketing's value. Most important, they miss out on the unique analytical skills and knowledge about customers and competitors that marketers bring to the table. Marketing professionals also pay a price: Marketing budgets, created to stimulate demand for a company's offerings — and thus generate cash — are nevertheless among the first to fall under the cost-cutting knife in difficult times. In many organizations, marketers are relegated to a support function, executing tactical elements of strategies designed by other functions. Equally frustrating, marketing executives in many companies face a revolving door: The average tenure of a chief marketing officer across a wide range of industries is only 23 months.[1]

In this book, we offer an array of techniques for combating these circumstances so that your company gets more from marketing and you get more from your company. However, in order to apply these practices strategically, you need a map of the landscape that marketing is operating in at most organizations today. To illuminate that landscape, our map starts with a description of common myths about marketing that prevent executives from perceiving the true value offered by this essential profession.

MYTHS ABOUT MARKETING

Myths about marketing reinforce a misunderstanding of how important marketing is to certain business processes or how marketing generates value for organizations. The following list of widely believed myths reveals the breadth of inaccuracy in business people's perceptions of marketing.

1. Spencer Stuart, "CMO Tenure: Slowing Down the Revolving Door," 2004, available at http://www.spencersturat.com/pdflib/CMO_brochureU1.pdf.

- Marketing is a line-item expense and should be cut when a company needs to show a short-term profit.
- To generate more revenue, it's better to hire more salespeople than to invest more in marketing because sales reps know a firm's customers best.
- Marketing attracts creative types with unquantifiable skills and shadowy methods.
- Marketing is all about advertising; therefore, it's important only for companies with large and discretionary advertising budgets.
- Marketing has no connection to execution of a company's strategy and growth plans.
- Marketing is about *creating* customer needs, not *fulfilling* those needs.
- Marketing generates qualitative results, but business is quantitative. Thus, there's no way to show a connection between marketing activities and business performance.
- Marketing can't develop well-informed action plans and programs because it can't measure the results of those plans and programs in objective business terms.
- Marketing strikes expensive deals with creative agencies that are more interested in winning awards than generating business results for their clients.
- Marketing is no help to research and development (R&D) in developing new products and services.
- Marketing is the entire purpose of the firm; consequently, everyone should be responsible for marketing.
- Marketing is the work to find and keep customers.

How did these myths win wide acceptance? Of course, stories of notorious marketing failures have fueled them. Among such legends, the doomed introduction of New Coke perhaps stands as the most infamous.

Marketing executives at The Coca-Cola Company had spent millions of dollars annually to build a brand identity touting Coke as "The Real Thing." Yet owing to stiffening competition, they began panicking about Coke's vulnerability. Their solution? Change Coke's secret formula. Risking the world's most powerful brand, the company launched the product — called *New Coke* — only to watch in horror as it fizzled. Blind taste tests notwithstanding, consumers (it turned out) still wanted "The Real Thing." Just 77 days after launching the new beverage, the company took New Coke off the market and brought back the original — now called *Classic Coke*. While then Chief Marketing Officer Sergio Zyman spins the story's outcome as a rekindling of customer loyalty to Coke, ordinary consumers could have told these professional marketers that New Coke would have been a colossal failure.[2]

More recently, Hewlett-Packard (HP) chief executive officer Carly Fiorina set out to make HP edgier, meaner, and — of course — more profitable. Fiorina's main achievement at HP was to shift the company's focus from manufacturing individual products to marketing integrated services, especially e-business solutions and innovations such as pay-per-use computing. The primary force behind HP's decision to acquire Compaq, Fiorina was ousted by HP's board in 2005 after the acquisition proved disastrous. The fact that she came from a sales and marketing background only intensified the "I told you so's" circulating through the company after Fiorina's ignominious fall from grace.

Stories about expensive promotion campaigns that generate questionable results have further fueled myths about what, precisely, marketing has to offer. Consider the *New York Times* article headlined "Marketers Relish a Good Recall." This piece decried the marketing profession for exploiting for fun and profit a serious grassroots movement that resulted in the recall of California's governor. Among the promotions linked to this recall election was a Taco Bell campaign inviting citizens to make their preferences for candidates known by ordering specific products: Arnold Schwarzenegger, represented by a crunchy beef taco; Cruz M. Bustamante (who is Hispanic), represented by a chalupa; and then incumbent

2. Sergio Zyman, *The End of Marketing As We Know It*, Harper Collins, 1999, p. 48.

governor, Gray Davis, represented by a soft chicken taco. Such promotions not only beg ridicule, but they also reinforce the view of marketing as frivolous and unimportant.

The way in which major business periodicals report on marketing further reinforces the myths described above. For example, *Business Week* is the only general business publication that regularly publishes a section titled "Marketing." However, the topics covered — such as retailing and consumer-goods advertising — suggest that the editors view marketing as something only large consumer products companies do.

Interestingly, many stories in the business pages of newspapers and magazines — whether they're about financial services, health care, automobiles, or technology — are, at bottom, marketing stories. These include case studies of customer-focused business strategies, articles about how companies compete, and analyses of new product innovations — all of which stem directly from marketing efforts. Yet few readers think of these pieces as related to marketing. As a result, marketing's value is obscured and the myths perpetuated.

Or consider the trade periodical *B-to-B Marketing*, which publishes an annual issue recognizing marketers of the year. The magazine almost exclusively selects winners from immense companies that boast multi-million dollar advertising budgets — reinforcing the mistaken impression that marketing equals advertising.

Business books provide additional grist for the marketing-myth mill. Take "The Books That Matter" feature story published in *Business 2.0* in September 2003. This article named the most important business books of all time and organized them into categories. The "Marketing" category listed six books that matter:

- *The Theory of the Leisure Class* (Thorstein Veblen, 1899)
- *Ogilvy on Advertising* (David Ogilvy, 1983)
- *PR!* (Stuart Ewen, 1996)
- *The Cluetrain Manifesto* (Rick Levine, Christopher Locke, Doc Searls, and David Weinberger, 2000)

- *No Logo: Taking Aim at the Brand Bullies* (Naomi Klein, 1999)
- *The Tipping Point* (Malcolm Gladwell, 2000)

Four of these volumes treat marketing as primarily a communication vehicle. One of them, *No Logo: Taking Aim at the Brand Bullies* by Naomi Klein, rails against marketers who, Klein argues, invent consumer needs so people will buy more products at high enough prices to offset the cost of branding campaigns.

Thorstein Veblen's *The Theory of the Leisure Class*, an analysis of economic growth in industrialized economies that most economics majors read as undergraduates, may have set the stage for marketing in the modern world. Nevertheless, this classic text hardly sheds light on the changing landscape of marketing today.

Only one book in the list, *The Cluetrain Manifesto*, comes close to illuminating marketing's necessary transformation in response to the shifting of power to the consumer that came with the advent of the Internet.

Where are the books elucidating how marketers are leading the drive to enhance profitability and growth in their organizations? Seth Godin, perhaps the most widely read marketing author today, has written several breakthrough books related to the new power of the consumer. His *Permission Marketing* (1999) and *Unleashing the Idea Virus* (2001) taught important insights about the type of marketing required to attract and retain customers in a time of mounting advertising clutter and the increasingly central role of the Internet in commerce.

However, the title of Godin's newest book, *All Marketers Are Liars* (2005), significantly tarnishes marketing's image in the eyes of nonmarketing professionals. The provocative title may sell books, but it also reinforces the perception of marketers as deceitful compared to their colleagues in finance, information technology (IT), and R&D, who only speak the truth.

Yet, in a strange irony, *All Marketers Are Liars* teaches an important lesson: The ability to tell stories in an ethical, authentic way constitutes a critical leadership skill. And storytelling counts among the valuable contributions marketers can make to their organization. Indeed, many CEOs depend on marketers to help them craft and communicate the company's story to stakeholder groups, including customers, employees, investors, and partners. For example, Apple Computer is all about technology that is easy to use and dressed in appealing and fashionable design. Just as marketers can craft stories about the companies they work for, they can develop stories about particular products and services their firms offer.

MYTHS AND CONSEQUENCES: MARKETING'S CONFUSED ROLE

Myths about marketing would be of no consequence if they did not shape reality. But they do — as we've concluded from our survey and follow-up interviews with marketers from all types of organizations. Drawing on this data, we maintain that myths about marketing have led to profound confusion over what marketing does. Unlike finance, for example, where responsibilities vary only slightly based on whether a company is public or private and small or large, marketing plays different roles in different companies. This variability and unpredictability makes marketing particularly vulnerable to misconceptions about its true purpose and value — a major barrier to effectiveness in the marketing landscape. Considering the breadth of roles that marketing plays, it's not surprising that nonmarketing executives cannot form an accurate picture of how marketing contributes value.

Indeed, in our survey of marketing's responsibilities inside organizations, we found wide variation in the incidence of specific responsibilities. From 16 different responsibilities listed, marketers report a high incidence for promotion and advertising (over 90 percent) and a low incidence for responsibilities such as revenue, profit, pricing, and customer service — all arenas critical to cash flow. We also found differences in responsibilities across business-to-business (B-to-B) and business-to-consumer (B-to-C) marketing. Figure 1.1 depicts our findings.

In addition to the B-to-B and B-to-C comparison, the survey reveals differences in marketing responsibilities depending on many other variables, including age of company, industry, size of marketing budget, size of company, number of marketers on staff, and so on. Virtually any variable we might choose reveals differences in marketing, but none alone is a very good predictor of differences. Clearly, marketing means something different in each organization — furthering the perception that it's unfocused and that it provides questionable value.

FOUR DISTORTED VIEWS

Based on our survey data and interviews, we identified four distorted views of what marketing does. Each view creates

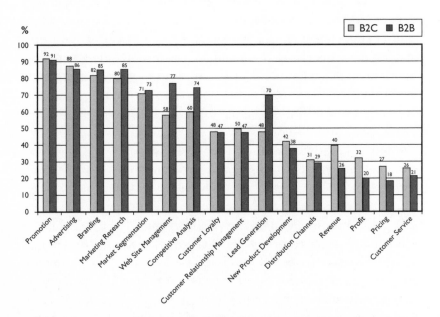

Figure 1.1 Responsibilities of the marketing mepartment (B2C vs. B2B). *Source:* Survey of MarketingProfs readers in organizations with 1,000 or more employees, 2005; question reads: "Which of the following activities is the Marketing Department responsible for in your organization?"

disadvantages that prevent others from seeing marketing's true potential — and that prevent marketers from fulfilling that potential.

Marketing Is Advertising

In many organizations, marketing only controls the *promotion* component of the *four Ps* in the traditional marketing mix — product, price, promotion, and place (distribution). That is, marketing is expected to increase customers' awareness of the company's offerings, motivate them to consider trying a product, and win their commitment to purchasing the offering.

To be sure, promotion is a critical function in many organizations — particularly companies where the business strategy calls for large mass-media ad budgets to build awareness and branding. However, the view that marketing is *only* advertising limits its perceived and actual value in several ways. For one thing, most companies treat advertising as a short-term expense. A firm's profit and loss (P&L) for the current period clearly reports advertising as an expense. Although the P&L also reports revenue, it does not and cannot show how the advertising will generate revenue beyond the current period. Thus, any longer-term consequences of advertising go unappreciated. And indeed, while almost all marketers manage promotion, just 25 percent have revenue responsibility. The upshot? The advertising budget gets slashed whenever top management wants to show improved earnings results in the short term.

In addition, nonmarketing managers tend to view advertising as something you do *to* a product specifically in order to sell it. Only after top management makes strategic decisions about what the company will sell and to whom it will sell should marketing supposedly step in to develop ad campaigns. Simply put, advertising is relegated to a tactical function rather than a strategic one.

Finally, advertising tends to draw creative and idiosyncratic people. Executives who are uneasy around such individuals conclude that anyone could create an ad campaign and that the business of advertising requires little business skill. Moreover, an ad's effectiveness is in the eye of its beholder. A particular advertisement may strike one observer as engaging and effective and another as bland or off point. Consequently, nonmarketing professionals conclude that marketers lack objective standards for measuring the effectiveness of their work.

"Marketing is not viewed as professional, since marketers typically migrate up from secretarial positions," said one marketer in a financial services company. "There is almost a stigma attached to it — the idea that anyone can do marketing. The bottom line is [that] we're seen as tactical rather than strategic. We're really just a service bureau [that gets a] you-do-what-I-tell-you-to-do mentality [from other executives]."

A marketing practitioner in the aircraft industry told us that "marketing, in the minds of many people, is synonymous with advertising and, therefore, is to be distrusted since advertising makes [consumers] do things [they] wouldn't ordinarily do if left to [their] own devices. Also, since there is a large element of psychology in marketing, people generally feel guarded in the presence of those who practice that black art."

When senior managers view marketing as *only* advertising — a short-term, tactical function performed by creative people with no true business sense — they conclude that marketing has no fundamental value to contribute.

Marketing Supports Sales

In many organizations — B-to-B as well as B-to-C — marketing serves the almighty sales function. Here's how the reasoning goes: Salespeople toil on the front lines in the field, while marketing people work comfortably in the office, at a computer, or in a meeting. Sales reps subject themselves to painful rejection every day in the hopes of generating revenues for their organization, while marketers remain shielded from the unsavory realities of sales work.

Particularly in B-to-B marketing, the sales function often

has more power in a company than marketing — that is, more control over resources and decisions. The reason? Everyone working within that firm recognizes that without sales, no one in the organization gets paid. Moreover, everyone can clearly see what salespeople do and how they create value: You close a deal, and the cash register goes "Ca-ching!" We can readily measure precisely how much noise a sales force makes by counting up all the cash flowing into the company's coffers. And we can easily tie budgets and compensation systems to sales quotas.

A marketer for a leading semiconductor manufacturer told us, "The sales function is very measurable and is typically viewed as the most important function at a company. Those executives tend to have the most political power and a poor understanding of the fundamentals of marketing and marketing processes."

When an organization develops a strong sales culture, top executives have a particularly difficult time understanding marketing's value. Many of them even believe that marketing materials and processes can be handled by administrative staff. That's the experience of another marketer we spoke with who works in the aviation industry. As he explained, "Granted, our job is to support sales and create marketing and advertising materials for the company to use. Unfortunately, we run into those who believe we are there to do as they want, when they want it. There is little understanding of what it takes to create these materials. We get folks who say, 'Just run down, take a picture, and print it. I'll write on it and send it with a letter.'"

As this marketing practitioner's company established its marketing department, it hired administrative staff who were intended to be shared between the sales and marketing groups. But in practical terms, these employees were *owned* by the sales function: It was sales managers — not marketing professionals — who conducted their performance reviews, supervised them, and defined their job priorities.

In this company, most of the salespeople have been around for 20 years or more. The sales force is the highest paid group outside of senior management (although some old timers out-earn certain executives). And great salesmen seem to have great egos. As our interviewee maintained, "Marketing [pro-fessionals are] nothing more than executive assistants to them." Clearly, the odds are stacked against marketing when the sales group runs things.

Further deepening the division between sales and market-ing, most organizations rely on sales to meet revenue goals in the present. But marketing is oriented toward the future. Marketing activities plant seeds that eventually become sources of revenue and thus profit. But planting and harvest-ing take time, and a company needs more than one reporting period to assess those results. In a trade-off between the pres-ent and the future, the present will win every time. Worried about short-term results, most top managers will give prefer-ential treatment to the work the sales department does in the present.

Marketing Isn't Needed for Product Development

Many organizations grow themselves by innovating break-through products or services or devising new processes for manufacturing and delivering their offerings. Leaders at these companies invest heavily in quality and process improvement methodologies such as Total Quality Management and Six Sigma. They also strive to generate revenues by continually innovating new products and enhancing existing offerings with new features. Their mantra is "If we build it, they will come. If we build it well, more will come. If we build it better than our competitors do, profits will come."

One of our survey respondents, a marketer in a high-tech manufacturing company, explained that "at companies where product R and D is a large component of the budget and the products are highly differentiated from competitive offerings, there tends to be more of an engineering culture, and those executives have a significant amount of political power. That's the case at our company. Engineering owns the processes and typically drives product development. Despite that, they never talk to customers."

In firms where R&D executives have scant interest in learning from customers, marketing stands little chance of demonstrating its value to the organization. When product development proceeds without an attempt to bring customers inside the organization and gather their input and the focus is on product or service features rather than on customer bene-fits, marketing practitioners have a meager role in shaping the company's offerings and identifying target customer seg-ments.

Another marketer we talked with articulated a similar view of marketing from within a durable goods manufacturer: "[In our] traditionally operationally excellent organization, individuals working in marketing were never really more than product managers. [Their job was to find] new products, make sure the new and old are available, resolve delivery and quality issues, maintain technical specs, et cetera, with little time remaining [for understanding] customer needs, position-ing a product line to the marketplace, promoting, and the like. As we've attempted to move into these areas, the general C-level sentiment is, 'Why do we need that? Go and find some more products.'"

Research and development– or operations-dominant cul-tures can also arise in service industries. One marketer from the hotel industry told us, "The marketing department in a ho-tel is not treated as part of the operational team. It is usually viewed as a department that goes out and builds relationships with the customer. The customer is external. Advertising and PR [public relations] are perceived as external. But senior management and general managers are usually promoted from operational departments and have little knowledge or exposure to what marketing is all about."

When the R&D or operations group leads, executives fo-cus *inside* the organization. They don't appreciate what their company might gain by gathering insights from outside. They therefore exclude marketing — with its external, customer focus — from strategy discussions on the assumption that marketing executives would have nothing valuable to add.

Marketing Has Nothing to Do with Revenues and Profits

Only in a few organizations do executives and peer managers view marketers accurately as generators of cash. That is, people understand that marketing practitioners not only identify future sources of cash by studying consumers and competitors but that they also harvest that cash by communicating the benefits of their company's offerings to customers.

But in most companies, people see little connection between marketing activities and financial results. Moreover, they assume (wrongly) that marketing outcomes cannot be translated into financial terms. These misperceptions are particularly damaging for both marketers and the companies they work for. Yet such assumptions are also understandable. The language of business is financial, and many marketers don't translate the lexicon of their profession (including *brand equity, segmentation,* and other discipline-specific terms) into financial terms used widely by other executives. Furthermore, when marketers track the outcomes of their work, they often use measures (such as number of trade shows attended or number of viewers reached by a TV ad) that don't translate into expressions of financial results.

As a marketer in the travel industry explained, "Revenue seems to be the number one measure by far, resulting in an underappreciation for the things being accomplished within marketing. Measures like awareness, impressions, and brand consistency are less understood and less important than revenue. Ultimately, revenue should be a key performance measure, but marketing should be recognized for the contributions it makes that ultimately have an effect on revenue growth, just not a direct, measurable effect."

As this individual suggests, marketing expenditures often have an indirect impact on financial results. And though other executives may beg to differ, that impact is crucial. Consider this example: Many consumer packaged goods companies invest enormous amounts of money on retail displays. Expenses include listing fees for products, slotting allowances, and trade promotions. Other executives tend to dismiss these as *nonworking* marketing expenses because such spending does not appear to directly incite demand or spur sales. These expenses, nonmarketing executives reason, are just the price of shelf space. Yet such expenses do ultimately generate revenue: Greater shelf space is frequently linked to greater velocity (or inventory turnover). And as we will see in subsequent chapters, velocity is a key driver of cash flow for any firm. It's up to marketers to trace these connections and make their financial implications explicit for peer managers and executives who don't see the links.

Though marketing expenditures have enormous potential to improve an organization's financial performance, top executives won't perceive that importance if the cause-and-effect links between marketing efforts and measurable business results aren't expressed in language they understand and regularly use. As you'll discover in later chapters, marketers can — and must — produce acceptable, quantifiable proof of their efforts' impact on financial performance if they hope to eradicate this damaging perception.

TRANSFORMING THE MARKETING LANDSCAPE IN YOUR ORGANIZATION: WHAT YOU'LL LEARN IN THIS BOOK

What will it take to change misperceptions of marketing? That won't be easy for one marketer or even for an entire marketing team, department, or unit. As we've seen, the marketing landscape presents some daunting obstacles. Yet regardless of where you work in your organization now, you can take steps to surmount those obstacles. This book provides potent navigational aids for doing so. In particular, we show you how to define marketing in terms of its outputs, not inputs; show

how each of your activities is connected to cash flow; and elevate marketing's role in your organization. Let's examine each of these more closely in the following.

Define Marketing's Two Outputs: Identifying Sources of Cash Flow and Producing Cash Flow

Though the marketing function handles different responsibilities in different enterprises, we define *marketing* as the *work designed to identify sources of cash flow and to produce cash flow.* All other business functions are defined in terms of outputs. Sales sells, R&D invents, operations makes and delivers, and finance funds. So what does marketing do? What is its outcome? That's what everyone in your organization wants to know. And that's what you must articulate. Explanations such as "We build the brand" and "We satisfy customers" do not represent business outputs that others will understand and appreciate.

Our definition of *marketing* recognizes two types of outputs. We call the work of identifying sources of cash flow *upstream marketing.* We refer to the process of producing cash flow (that is, bringing offerings to market) as *downstream marketing.* We like the phrase *upstream marketing* because it implies efforts to understand the sources of future demand and to lead the organization to manage that demand. Downstream marketing — the efforts required to sell the organization's products and services in their intended markets — is what marketing is traditionally known for.

Through upstream marketing, you continually analyze your company's strengths and weaknesses, its existing and potential customers, and its current and emerging competitors. You study customers' purchasing behavior, their motivations, their perceptions of products and services and companies, and their preferences. This analysis hinges on segmenting the market correctly so that your company does not waste resources on inappropriate prospects. Segmentation, in turn, requires a profound understanding of customer attitudes and emotions.

In addition, upstream marketing generates a solid understanding of a company's competition. Simply identifying your competitors isn't enough. You must also anticipate rival companies' responses to your firm's pricing and product strategies as well as discern competitors' objectives and capabilities. Consider the dot-com boom. How many start-up Internet companies took time to calculate the potential immediate and long-term responses of their rivals — the entrenched players? How many devised plans to counter competitive moves from incumbents? Those who didn't conduct such analyses went belly up during the infamous dot-bomb.

Finally, upstream marketing requires you to assess your company's ability to survive in the market. You gauge not only your firm's financial strength but also its organizational culture, compensation systems, relationships with distributors and suppliers, and other intangible assets. Lack of alignment among any of these elements can prevent the company from achieving its goals. For instance, suppose your firm wants to generate more revenue from new products sold to new types of customers, but its incentive system rewards salespeople for quick sales. In this case, sales reps may (understandably) focus on selling existing products to current customers as those sales are easier to close. Result? The intended shift to generating revenues from new sources won't happen.

In sum, upstream marketing entails analyzing customers, competitors, and company characteristics; identifying strengths and opportunities as well as weaknesses and threats; and targeting the most profitable customer segments — thereby identifying sources of potential cash flow.

Downstream marketing involves differentiating the firm's products in consumers' minds and delivering the unique value promised by those offerings — thus harvesting cash flow, covered in detailed in the next section.

Link Your Activities to Cash with Downstream Marketing

As we've seen, distorted views of marketing's role have placed unnecessary limitations on what marketers can accomplish in their organizations. Yet no matter what role *your* company has

relegated you to, you can still strengthen the connection between marketing and the harvesting of cash flow —thereby
dispelling those myths and expanding others' perceptions of
what marketing is capable of.

To show how this works, we've developed a hierarchy of
cash-flow responsibilities, shown in Figure 1.2. In this model,
the responsibilities have more direct connections to cash flow
the higher they are in the pyramid. Let's start at the bottom to
see how these responsibilities gradually build in their relevance to cash flow. As you read the descriptions, consider
which of these responsibilities *your* marketing team or department fulfills in your organization and determine which one is
marketing's primary responsibility.

Communications

As their most basic responsibility, marketers get the word out
about their company's offerings. They do so through PR cam-

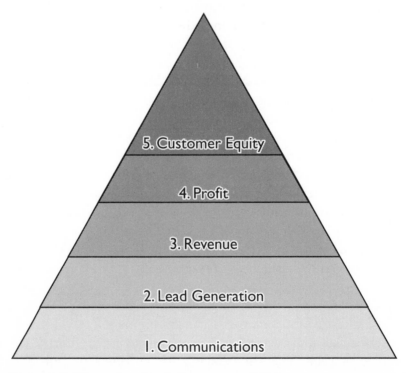

Figure 1.2 Hierarchy of cash-flow responsibilities.

paigns, mass-media advertising, corporate brochures, company web sites, and other communication vehicles.

Lead Generation

Business-to-business organizations, in an effort to support the sales function, commonly cast marketing professionals in the role of lead generators: These practitioners identify people or organizations who are likely to buy the firm's products or services in the near future. Lead-generation activities include typical marketing communications as well as direct-response campaigns, trade shows, and online seminars (known as "webinars").

Revenue

Some top executives perceive marketing as a function that generates sales. Indeed, many marketers' job performance is evaluated based on how much revenue they've generated directly. Often, however, executives don't fully grasp the costs that marketers must incur in order to produce the required revenues. Thus, the ultimate cash flow generated is not included in estimations of marketing's value.

Profits

Few marketers are accountable for generating profits — cash left over *after* costs are subtracted from revenues. Marketing practitioners who do have profit responsibility often manage a product or service as a business. In other words, they act like general managers. We find these marketers typically in the packaged-goods industry, where they manage the demand and supply side of a product or product line. However, few organizations outside of this industry have defined the role of marketing as including full P&L responsibility.

Customer Equity

The highest role for marketing in any organization — and the one that has the closest links to cash in both the short-term and long-term — centers on managing and investing in customers as assets that produce cash flow. Marketers who fill this role are responsible for customer acquisition, customer profitability, and customer retention, the primary sources of cash now and in the future.

While reading these descriptions, you may recognize some similarities between several of these responsibilities and the distorted views of marketing discussed in the preceding. For example, *Communications* reflects the view that marketing is advertising, and *Lead Generation* suggests the view that marketing supports sales. Clearly, we're not denying the reality of the constrained roles marketing plays in many organizations, and we accept the fact that you may not be able to change your role in your company. If your firm uses marketing primarily for advertising, so be it.

But by understanding the cash-flow hierarchy — and identifying where your marketing function fits in it — you can show others that your activities have a stronger connection to cash flow than they may have assumed. Even if your team's or department's primary responsibility is to coordinate marketing communications or generate sales leads — the bottom rungs on the cash-flow hierarchy — you can help executives and managers throughout the firm see the connection between these activities and cash flow. For instance, by using communications to build a brand, you strengthen customer loyalty — which translates into cash as customers spend a premium on your products and buy more frequently from your company.

But to be a true marketing champion, you must do more than just open people's eyes to your connection with cash. You must also influence other parts of your organization, notably R&D, to think in terms of cash flow and to generate the dollars needed to achieve the firm's mission. In other words, you must be a cash-flow leader.

Taking these two dimensions together — the connection between marketing activities and cash flow and cash-flow leadership — we developed the Cash-Flow Driver Index, shown in Figure 1.3.

Marketing champions not only help people make the marketing–cash-flow connection but they also win reputations as

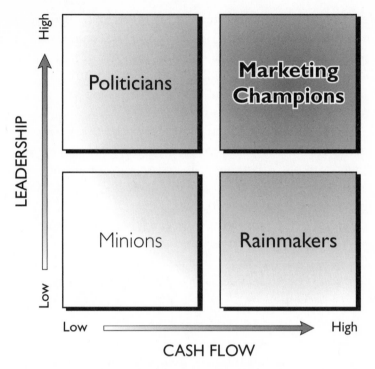

1. **Marketing Champions** (high on Cash Flow and high on Leadership)
2. **Rainmakers** (high on Cash Flow but low on Leadership)
3. **Politicians** (low on Cash Flow but high on Leadership)
4. **Minions** (low on Cash Flow and low on Leadership)

Figure 1.3 Cash-flow driver index.

cash-flow leaders throughout their organizations. They dwell in that rarified but oh-so-valuable realm: the upper-right quadrant of the Cash-Flow Driver Index. You'll learn more about this Index in Chapter 9.

Elevate Marketing's Role in Your Organization

By enabling people throughout your organization to see the links between your current activities and cash, you begin elevating marketing's role. In particular, you help senior management grasp the real value that marketing delivers. And as executives begin *perceiving* marketing more correctly as a cash-flow driver, they will likely invite you to take on more responsibilities residing at higher levels in the cash-flow hierarchy. The strategies for managing North, East, South, and West that you'll find throughout this book will help you with this elevation process.

But before we venture North into the marketing landscape, we want to provide you with a powerful tool to include in your backpack: language. In particular, the more you can master and speak the language of business — including translating marketing terminology into commonly used business vocabulary — the more influence you'll have with your executive team and peer managers and the more support you'll win for your marketing efforts. Result? The more actual, measurable value you'll deliver for your company. Because every strategy presented in this book hinges on savvy use of communication, we give language special attention in Chapter 2.

2

Clean Up Your Language

To shatter the marketing myths we laid out in Chapter 1 and create a new reality for marketing in your organization, you are going to have to clean up your language. Myths are dispelled with clarity, and to communicate clearly with others, marketers need a consistent and relevant language whose meaning is shared by everyone in the organization. In this chapter, we assess marketing professionals' current use of language (including oft-used marketing terminology) and explain how to translate it into the more widely spoken language of business.

As a marketer, you probably talk frequently about *segments, quality, value, strategy, performance, image, position, branding,* and *brand equity* — all important concepts. However, your president, CEO, chief financial officer (CFO), and other members of the executive committee are talking about *assets, return on assets, velocity,* and *leverage.* If you work in a publicly traded company, they're probably also discussing *P/E multiple* and *shareholder value.* And if you work in a not-for-profit organization, they're likely discussing terms such as *contributed collections and services* and *promises receivable.* For better or worse, financial terms and metrics are every company's common language. Organizations use these terms to satisfy reporting requirements. And executives use them to evaluate the potential payoff of strategic moves they're considering, to evaluate performance, and to determine how to compensate employees.

Of course, every business function has its own specialized

vocabulary, and the marketing language you regularly speak has its place and value. Moreover, many of the terms you use may even have similar meanings as words used by other executives — but you and these other professionals aren't aware of the shared meaning. For example, some nonmarketing executives may not realize that *brand equity* is a valuable type of *asset*. Part of your task will be to translate your marketing language into the language of business so people throughout the organization can see that you're all talking about the same things after all. But before you can conduct that translation process, you need to clear up any ambiguity regarding the discipline-specific words you're using.

CLARIFYING THE LANGUAGE OF MARKETING

You're sitting around a conference table with managers and executives from marketing, sales, R&D, and other functions in your organization discussing strategy. Someone says, "We really need to be more strategic about our segmentation targeting." What does he mean? If he's from marketing, you may assume that by *segmentation* he means grouping customers together according to specific characteristics. But if he's from R&D, he may well mean grouping products together instead. If the people in the room don't agree on the meaning of the word — and aren't aware that they don't agree — then you can well imagine the uselessness of the resulting conversation.

Unfortunately, such cross-functional ambiguity about terms is all too common in organizations. But confusion over the meaning of a word or phrase can also arise *within* the marketing function. When marketers themselves don't agree on the meaning of a word, they worsen other executives' misunderstanding of what marketing is, what it does, and why it's important.

The very term *marketing* provides a case in point. If marketing professionals from different parts of your organization define *marketing* in different ways, you can count on creating confusion and skepticism in the minds of others in your organization. Nothing frustrates senior managers more or destroys credibility for marketers more than when marketing professionals from two different divisions use the same words but mean different things by them. The resulting confusion becomes especially harmful when marketers interact with managers from other parts of their organization (such as R&D, finance, and sales) and even other companies (for example, advertising agencies).

Simply put, confusion over the meaning of terms leads to confusion over what the marketing department's strategy is and how that strategy should be executed. For example, a marketing practitioner may say, "Let's put our value proposition in that product brochure." But in many companies, *value proposition* means different things to different groups. For a particular product, the sales head might view the value proposition as the price of a product or service relative to the price of competitive offerings. The vice president of engineering might offer yet another understanding of the product's value proposition — such as how efficiently it can be produced relative to competitors' offerings.

Here's another example. For a number of years, we consulted with a major electronics company. Every time the issue of segmentation came up, the firm's research director said: "We don't do segmentation here." As it turned out, they didn't do *demographic* segmentation. They *did* do segmentation — but they based it on criteria other than demographics, such as applications used, end users, and product requirements. Yet the R&D group didn't call this process *segmentation*. In fact, they considered the notion of demographic segmentation objectionable because they believed it was more important to classify products based on applications and uses, not people. As a consequence, marketing lost credibility with senior management when high-powered external consulting firms recommended a segmentation strategy.

The same confusion arises when people use the word *quality* to mean different things. When you say *quality* in your company, what do you mean? Product reliability? The attractiveness of a product brochure? Something else entirely? Moreover, do other managers with whom you discuss *quality* give the term the same meaning you do? And what about your customers: How would *they* define *quality?* Often, the word means something different to each customer — further muddying the waters about what constitutes a quality product or service.

Another confusing expression is *brand equity.* To some managers, *brand equity* signifies what a brand stands for — for instance, safety (in Volvo's case), irreverent fun (in Virgin's case), and reliability (in the case of HP printers). To these managers, *brand equity* is a characteristic of the brand itself. But to other managers, *brand equity* is a characteristic of the *consumer* — it represents the mind share and share of wallet consumers devote to the brand as opposed to competitors' offerings. To still other managers, *brand equity* is an asset that resides within the *company* — it is the financial value the brand generates for the firm.

Image is another tricky term. Some managers use *image* to refer to the picture consumers see in their heads when they think about the brand (for example, the physical product or its logo). Other managers talk about *image* in terms of advertising. For instance, an *image ad* doesn't contain much information about the product; rather, it associates the product with a certain type of person or lifestyle.

◆◆◆◆◆

Spotlight on *Branding*

Because the word *branding* causes an unusual degree of confusion, let's take a moment to talk about it at some length. Many managers wrongly view *branding* as merely creating a slogan for a company, product line, or service. Even many advertisers (and advertising agencies) mistakenly assume that a brand is simply a slogan or tagline. They point to such examples as FedEx's "When it absolutely, positively has to be there overnight" and BMW's "The ultimate driving machine."

Yet while a slogan or tagline can sometimes *capture the essence* of a brand, it cannot *create* that essence. To create the essence, you must ensure that consumers understand the brand first. Then the right tagline can reinforce that understanding. But unless current and potential customers already understand the brand, a slogan or tagline is meaningless to them. Indeed, some of the best-regarded brands in the U.S. business arena—Starbucks and Nordstrom's, to name two—don't even have slogans.

So if a brand isn't a slogan or tagline, what is it? We agree that *a brand is a unique collection of values that a product or service brings to the marketplace.*[1]

If Starbucks merely sold coffee at ridiculously high prices, it would have a lot of competition and might not have survived, let alone prospered. But the unique collection of values that Starbucks brings to the marketplace far exceeds the coffee alone, tasty as it may be. These values include such intangibles as social interaction, feelings of sophistication, personal gratification, and perhaps even the sense that one is better than others who get their coffee at Dunkin' Donuts. Customers get all these forms of value when they sip their coffee at a Starbucks. It's why Starbucks can charge $1.60 for a cup of coffee, with no refills, while the same cup of coffee can be made at home for 25¢ or bought at a mom-and-pop coffee shop for 75¢.

Clearly, to build a brand, you must change customers' mind-set so they view your product or service in terms of the total collection of values—intangible and tangible—that the offering brings to them. Because brand building is a process, it must start inside customers' minds—with what they know and don't know, what they believe, and what qualities and values are important to them.[2] Skillful brand building generates a particular final result: a customer's willingness to choose that brand over competitors' offerings, even if doing so means paying a premium price.

In fact, that's why marketers must understand the brand to be an intangible asset. While brands don't appear on the balance sheet because of standard accounting practices, most business leaders today understand how the brand is an asset that produces real—tangible—returns.

◆◆◆◆◆

1. Kenneth G. Lauerer and William R. Markin, "Focus on Marketing Strategy, Not Just Tactics," http://www.marketingprofs.com/5/LauererMarkin1.asp.
2. Ibid.

You use terms like *value proposition, positioning, attributes, benefits, branding, brands,* and *target market* every day. But if other people in your organization — within marketing and outside of marketing — don't agree on what these words mean, how can you communicate a coherent marketing strategy? You, your marketing colleagues, and managers from other parts of the organization won't be able to arrive at a shared understanding of how best to proceed with your marketing efforts.

In addition to outright confusion, failure to use particular terms in the same way spawns mistakes and inefficiencies. For instance, people may approve a certain marketing strategy but then implement it in different ways — because those executing the strategy understood it differently from those who formulated it. Segmentation is a classic example of this problem. One does not segment a market; one segments in a particular way and for a particular purpose. To suggest that a market be segmented provides incomplete information at best and misleading information at its worst.

SAY WHAT YOU MEAN, AND MEAN WHAT YOU SAY

How do you avoid the preceding problems? Start by gathering your marketing team together and listing the marketing terms you use every day. Then arrive at agreed-upon definitions. To persuade people to invest time in this meeting, explain to them beforehand the importance of clarifying confusion. Cite the benefits that will arise from developing shared understanding of each term's meaning — such as more generous support for marketing initiatives or greater willingness to provide feedback on proposed marketing strategies.

Here's another useful exercise. Gather the same group together and ask "What does our company's offering stand for? If we could name just two benefits our product or service provides, what would those benefits be? How would our *customers* answer these questions?" If your company is like most, you'll get different answers to these questions from different people. If participants in this exercise can ultimately agree on the answers, this shared understanding will help you design more focused marketing initiatives that stand a greater chance of success.

Consider this suggestion as well: Avoid using terms like *value, quality, reliability,* and *strategy* (pick your favorite ambiguous terms) if they have different meanings for different people in your company and can be interpreted in a broad and confusing way. Instead, use words for which people across the organization can agree on their meaning.

By creating a common language of marketing, you save your company money and time (always important to top management). You also introduce efficiency in your marketing meetings. Equally important, you generate coherent marketing strategies that everyone can understand *and* execute as intended. Finally, you will find it easier to translate the vocabulary of marketing into the language of business used by high-level executives in your firm.

Even if you've established a consistent marketing language, you need to do still more to become a marketing champion: You have to establish and communicate transparent, repeatable processes and translate your specialized vocabulary into the common language of business. When you do so, you build credibility and help others see marketing's connection to cash. You also boost your chances of gaining a seat at the executive table and qualifying for senior management roles in your organization.

STANDARDIZE YOUR PROFESSIONAL PROCESSES

It's not enough that all marketers in your organization use the same terms; they must also mean the same thing when they use these terms. And this shared meaning needs to capture both the concepts *and* the processes that give rise to the concepts. For example, a term like *market segmentation* should mean the same thing to everyone — say, a recognition that customers differ in their needs and the benefits they seek to gain from using a product. But even this shared conceptual understanding is insufficient if it does not also recognize a common process that gives rise to the definition. For this reason, it's also important to standardize the professional processes you carry out in order to accomplish your work — and to communicate those processes to others.

Many marketing departments carry out their processes — including evaluating success, segmenting customers, and developing marketing campaigns — in an undisciplined, ad hoc way. For example, even in the same company, one marketer may emphasize the importance of measuring changes in brand consideration based on customer surveys, while another will stress lead generation as the most important indicator of success. In a company that sells computers, printers, and scanners to the same customers, each division may take its own approach to segmenting those customers — even though many customers buy all three products at the same time.

Nonstandardized processes waste time and money as people duplicate one another's efforts or work at cross-purposes. Yet some marketers chafe at the notion of standardization because they believe it reduces creativity. These managers don't realize that under the right conditions, process standards actually enhance creativity. A mystery writer, for example, can create much more appealing cliffhangers when he or she employs the established style and tried-and-true formulas that define the genre in which the writer works. Even creative people who depart radically from conventional processes can benefit precisely because there *are* standards that serve as points of comparison for their work.

In our survey of marketing professionals, we asked "For each of the areas that your department handles, would you characterize the process you use as 'highly systematic and repeatable' or 'unsystematic and ad hoc'?" Figure 2.1 shows the responses.

Fifty-nine percent of our respondents said that their de-

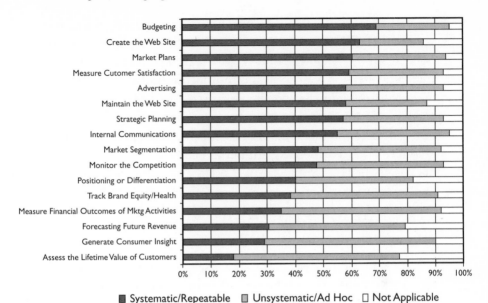

Figure 2.1 Extent processes used in marketing are systematic/repeatable or unsystematic/ad hoc. *Source:* Survey of MarketingProfs readers in organizations with 1,000 or more employees, 2005.

partment's "measure of the financial outcomes of marketing activities" was unsystematic and ad hoc. Fifty-eight percent described the department's processes to "monitor the competition" as ad hoc. Even larger percentages saw processes to "measure the financial outcome of marketing activities" and to "assess the lifetime value of customers" as unsystematic and ad hoc.

On the other hand, 61 percent described the budgeting process as highly systematic and repeatable. More than half of these respondents also claimed that their company has systematic processes to prepare market plans and to maintain the organization's web site.

Remember: Different companies handle marketing activities through different processes. In fact, to determine how best to establish prices, segment markets, build a brand, or carry out any number of other marketing activities, you could consult numerous books and other resources — and you'd find a wealth of different (and often conflicting) suggestions. The point is not to select the one "right" process for each activity: Instead, settle on a process, communicate it clearly to others in your firm, and use it consistently. You'll build credibility — a key achievement for marketing champions. Equally important, you'll help your company avoid the wastage of time and resources that happens when people work at cross-purposes because processes are unclear.

TRANSLATE MARKETING INTO THE LANGUAGE OF BUSINESS

Of all the marketing processes you use to carry out your work, the most ad hoc among them tend to be those related to linking marketing activities to financial results. For example, marketers within and across organizations may disagree on how best to express the value of, say, brand equity in terms of future cash. For this reason, it's vital to develop a shared understanding of how key marketing terminology translates into the business vocabulary that matters most to your executive team. This takes some thinking, but the payoff is well worth the effort:

- Other executives view your work as relevant and central to the business.
- Your peers throughout the organization understand how marketing can help them achieve their goals.
- Nonmarketing executives see precisely how the results of your efforts improve the company's financial performance and competitive position.
- You develop business acumen and become known as a leader in spurring the enterprise's growth and prosperity.
- You master a language that is used across industries and organizations, so if you move to a different employer, you can expect to retain your newly acquired business acumen.

Despite many marketers' assumptions, it's not a difficult stretch to translate marketing terminology into the language of business. The key is to gain familiarity with this vital language and see examples of the translation process. To those ends, the next section introduces and defines five important business terms you should understand and shows how to use them while communicating about marketing with other managers and executives in your firm.

Assets

A company produces and distributes its offerings using both *tangible assets* expressed in the firm's balance sheet (stores, factories, manufacturing equipment, computers, office buildings, inventory) and the *intangible assets* (web sites, brands, workers' knowledge, copyrights, patents, intellectual property, goodwill) that the organization has amassed. Assets are the concrete matter and hard-to-measure yet vital qualities the organization owns and uses to compete. The value of an asset, tangible or intangible, is directly related to its ability to generate cash flow. Some managers believe that a company's total assets determine its value — the amount of money it would fetch if it were acquired.

But such managers misunderstand the real value of assets. It's how assets are *managed and used* that determines a company's value. Empty buildings aren't assets — they're liabilities because they're not producing anything that can be sold. Similarly, a pocketful of patents has no value unless a company uses those patents to produce products that sell.

A study comparing market value (the value of all the outstanding stock) to the book value (the total assets minus the intangible assets and liabilities) of 3,500 U.S. companies over a period of two decades shows a dramatic upward rise in the importance of intangible assets. In 1978, market value and book value were pretty much matched: Book value was 95 percent of market value. Twenty years on, book value was just 28 percent of market value. Baruch Lev, an accounting professor at New York University's Stern School of Business, reckons that in the late 1990s businesses invested a staggering $1 trillion per year in intangible assets.[3] Yet accounting rules have not kept pace with this rise in importance of intangible assets. For instance, if a pharmaceuticals company's R&D efforts create a new drug that passes clinical trials, the balance sheet does not reflect that development's value. The value does not show up in financial statements until the firm actually begins selling the drug, when that value is expressed as revenues in the company's income statement. But that could be several years down the road. The asset's value lies in its *potential* to generate cash flow in the future.

Or consider the value of an e-commerce retailer. Arguably, almost all of its value comes from software development, copyrights, and its user base. While the stock market reacts immediately to a pharmaceuticals company's clinical trial results or an online retailer's customer churn, intangible assets such as the e-tailer's slip through financial statements.

Thus there is a serious disconnection between what happens in capital markets and what financial statements reflect. Accounting value is based on the historical costs of equipment and inventory, whereas market value comes from expectations about a company's *future cash flow* — which derives in large part from intangibles such as R&D, patents, workforce know-how, and the way in which important assets such as brands are actually managed.

As you know, much of marketing's work centers on building intangible assets, including brands, information and knowledge, web sites, customer lists, and so forth. Thus, you have numerous opportunities to express the results of your marketing activities as valuable intangible assets — and to point out the growing importance of such assets in today's knowledge economy.

3. Baruch Lev, "Sharpening the Intangibles Edge," *Harvard Business Review*, June 2004.

Return on Assets

A business uses its own money or someone else's money to grow. For example, it may use its savings to invest in assets or borrow from a lending institution to do so. The money (or cash flow) the business produces by using these assets is its *return on assets* (ROA). You can get some sense of ROA by dividing your company's net income (from its income statement) by its total assets (from its balance sheet) — though recall that the balance sheet does not show intangible assets.

How do you translate the language of marketing into this oft-used financial expression? Use the assets you control to generate a greater return for the company — and express the results as a return on assets. Consider Procter & Gamble (P&G). Marketing experts at this consumer-products giant extended the company's mighty Tide brand into a whole range of cleaning-related products — from detergents (powder, liquid, cold water) and the Tide Stain Brush (an electric brush for removing stains) to Tide Floor Cleaner. You might be saying to yourself, "That's a brand extension." You're right. But it's also a return on assets (the Tide brand). By describing the cash generated by a brand extension as a return on assets, you make the translation between marketing terminology and the language of business — using vocabulary that matters most to the executive team.

The retail industry offers additional examples of how to translate. Cross-selling and up-selling — two important marketing activities — enable your company to generate more value from its investments in acquiring customers. Thus these activities improve return on assets, where the assets in question are the company's customers and its relationships with them. By framing cross-selling and up-selling as activities that improve return on assets, you build credibility and help others throughout your company see the connection between your work and a key measure of your firm's performance.

Velocity

Velocity, also called *inventory turnover,* is the number of times a company's products or services are sold and replaced with new inventory in a given time period. You can calculate velocity by dividing cost of goods sold (from your company's income statement) by average inventory cost for that period. (If inventory cost has significantly changed from the beginning to the end of the period, you can estimate an average by adding the beginning and ending inventory amounts and using half of that total as the average.)

Generally, high velocity indicates a healthy liquidity — the ability to convert inventories to cash quickly if needed. By contrast, low velocity suggests that the company has too much capital tied up in inventory — which can cost money and result in obsolescence of the products sitting in the company's warehouse. Profits perk up when a company can move inventory out the door quickly.

Consider Dell Computer Corporation: This company assembles products to customer specifications in less than a week — a remarkable velocity. As a result, it generates cash quickly and keeps costs low — both of which translate into higher profits.

In addition to using Dell's business model, a company can increase velocity by establishing an extensive distribution network so that it can sell its offerings wherever consumers want or need them. Coffee behemoth Starbucks, for example, has planted a store seemingly on every street corner, in every airport, and at every hotel. It even sells bags of coffee for people to brew up at home. Any time a consumer wants a cup of coffee, and anywhere he or she wants it, Starbucks is there.

You can improve your company's velocity through numerous marketing activities — including well-thought-out promotions and price reductions. Indeed, a major objective of your role is to help your company sell more of its products and services, as quickly as possible. The more you can show other executives how your work enhances velocity, the more they'll see the connection between marketing and measurable financial performance.

Leverage

Leverage is a company's ability to use someone else's assets to produce cash for itself. European fashion retailer Benetton, for instance, owns no stores and no manufacturing plants. However, it does own a powerful brand and possesses a workforce renowned for its creativity. Benetton uses its brand and innovativeness to control the assets of distributors (retailers) and manufacturers without having to own (and thus pay for) those assets. Consequently, its relatively small asset base produces a large return.

In financial markets, investors who borrow someone else's money and then invest it for their own gain are said to be leveraged. The key to leveraged investing is to be able to obtain a return on the investment that is greater than the cost of borrowing the money. For example, Frank, a homeowner, may take out a second mortgage on his home at, say, 7 percent interest per year and invest the loan in a stock that returns 10 percent a year. After paying the interest on the loan, Frank can pocket a 3 percent return on the bank's money that he borrowed. Yet leverage can prove even more complex than this scenario suggests. For example, suppose Frank buys the stock on margin; that is, he purchases it by borrowing half its value from the stockbroker. This move doubles the return on his investment. Of course, the broker has to be paid interest, too, which means that the rate of return on the investment has to be sufficient to cover these costs. If the investment does not produce the necessary returns, it begins to shrink in value.

Clearly, leverage can be risky. Imagine that the interest on Frank's second mortgage is due as is the interest owed to the stockbroker (which Frank must pay regardless of the stock's performance). Because stock returns are volatile, Frank must spend substantial time and effort finding investments that provide the returns he needs to repay his costs of borrowing — or suffer the consequences of not having the money to pay his broker.

Owing to the risk inherent in financial leverage, analysts become concerned when firms are overleveraged. You can help your firm use leverage *and* reduce risk at the same time. In your organization, the intangible assets you create — brand equity, customer equity, workforce knowledge and productivity — can all provide leverage by enabling the company to exercise control over assets it doesn't have to own. For example, every time Disney creates a new animated movie character, it creates opportunities for leverage. It can license use of the character to toy manufacturers, merchandisers, and others. Disney collects a royalty on such licenses and does not have to tie up its own money in manufacturing and inventory. The license allows Disney to obtain the benefits of the licensee's assets without having to actually own the assets. Therefore, the organization does not have to invest as much of its own money to get the benefit of substantial assets. Result? It keeps more of its cash.

Moreover, intangible assets in the form of brands permit the company to charge a premium for its offerings. A trip through your local grocery store is all it takes to see how this works: A six-pack of Coca-Cola costs significantly more than soda carrying the grocery store's label or the generic label.

Though many marketing investments create intangible assets, the return on such assets is not as immediately apparent as it is for tangible assets. Build a new production line, and products can start rolling off it (and generating revenues) as soon as the line is up and running. Build a new brand through a marketing campaign, and your company may not see the full impact on sales for a while. That's because the marketing campaign creates both immediate sales and sales in the future. Your task is to explicate how marketing actions will provide financial benefits for your firm in the long run.

The good news is that marketing leverage is almost always positive. Unlike financial leverage, which can be a problem if taken too far, the positive results of marketing leverage are bounded only by the creativity of your marketing team.

Risk

While the language of business includes a variety of risk-related terms (*business risk, financial risk, risk averse, risk neutral*), for our purposes, the word *risk* refers to the possibility that a marketing investment's actual return will differ from the expected return. Companies usually measure risk using the historical or average returns for a specific investment. Chief executive officers and CFOs are particularly concerned about risk, so they may limit the programs proposed by their marketing and other departments in an attempt to mitigate risk. Marketers can help reassure risk-wary top management by demonstrating that they've analyzed the risks for a particular program and have ideas for mitigating those risks.

For example, when you're deciding how to respond to a competitor's price cut, consider and articulate the risks of starting a price war. If dropping your price has the potential to spark a long and costly price war, with round after round of price cuts that erode everyone's profits, your firm will not be well served by this action. By acknowledging such a risk, you help yourself and others in your organization to generate ideas for less risky responses — such as stepping up your advertising.

Once you gain familiarity with the preceding five finance terms, you can more easily frame your conversations with marketing presentations to top management using this language. Your reward? You'll help them see how your efforts enhance your company's financial performance — thus demonstrating your strategic value to the firm. And you'll have greater influence with your executive team and peer managers.

TIPS FOR TALKING BUSINESS

So you've mastered the key business terms every marketer should know. And you've worked to develop a common marketing language and to standardize marketing processes. Now how might you put your knowledge to work in your discussions with senior executives and peer managers in your organization? You'll find extensive recommendations in Parts 2 and 3 of this book. But the following suggestions can help you get started.

Shift Focus from Marketing Activities to Business Results

Not long ago, we consulted to a mortgage company. The marketing staff laid out all the activities they had planned for 2006. "We're going to do this webinar. And this brochure. And we're planning a trade-show exhibit." All significant activities, but you could see the CEO's eyes glaze over. His reaction was, "It's great that you guys can manage these things, but I don't know what they're going to do for me or why I'm at this meeting."

These talented marketers neglected to take their presentation one step further: explaining the business results that each activity would generate. They should have explained, for example, that the brochure and webinar would generate leads. Leads would point the way to new sales. And sales would generate cash flow — which would help the CEO fulfill his promise to shareholders to grow the company 10 percent in the coming fiscal year. *That* would have grabbed their CEO's attention.

Prioritize Your Marketing Activities

Identify those marketing activities that have the most potential to stimulate the growth your company is after and to generate the best returns on its investments. You've got only so much budget, energy, and time — so invest those limited resources in the activities that will give your company the biggest bang for its marketing buck.

Those activities may be developing new products or services or using a different distribution channel. They may be participating in more trade shows while making fewer brochures. Each marketing department's situation is unique, but the goals remain the same: Improve your firm's cash flow, generate fatter profit margins, increase returns on assets, turn over inventory faster. Examine each marketing activity you're considering, and ask yourself which ones will generate the best business results described in this chapter.

Demonstrate Your Business Acumen

If you're currently operating at the bottom level of the hierarchy of cash-flow responsibilities we described in Chapter 1, you probably have limited opportunities to affect your company's overall marketing strategy. Nevertheless, you can — and should — learn the language of business and use marketing terms (such as *segments* and *positioning*) for which everyone agrees on the meaning. And although you may not be accountable for sales results, you should still demonstrate your awareness that what you do affects those results. Moreover, you should express your commitment to improving them.

As you move up in the hierarchy, you'll have more opportunities to affect marketing strategy. And it will become even more important that you express what you do and what you want to accomplish in the language of business. For instance, you don't want to "spend two million dollars on newspaper inserts"; you want to "invest two million dollars on inserts that are projected to offer a ten percent return — we expect to see one dollar and ten cents in sales for every dollar we spend on the inserts."

Help Others "Talk Business"

Ensure that everyone else inside and outside your company who's involved in marketing — including advertising agencies, freelance copywriters, trade-show exhibit designers, and so forth — are all using key marketing words and phrases the same way, to mean the same thing.

Learn How Wall Street Talks Business

Take time regularly to review stock analysts' reports — you'll learn a lot about how Wall Street evaluates companies and translates marketing-related and other activities into financial language. Consider the following excerpt from one such report:

> We think Johnson & Johnson is an exemplary wide-moat company. It boasts trusted brand-name products, world-class R&D and marketing capabilities, and global scale and reach. We would eagerly buy the shares at a slight discount to our fair value estimate. . . .
>
> J&J is a model of consistency and stability. The firm has delivered 19 consecutive years of double-digit earnings increases and 42 consecutive years of dividend increases. Cash flow from operations covers the dividend . . . nearly 3 times. J&J has an excellent record of capital allocation and generation. Returns on invested capital averaged 22% during the past five years.
>
> A key reason for J&J's success is its decentralized management structure. The company encourages entrepreneurship among local managers to stimulate creative new product development. . . Sales and marketing expertise and quality manufacturing skills are [also] important distinguishing core competencies.[4]

Notice this analyst's attention to J&J's brand power, marketing prowess, and cash flow. Such reports speak volumes about how Wall Street weighs these factors in order to put a financial value on companies — and deliver opinions that powerfully influence investors' choices. The more you understand how Wall Street "talks business," the more you can see how the investment community evaluates marketing and other important activities in your company and industry.

4. Tom D'Amore, "The Guidant Deal's Impact on J&J," morningstar.com, accessed November 11, 2005.

Once your CEO and other senior managers understand your work's connection to measurable business results that they care about, they'll gain a deeper appreciation for the value that your marketing department delivers. The preceding tips can help you start laying the foundation for Managing North, which we cover in Part 2 of this book. In the coming chapters, you'll learn how to make marketing matter to your CEO; prove your business prowess to your CFO; and develop metrics that enable you to monitor, enhance, and demonstrate the business value your work creates. So set your compass to true North, and let's venture into this frosty but promising landscape.

PART TWO

Manage North

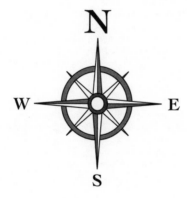

3

Make Marketing Matter
to Your CEO

"There are two types of CEOs," contends marketing guru Philip Kotler, "those who know that they don't understand marketing and those who don't know that they don't understand marketing."[1] Whether Kotler overstates the problem, if your CEO does not understand the value marketers bring to your organization, you and your marketing colleagues stand little chance of exerting influence in the company, making a measurable difference, or advancing in your career. You *and* your company will pay a heavy price.

To demonstrate the value that marketing creates for your firm, you need to Manage North—and that starts with understanding your CEO, your number-one internal customer. What does he or she know and appreciate about marketing? What role has this top executive assigned to the marketing function? What does he or she need from marketing in order to make strategic decisions? And how can marketing help improve performance on your company's *key performance indicators* (KPIs)—those vital measures that your CEO has defined and that managers throughout the firm use to assess their progress toward business goals? Just as you strive to understand the needs of the customers who buy your company's products or services, you must grasp your CEO's needs and priorities. Otherwise, your chief executive may continue to look to functions that are more clearly defined by their output—sales, R&D, finance, accounting, and so forth—for infor-

1. Philip Kotler, *Marketing Insights from A to Z*, John Wiley & Sons, 2003.

mation with which to set the company's direction. And you
won't likely gain a seat at the strategy table.

SLEEPLESS IN THE C SUITE

As your first step to building credibility with your CEO, discern what keeps him or her awake at night. Once you understand the CEO's primary concerns, you can identify the marketing activities that will help address those priorities. *The
CEO Challenge,* a report based on an annual tracking survey of
CEOs worldwide by The Conference Board,[2] can shed light
on your CEO's top concerns. According to this publication's
executive summary, CEOs are asked to "rate the magnitude of
challenge that each of 91 challenges poses over the next 8 to
12 months." The analysis ranks the challenges by those with
the largest percentage saying it is "my greatest concern."

The survey results indicating the leading challenges of
CEOs aren't surprising: Thirty-eight percent of CEO respondents identify "sustained and steady top-line growth [reve-
nues]" as their greatest concern. Thirty-six percent select
"profit growth [revenues minus expenses]" as their biggest
challenge. And 33 percent choose "consistent execution of
strategy by top management" as their most pressing difficulty.

These findings are good news for marketers — because the
top three challenges that most keep CEOs up at night are precisely where marketing contributes value. To make marketing
matter to your CEO, you can focus your energies on the mar-

---

2. Linda Barrington,"CEO Challenge 2006: Top 10 Challenges," based on a
three-page survey of CEOs conducted in July 2005, with 658 respondents worldwide, from a sample of over 11,000 surveys e-mailed, for a response rate of almost
6 percent. The survey is conducted regularly to update an understanding of the
CEO agenda. According to the executive summary, CEOs were asked to "rate
the magnitude of challenge that each of 91 challenges poses over the next 8 to 12
months." The analysis ranks the challenges by those with the largest percentage
saying it is "my greatest concern," from the following six response options: "not applicable to my business," "applicable but not important," "somewhat important,"
"important but not a priority," "among my chief concerns," and "my greatest concern."

keting activities that directly address top-line revenue growth, bottom-line profit growth, and strategy execution. But before we say just how, let's explore ways to find out what specifically keeps *your* CEO up at night.

An especially useful source of information about your CEO's concerns is your organization's annual report. This document often lists specific commitments to performance your CEO has made. For example, in Procter & Gamble's 2004 annual report, CEO A. G. Lafley made a public commitment to deliver 4 percent to 6 percent sales growth (excluding the impact of foreign exchange), 10 percent or better earnings-per-share growth, and free cash flow equal to 90 percent or more of net earnings.

How did Lafley intend to fulfill these commitments? It seems he promised to build existing core businesses into stronger global leaders, grow leading brands, and develop faster-growing, higher-margin, more asset-efficient businesses with global leadership potential. In addition, he planned to regain growth momentum and leadership in Western Europe as well as drive growth in key developing markets. These commitments suggest Lafley's key priorities and the strategies he may have had in mind for fulfilling the priorities listed in the company's annual report.

In addition to perusing your firm's annual report, consider asking to meet with your CEO to discuss his or her top priorities. Many CEOs also communicate their goals — that is, the company's strategy — through their speeches, articles in the company newsletter, and other vehicles of public address. Your company's performance management system — whether it's Six Sigma, TQM (Total Quality Management), Balanced Scorecard, or some other formal methodology — also reveals information about the CEO's priorities. For instance, if the organization uses the Balanced Scorecard and has created a corporate-level strategy map, the map would lay out top management's thinking about what steps are needed to achieve the highest-level performance objectives.

Of course, you may be lucky to have a CEO who has previously worked for marketing powerhouses like P&G and who knows full well that marketing matters. Consider two P&G alumni: Meg Whitman of eBay and Jeffrey Immelt of General Electric (GE). Whitman recognizes marketing as the leading source of her organization's growth. In response to recent lagging sales in Germany, for example, she advised the marketing staff to *increase* investment in advertising.

Immelt recalls building the Duncan Hines brand at P&G on "two or three hours of sleep."[3] In his first year at GE as successor to the legendary Jack Welch, Immelt appointed a chief marketing officer — the first person to hold that title at GE for nearly a decade. He set out to make GE's marketing function as great as its finance and human resources operations. "At first no one knew what he was talking about," acknowledges vice chairman Dave Calhoun. General Electric wasn't known as a customercentric company. "Marketing had become a lost function during the 1990s," notes Immelt. Breathing new life into the marketing function presented a valuable opportunity to make GE more competitive. In his view, restoring marketing to its rightful place would transform GE's culture. The company would turn its attention outward and begin measuring its success according to its customers' success. As Immelt puts it, "The purpose of this generation of GE leaders is to make the company as good externally and commercially as it has always been operationally and financially."[4]

CEOs like these are rare, however. Indeed, only 20 percent of *Fortune* 500 CEOs come through the ranks of marketing,[5] and that number is far lower for small and midsized companies. So it's likely you must educate your CEO.

MARKETING TO THE RESCUE

As a marketing practitioner, how can you show how marketing addresses your CEO's most daunting challenges? How can you provide ongoing input that helps determine your

3. *Fortune*, May 12, 2003.
4. Geoffrey Colvin, "The Bionic Manager," *Fortune*, September 19, 2005.
5. Spencer Stuart, "Route to the Top," 2003 study in CEO career trends.

organization's strategic direction? As we saw in Chapter 2, speaking the language of business will enhance the credibility you need to alter your CEO's thoughts about marketing. And as we'll explain in Chapter 5, defining a set of metrics that enables you to show how your marketing activities translate into cash flow further builds your credibility and influence. But you also need to change your relationship with your CEO. The remainder of this chapter provides potent guidelines.

To adopt the mind-set needed to show marketing's effectiveness in generating financial results, you might find it helpful to familiarize yourself and your CEO with a definition of *marketing* that builds on our earlier definition and that focuses on the outputs that matter most to the CEO: *Marketing is work designed to identify sources of cash flow and to produce cash flow by solving customers' problems profitably.*[6] This definition speaks to CEOs' primary concerns: steady top-line growth, profit growth, and consistent execution of strategy. Notice that it expresses what marketers do in terms of the most important result to any chief executive: *how the organization gets paid*. It also articulates what marketers need to do to be *effective*: They must apply their knowledge of customers and the competition to generate cash flow now and in the future.

To deliver the current and future cash flow promise of marketing, you can address your CEO's primary concerns and win his or her support for your initiatives through these means:

- Upstream marketing: identifying sources of money (profit growth)
- Downstream marketing: making money (top-line growth)
- Leveraging marketing drivers: tying marketing outcomes to your company's key performance indicators (execution of strategy)

6. Adapted from definitions by Tim Ambler in *Marketing and the Bottom Line*, Financial Times Prentice Hall, 2nd edition, 2003, and Peter Doyle in *Value-Based Marketing*, John Wiley & Sons, 2000.

- Striking fear of failure in your CEO's heart

Let's take a closer look at each of these practices.

Upstream Marketing:
Identify Sources of Future Cash Flow

Chief executive officers have an intense interest in *where* their organization's money comes from. You can satisfy that interest by explaining to your CEO that your ability to articulate and serve current and potential customers' needs generates the cash that drives your company's growth. Effective marketers identify the most profitable current and potential customers, discern their needs, and envision the products and services that will meet those needs.

Effective marketers also can answer the following questions about customers, their organization, and the competition:[7]

1. How can we give value to the customer? What problems do our offerings solve for customers? How can we help customers solve these problems more easily or efficiently, with more gain for our organization?
2. Are all our customers alike, or do they differ in important ways?
3. Which customer groups produce the greatest profit for us? Why do they buy from us? Do we have the unique assets or skills needed to serve these groups?
4. What does it cost us to serve different customer groups? Do we enjoy unique cost advantages in serving some of these customers? If so, which ones?
5. What are our customers' purchasing frequencies and amounts, and what explains these patterns?
6. How do our current customers differ from our potential customers?

---

7. *Marketing and the Bottom Line.*

7. What aspects of our products and services and our competitors' offerings satisfy and dissatisfy customers?
8. How do our customers perceive our offerings? How do they perceive our competitors' products and services? How do these perceptions differ? What improvements to our offerings do customers want?
9. What is our strategy on pricing for the trade and for end users? What impact can we expect from price changes?
10. How will our competition likely respond if we introduce a new product, go after a new market, launch a radical new promotion, or make some other move?
11. Exactly how are our customers changing? What shifts might arise in the market that would radically alter our customers' needs and purchasing behavior?
12. How do our company's assets, skills, and competencies map onto the needs of the customers we serve or want to serve?

As a marketer, you are uniquely qualified and positioned to provide reliable answers to these vital questions. Using your expertise in customer research, competitive analysis, environmental scanning, target segmentation and positioning, and sales forecasting, you and your team can generate answers to these questions and use that information to identify current and future sources of money.

The results of your upstream marketing guide are your conclusions about whom your company should sell to and what to sell them. Thus, your insight strongly informs the enterprise's strategy.

For example, upstream marketing has provided critical insights leading to profitable growth at GE Plastics. In an industry battered by low-cost competition from China and dramatic price reductions due to excess supply, GE Plastics uses its technology expertise to create applications customized to address the most pressing concerns of individual customers (who include automobile manufacturers and other large businesses). As Ram Charan writes in *Profitable Growth Is Everybody's Business,* "In the automotive industry, GE Plastics could show a manufacturer like Ford how applications of its technology could reduce the weight of a car, improve gas consumption, reduce cost, or otherwise improve the customer's differentiation against the competition." GE Plastics has demonstrated that customer-needs segmentation — along with a pricing structure that supports the positioning of attributes customers prefer — make up the upstream-marketing effort that is critical for profitable growth.[8]

The Thomson Corporation provides another example. Chief executive officer Dick Harrington asked the company's Prometric division (which provides technology-based employee assessment and testing services) to describe the unit's customers and their needs. In addition to its current customer segments, Prometric identified the growing, but highly fragmented, corporate market as a source with great potential. Again, according to Charan:

> They're placing the tools of Upstream Marketing at the center of their organization so they can understand the needs of major customers and create attractive value propositions for them. . . . Prometric's marketing segmentation . . . found that pre-employment testing is not limited to relatively lower-level positions in businesses like retailing [in such companies as Home Depot, Wal-Mart, and Lowe's] but extends to the needs of sophisticated financial services firms like Capital One. . . . Once a new segment has been discovered, [Prometric] designs the right product with the right pricing structure. . . . Prometric's value proposition would show companies like Capital One how it can help them select people with the requisite analytical skills that lead to the development and introduction of the right new credit-card offerings.[9]

8. *Profitable Growth Is Everyone's Business.*
9. Ibid.

And consider this additional example from Disney illustrating how upstream marketing helps companies identify and realize profitable growth opportunities. In his early years as CEO of Disney, Michael Eisner asked himself how much a family spends on a vacation, and what percentage of that amount Disney could capture. To answer that, Disney had to move from a product focus to a customer focus. Even though its theme parks were quite profitable, Disney was capturing only 25 percent of visitors' vacation dollars. A new customer-focused metric — share of vacationers' total spending — generated insights that helped Disney to formulate innovative growth strategies. Disney began building hotels and teaming up with airlines to offer travel packages to tourists — new offerings that reduced the hassle of family vacation planning. The payoff? Disney's share of Orlando vacationers' spending increased from 25 percent to a whopping 75 percent.[10]

Using upstream marketing to identify sources of money isn't easy. We'll talk about these challenges and ways to surmount them in subsequent chapters. Moreover, effective upstream marketing requires training and expertise in analytical processes unique to marketing. It also hinges on the ability to translate the insights derived from these analyses into meaningful actions that you and your team can carry out in order to generate results for your company.

Some marketers also face a challenge in CEOs who are so internally focused that they don't recognize the importance of analyzing customers and competitors. Management guru Peter Drucker long ago recognized executives' tendency to focus on internal matters as a major obstacle to both management and organizational effectiveness. As far back as 1967, Drucker wrote, "Unless he [the top executive] makes special efforts to gain direct access to outside reality, he will become increasingly inside-focused. The bigger and apparently more successful an organization gets to be, the more will inside

---

10. "When Art Meets Science: The Challenge of ROI Marketing," *Strategy + Business*, 2003.

events tend to engage the interests, the energies and the abilities of the executive to the exclusion of his real tasks and his real effectiveness in the outside."[11]

But despite its challenges, upstream marketing generates *knowledge* about profitable growth opportunities for your firm. Armed with that knowledge, you can take effective *action* to make money for your organization — through downstream marketing.

Downstream Marketing: Make Money Now

Through downstream marketing, you manage resources and programs to generate sales today — including communications (promotion, advertising, and public relations), pricing, sales, distribution, and customer service. Downstream is where a skilled marketer uses his or her knowledge of customers to make them aware of and favorably disposed toward the company, its products, and its services.

Three unique attributes of downstream marketing will have particular significance for your CEO:

Downstream Marketing Helps Your Company Stay Effective in Today's Marketplace

Organizational leaders, like any of us, tend to see what they expect to see. Yet markets today change faster than ever before. As a marketer, you're among the first to learn how well a new offering performed in the marketplace. You assess consumers' *and* competitors' responses to newly introduced offerings, and you communicate these analyses to your CEO. Your interpretation of short-term changes in the external environment gives your department license to challenge the prevailing views of the market within your organization.

Downstream Marketing Helps Your Company Act Today

Effective downstream marketing enables you to put your knowledge of changing consumer and competitor behavior

11. *The Effective Executive*, HarperCollins, 1967, republished in 2002.

into action in ways that give your firm a competitive advantage. Moreover, downstream marketing helps you identify which information about shifts in the external business landscape are important and which information is irrelevant. As Lee Iacocca wrote in his autobiography: "The biggest problem facing American business today is that most managers have too much information — it dazzles them, and they don't know what to do with it all."[12] Jeffrey Pfeffer and Robert Sutton, Stanford Business School professors of organizational behavior, add that "knowledge and information are obviously crucial to performance. But we now live in a world where knowledge transfer and information exchange are tremendously efficient, and . . . numerous organizations [are] in the business of collecting and transferring best practices. So, there are fewer and smaller differences in what firms know than in their ability to act on that knowledge."[13]

Downstream Marketing Helps Your Company Adopt an Entrepreneurial Mind-Set

Marketers are in the best position to model how managers can move beyond habit and turf protection to adopt an entrepreneurial stance instead. Marketers embody how to be hungry and fast. You can demonstrate how to combine the necessary resources from all areas of your company to respond quickly to new opportunities in the marketplace.

Marketing Drivers and KPIs: Focus Your Company's Performance

As your third tactic to address your CEO's most pressing concerns, show *how* upstream and downstream marketing support consistent execution of your company's competitive strategy. In short, demonstrate marketing's impact on your company's KPIs — the metrics reflecting your firm's most important strategic objectives.

12. *An Autobiography*, Bantam, 1984.

13. Jeffrey Pfeffer and Robert Sutton, *The Knowing-Doing Gap: How Smart Companies Turn Knowledge into Action*, Harvard Business School Press, 2000.

Usually defined by the executive committee, KPIs are the measures CEOs can recite in their sleep. Examples include share of revenue from new products or new product categories, same-store sales, revenue from new distributors, price increases, market share, profit margin, employee turnover, customer loyalty, new-customer acquisition, revenue growth, and sales staff production. Key performance indicators differ across organizations. What one organization finds a critical measure of how well it's executing its strategy, another organization finds unimportant. Key performance indicators differ not only by industry but also by firms within the same industry.

Therefore, you need to find out what your company's KPIs are, how performance on each KPI is measured, and what each KPI's target is. For instance, if your company's KPIs include customer loyalty, perhaps the marketing department measures loyalty by percentage of customers who make repeat purchases over a certain length of time. And maybe your company has set a target of improving customer loyalty 10 percent over the coming year. To get a complete list of your company's KPIs and the sources of their data, talk with your CEO and CFO.

Once you're familiar with your company's KPIs, find ways to demonstrate how the marketing department's activities — both upstream and downstream — support positive performance on those indicators. And show how that performance translates into cash flow for your company. For example, again, if customer loyalty is one of your company's KPIs, you could explain: "Our recent campaigns have improved customer loyalty ten percent. This increase in customer loyalty has in turn meant a seven percent jump in revenues as loyal customers have bought more of our higher-priced offerings. Greater loyalty has also lowered our expenses: We've been able to spend twelve percent less than usual on customer acquisition. The combination of higher revenues and lower costs has improved profitability by six percent and boosted cash flow eight percent."

Marketing activities that exert the largest impact on your company's KPIs and, ultimately, its cash flow are often called *marketing drivers.* Thus, a marketing driver is a leading indicator of revenue growth. The most effective marketing drivers are related to customers and competitors, not products and sales. The following are two examples.

For some time, Starbucks focused on the introduction of new beverages as a leading force in improving frequency of customer visits. Yet research found that while Starbucks' customers loved innovative drinks, they tended to value fast and friendly service more than the opportunity to try new beverages. Management knew that a satisfied customer spent more and visited more frequently. Realizing that speed of service was more powerful than new beverages for increasing customer satisfaction, management set out to raise the share of customers served in less than three minutes. By adding frontline staff and investing more in training them, the chain boosted the percentage of those served in less than three minutes from 54 percent to 85 percent. Customer satisfaction rose demonstrably. As a result of this improvement in customer satisfaction, the average amount spent on each purchase and the frequency of visits increased.[14] Velocity (inventory turnover) thus increased, further improving cash flow.

The experience of a nationwide mortgage bank offers another illustration. Management at the mortgage bank had identified loan-officer production — the number of loans written by loan officers — as a KPI. The company could improve future growth, management reasoned, by increasing the number of loan officers as well as the number of loans written on average by each. The question management needed to answer was, what drives loan-officer productivity? That is, what enables these employees to write more loans?

Not surprisingly in this relationship-driven business, marketers discovered that the size of a contact list is critical.

14. McGovern, Court, Quelch, and Crawford, "Bringing Customers into the Boardroom," *Harvard Business Review,* November 2004.

Therefore, the mortgage bank's key marketing drivers included helping loan officers to grow their lists of end consumers and realtors who refer home buyers. The company therefore channeled its marketing resources into developing an automated system of communications programs and instructional materials to help loan officers expand their contact lists and solidify relationships with prospects. As a result, loan-officer productivity rose dramatically. This jump in productivity also increased velocity (in this case, sales of mortgages) and, hence, improved cash flow.

As these examples illustrate, marketing drivers demonstrate marketing effectiveness through three means. They provide information about current and future sources of money (i.e., customers and prospects). They guide resource-allocation decisions. And they burnish marketing's credibility and accountability.

Fear: Scare Your Way to Success

So far, we've explored positive ways of helping your CEO see the value of your marketing activities and win his or her support for your proposals. But there's one additional strategy that bears mentioning: citing examples of colossal failures that reveal what can happen when CEOs ignore marketing's value.[15] Jack Trout, former president of Trout & Ries and co-author of *Positioning: The Battle for Your Mind*, told us:

> When you're trying to sell a CEO on a course of action and you think he might be doing the wrong thing, you don't go in and tell the guy he's doing the wrong thing. You go in there and say, "Let me tell you what happened to a company that was doing a similar thing, and they went into the toilet. Now, this might not happen to us, but this is the kind of stuff that can happen." That's how you introduce the element of fear and doubt. And the guy said, "Whoa, is

15. These examples and many others can be found in *Big Brands, Big Trouble: Lessons Learned the Hard Way*, by Jack Trout, John Wiley & Sons, 2001.

that what happened?" I said, "Oh yeah." You need that fear analogy. That's the best way to get somebody not to do something that you feel, as a marketing guy, shouldn't be done.[16]

The bursting of the dot-com bubble provides one apt example of what can happen when companies ignore customers' perceptions and preferences — information typically provided by marketing practitioners. Assuming that technology was the be-all, end-all, many Internet companies forged ahead with business plans built on the assumption that consumers would leap at the chance to buy things like groceries or pet supplies on the web — and that they'd be willing to pay the prices required to generate a profit for these companies. Beguiled by technology and dismissive of marketers' warnings, many of these organizations failed spectacularly. For instance, as it turned out, numerous consumers didn't trust an online grocery service to pick out just the right cantaloupe for them or to substitute just the right alternative if their favorite brand of toothpaste was out of stock. And after weighing factors such as convenience, price, and ability to choose products, consumers decided they weren't willing to pay more for groceries to be packed and delivered to them by an online service.

Here's another well-known example: Digital Equipment Corporation (DEC), the inventor of the minicomputer and for a time the second-largest computer manufacturer in the world, ignored the appeal of personal computers for consumers. Ken Olsen, DEC's founder and CEO said, "The personal computer will fall flat on its face in business because users want to share files and want more than one user on the system."[17] What Olsen failed to realize is that, when it comes to technology, consumers value independence and early adopters eagerly anticipate the next generation of products. Digital Equipment Corporation missed the opportunity to intro-

16. Telephone interview on December 16, 2003.

17. *Business Week*, May 2, 1983; quoted in *Big Brands, Big Trouble: Lessons Learned the Hard Way*.

duce the next big thing after IBM dazzled the market with its 16-bit office computer. "When the moment passed," Trout writes, "[DEC was] in more than big trouble. They were toast."[18]

Some business leaders make savvy use of graphic imagery to strike fear of failure in colleagues' hearts. Take the legendary Brad Anderson, CEO of retail giant Best Buy. Outside Anderson's office is a mock hospital scene: a row of beds containing effigies of struggling or failed retailers such as Kmart and Woolworth. These companies' corporate logos are propped up on the beds' pillows, while bedside charts display their dismal vital signs in the form of rock-bottom financial results. A nearby sign reads, "This is where companies go when their strategies get sick." Such imagery provides a constant reminder to executives and managers from all functions of what can happen if they lose touch with market changes.[19]

Show your CEO how the company's successes hinge on solving *customers'* problems and differentiating the organization and its products from *competitors*. As we've seen, CEOs who don't acknowledge the value of marketing's external focus put their companies at risk and waste the promise that their marketing experts bring to the organization.

A WORD ABOUT THE BOARD AND WALL STREET

No discussion of marketing's relationship to the CEO would be complete without acknowledgment of the role of the board of directors and Wall Street (for publicly owned companies) in the CEO's life. These two stakeholder groups are of primary importance to any CEO. The board of directors hires and fires the CEO. And CEOs typically spend as much as 75 percent of their time meeting with Wall Street analysts to explain the company's strategy and its prospects. Why such

---

18. *Big Brands, Big Trouble: Lessons Learned the Hard Way.*

19. Matthew Boyle, "Best Buy's Giant Gamble," *Fortune*, April 3, 2006, pp. 69–75.

extensive attention to analysts? Stock price has become a critical measure of companies' financial performance.[20] And analysts issue reports about companies' prospects and health (as well as buy and sell recommendations) that greatly influence share price.

Like CEOs, most board members and Wall Street analysts don't understand what marketing does or why and how it does it. Indeed, few directors and analysts have professional backgrounds in marketing. Therefore, just as you must prove marketing's value to your CEO, you need to do the same for these two additional Northern constituencies.

As a marketing practitioner, you may not have direct access to directors and analysts. However, that doesn't mean you can't influence them indirectly, through your CEO. Here's how: Regularly update your CEO on your company's relationships with customers, with a decided focus on future opportunity rather than past performance. Wall Street is especially future oriented — and that's where *your* strength lies. Know why your company's future is brighter than its competitors', and describe this future and its related opportunities in compelling terms to your CEO. As always, translate these prospects into the language of business by explicating the links between marketing activities and your firm's financial performance.

Ensure that whenever you unexpectedly meet your CEO in the elevator, you update him or her quickly through one or more of the following means:

- A visual hand signal — such as a V for victory or one or two fingers — representing your company's position in the marketplace[21]
- A recent quote from a customer ready on your lips

---

20. According to Leslie Gaines, *CEO Capital,* John Wiley & Sons, 2003.

21. The V for victory, the symbol used by Winston Churchill, is suggested by Bradford Kirk in his book, *Lessons from a Chief Marketing Officer* (McGraw-Hill, 2003), giving advice to marketers in the consumer packaged goods industry.

- A performance update on a marketing-related KPI — such as revenue growth from new customers, customer retention, customer lifetime value, or customer wait times
- A description of an important opportunity for your company — for instance, refer to the latest developments in Internet marketing, e-commerce, or digitalization

Convincing your CEO of marketing's value pays big dividends — as the box "Rejuvenating a Faded Brand: Lessons from Travelocity" reveals. But the CEO is not your only Northern constituency. You also need to forge a mutually beneficial relationship with your CFO — that executive who has your company's purse strings firmly in hand and who decides which functions get the lion's share of the organizational resources. In the next chapter, we shift focus to this equally crucial Northern constituency.

⸻⸻⸻⸻⸻ ◆◆◆◆ ⸻⸻⸻⸻⸻

Rejuvenating a Faded Brand: Lessons from Travelocity

Following a period of financial losses and declining market share in a highly competitive industry, a new management team at Travelocity led a turnaround to realize eight straight quarters of over 25 percent growth and profitability—music to any CEO's ears. Chief marketing officer Jeffrey Glueck reveals the key to this success: revitalizing the Travelocity brand. The following excerpt, from an interview with Glueck, offers lessons for any marketing professional seeking to make marketing matter to his or her CEO.

ROY YOUNG: Tell us about your role and responsibilities as CMO of Travelocity.

JEFFREY GLUECK: The chief marketing officer role at Travelocity covers a wide range of things. It's advertising obviously, but also our customer relationship management [CRM]; all of our editorial, site design, and production; loyalty programs; online search marketing; and the like. The CMO reports to the CEO.

YOUNG: What key advice do you have for other marketers?

GLUECK: You can take a faded pioneer brand like Travelocity and completely reenergize and revitalize it. We did so by building high-margin products, creating a unique positioning in a commodity industry, and building emotional brand connections. We also used personalization technology to become a real retailer and customer service provider.

YOUNG: What are some steps you recommend to make such a turnaround successful?

GLUECK: As a company, we think about three steps to reenergizing toward profitable growth. First, you have to have your economic engine in line—you have to know how you are going to make money. For us, that was moving away from air tickets toward high-margin products like hotel reservations and vacation packages and cruises. In two years, we [shifted] from a company that made almost seventy percent of its revenue from just plain old airline tickets to a company that makes over seventy percent of its revenue from everything *but* airline tickets, which is a pretty remarkable transformation for a company that this year sold about seven point four billion dollars worldwide in travel.

Second, you have to attack commoditization. For us, that means knowing what you stand for. We set out to be the premier advocate and champion for travelers—to say, sure, everyone has to have competitive prices—that's a given. But we realized that most customers really cared that there was someone standing behind their travel—there was a real human being to call twenty-four seven for help or advice, if they needed it. Our tag line—which is "You will never roam alone"—really brought home the human element. We also redesigned the web site completely to be human-oriented—not techno-oriented.

Third, you have to be a smart retailer. That means delivering on your customer service promises and offering good merchandising of products that will save customers money but also be high margin. It also means touching people in a relevant way through e-mail as well as on the web site and being consistent in all of your communications.

YOUNG: Does your CEO understand marketing?

GLUECK: Absolutely. She has complete faith in our marketing team. We check in frequently with our CEO. We have proven through econometric modeling and (more obviously) our market share and gains that the marketing team can be a strategic leader for Travelocity. Three years ago, no one really thought of marketing as a strategic catalyst for the business. Now there is a lot of faith, including [that of] the CFO and CEO. We have tremendous support.

YOUNG: When you speak about econometric modeling and the metrics that chart your effectiveness, how important are these?

GLUECK: We have built very sophisticated econometric models that allow us to track our large investments by channel—network TV, DRTV [direct response television], network radio, national newspaper, local newspaper, online banners, search, e-mail, et cetera. And we have refined it with three years of data on us and all sorts of economic indicators and industry indices and competitor advertising spending . . . you name it. Now, after three years into the modeling, we have a model that lets us forecast acquisition costs and traffic levels to a high degree of accuracy. We try to be very scientific and disciplined about all of our ROI [return on investment] in every channel.

YOUNG: In what respects do you encourage a longer-term focus?

GLUECK: We are launching a loyalty program, [currently] in beta form. I am not talking too much about it in detail, but it is something we've mentioned that we are doing for several hundred thousand of our best customers, giving them special recognition, special service, some extra discounts, a little love, various perks. It's very early, but so far we are seeing a great response.

My goal is to prove that an online company can be more than simply online software. It can really be a trusted partner that you build a relationship with and that serves you well. It points out ways customers can save money but also points out when it's worth spending a little extra to have a nicer hotel right in the middle of town convenient to all the attractions.

So being a good advisor and coming through when things go wrong in travel—that's another way that we really are earning loyalty. We are seeing a tremendous response. Our agents have even gotten marriage proposals for helping people out in their hour of need while traveling!

YOUNG: What makes you personally successful at Travelocity?

GLUECK: It helps to have a great team and to work with a tremendous group of people across the whole organization. We have a CEO and CFO who believe in the strategic vision of being the premier advocate for travelers, so that helps. I don't know if it's possible to do that without complete alignment.

One of the things I've been surprisingly fortunate to find over the last couple of years is that in working with all these specialists, my own specialty is integrating—so I have a good sense of how to be creative and keep creative people motivated but also how to be pragmatic and technical when that's called on. Also, I know how to be ROI-focused when that's called on, too.

So it's stringing together that—listening to the customer, showing creativity, the visual and aesthetic elements of making complex things easy for real people to use, and then bringing that all together with a focus on strategy and differentiation and financial returns. That kind of integrative thinking is what it takes to keep the whole team growing in the same direction.

Source: Telephone conversation with Roy Young, February 13, 2006.

◆◆◆◆◆

YOUR CEO STRENGTHS, WEAKNESSES, OPPORTUNITIES, AND THREATS (SWOT) ANALYSIS

Use the following tool to regularly evaluate your strengths, weaknesses, opportunities, and threats in your relationship with your CEO.

For each statement in Table 3.1, check whether you agree or disagree.

Table 3.1
Your CEO's Views of Marketing

My CEO . . .	Agree	Disagree
Thinks of marketing as more than a set of inputs (expenses) to help sell products and services.	_____	_____

(continued)

Table 3.1 (*continued*)

My CEO . . .	Agree	Disagree
Depends on marketing for more than just communicating about our offerings to consumers.	_____	_____
Sees marketing as accountable for developing and implementing plans that support corporate strategy.	_____	_____
Understands marketing as a professional discipline.	_____	_____
Values marketing's insight about customers.	_____	_____
Values marketing's ability to help clarify how the company differs from the competition.	_____	_____
Understands marketing as the driver of cash flow.	_____	_____
Understands marketing as an important voice in discussions about profitable growth.	_____	_____
Advocates for marketers to participate in or lead cross-functional teams.	_____	_____
Depends on information from marketing to develop accurate and useful reports to the board and Wall Street analysts.	_____	_____

Any statement to which you checked "Disagree" represents an area for improvement in your relationship with your CEO — and an opportunity to ensure that marketing matters to the CEO. How you address these areas will depend on your CEO's personality, your company's markets and strategies, and your knowledge and diplomacy. The following guidelines can help:

1. What actions would best help you address each area for improvement in your relationship with your CEO? For example, if your CEO hasn't advocated your participation in or leadership of cross-functional teams, how might you turn this situation around? Ideas include networking with peer managers and executives to learn about important cross-functional initiatives, offering your assistance to project sponsors, and casually mentioning your participation in such projects to your CEO whenever the opportunity arises.

2. What allies do you have within the organization, but outside of marketing, who can help your CEO understand the unique importance of marketing? How might you enlist these allies' help? For example, does your sales organization regard marketing as an important source of leads and as a contributor to closing sales? If so, how might your colleagues in sales communicate this important role to your CEO?

3. Has your organization begun using customer-focused performance metrics? If so, what performance data might you provide to demonstrate marketing's value to your CEO? For example, is customer retention or satisfaction on the rise? Are customer complaints decreasing? Look for opportunities to share these data with your CEO.

4. How well are you translating marketing outcomes into the language of business? Examine each marketing outcome your group has generated, and think about how you might express them in one or more of the five key business terms — *assets, return on assets, velocity, leverage,* and *risk* — that you learned about in Chapter 2.

5. How is marketing helping your CEO sleep soundly? Consider how you might express each marketing outcome in terms of your company's KPIs — those vital few performance measures that keep your CEO awake at night.

4

Forge a Friendship
with Your CFO

Like your CEO, your company's CFO is another key internal customer in your efforts to Manage North. By forging a close relationship with the CFO, you stand a better chance of obtaining the financial fuel (in the form of project approval and funding) that you need to run your company's marketing engine. Yet CFOs often seem like gatekeepers — nixing funding for major initiatives, tightening departmental budgets, demanding documentation of expenditures, and requiring extensive proof of a proposal's potential benefits before giving the financial green light.

On the other hand, your CFO needs you in order to carry out his or her job responsibilities. If your organization is like many, the CFO not only reports quarterly financial results to the CEO but also paints the financial picture of the firm's future for top management as well as the board of directors and other constituencies. And for all of this, he or she needs input from marketing in the form of updates on actual sales, projected sales for the future, and likely growth opportunities, among other things. By providing this information, you help your CFO become a true strategic partner to the CEO — rather than someone who merely guards the till.

The finance and marketing functions also share an important purpose. Both play a vital role in communicating information about the company to external constituencies. Marketing communicates with customers about the firm's offerings. The CFO conveys information to the company's financial stakeholders — current and potential investors, bankers, industry analysts — about how the firm is generating cash flow now and how it expects to do so in the future. And as we've seen, marketing's role is to identify sources of cash flow (through upstream marketing) and to harvest the cash (through downstream marketing).

Forging a positive relationship with your CFO is similar to building mutually beneficial bonds with external customers: You identify your CFO's needs, deliver something of value to him or her, and regularly communicate information of interest to him or her. We examine these activities in detail in the following.

UNDERSTAND YOUR CFO'S NEEDS

If your CFO is like most, he or she likely has five primary needs:

- Healthy and predictable cash flow
- Steady earnings growth, year after year
- Increasing shareholder or financial value
- A credible story about future earnings to tell the CEO, board of directors, and external constituents, including industry analysts
- A defensible set of controls on company expenditures

You already understand many of these needs. But if you have any questions about these five concepts, consider inviting your CFO to lunch to learn more about them. Ask, "What are your top priorities in your role?" "What do you worry about most?" or "What are the latest pressures on you?" Explain that you want to better understand your CFO's needs so that you can help him or her meet them through the activities you carry out in marketing.

GIVE YOUR CFO SOMETHING OF VALUE

Whether your CFO knows it, you're probably already helping to meet most of his or her needs. For example, you're likely generating healthy and predictable cash flow by catalyzing short-term profits through sales of products to current customers. To fuel steady earnings growth over the years, you drive long-term demand growth through developing new markets and acquiring new customers. This combination of short-term profit and long-term growth in turn enables your CFO to go to the CEO, the board of directors, and industry analysts with a compelling, clear story about how your firm is increasing shareholder or financial value.

You can deliver additional value to your CFO by providing the following information:

Revenue Forecasting

Finance professionals need to know how marketing efforts such as new-product launches and promotional campaigns will produce revenue and over what time horizon. To provide this information, you'll need to develop accurate and reliable revenue forecasts for each of your initiatives and programs. It's not enough to look backward for examples of previous marketing successes as justification for proposed future expenditures. Especially in complex organizations with large portfolios of products, served markets, and customers, you'll need forecasts that estimate which marketing expenditures will generate the greatest return. For example, should more of the budget be spent in Brazil or Indonesia? Should some products receive greater marketing support than others? Will there be a greater return on a trade promotion or on an increase in advertising? Work with the finance team to blend their and your experience and intuition with scientific methodology to produce informed forecasts.

Risk Assessment

Every time you prepare a revenue forecast for a proposed marketing expenditure, also provide an assessment of risk: State everything that might go wrong — from revenues falling short of budget to utter failure of your initiative — and explain how you'll mitigate those risks. For instance, what might happen if a major hurricane hit several important markets? What might occur if a competitor launched a new product?

Also acknowledge the risks that can come with successful execution of an initiative. For instance, a trade-show exhibit might create so many leads that the company can't process them all or provide every potential new customer with the promised product or service. Successful generation of leads may also cause competitors to start sniffing around your business. As you do in assessing risks associated with problems, explain in your forecast how you'll deal with risks associated with success.

Perhaps the most important type of risk assessment to include in your revenue forecasts is recognition of market discontinuities. These are radical changes in technology or customer behavior that threaten your firm's core businesses or create opportunities for development of new businesses. To illustrate, consider the impact of the Internet and eBay more specifically on the collectibles market. Now that consumers can readily go to the Internet to find that ceramic Elvis ashtray, sellers of collectibles must today go head to head with an efficient new competitor (eBay). Or consider another discontinuity, the mobile telephone. Even as some consumers replace their standard landlines in their homes with a telephone they carry with them at all times, the advent of mobile telephones has also created new opportunities for companies to provide local information and advertising.

To recognize market discontinuities, you need to do more than just extrapolate historical trends: You must understand how and why customers behave as they do and what role existing and potential products and services play in this behavior. The best way to gain this understanding? Acquire an intimate understanding of your customers' worlds and the ways in which those worlds may be changing.

Drawing on your understanding of why technology and customer behavior are changing — and how — propose implications of these changes in your revenue forecasts. For any discontinuities that pose threats, explain how you plan to de-

flect those threats. For any discontinuities that present opportunities, present your ideas for exploiting those opportunities.

Pricing

Of the *four Ps* of the traditional marketing mix, price has the
most direct and obvious link to cash flow. Price too high, and
customers won't buy; price too low, and your firm leaves
money on the table and perhaps damages the perceived quality of the product. A one-time discount may spur sales and inventory turnover in the short term but may prevent you from
charging higher prices in the future if consumers decide to
hold off buying until the next sale. By communicating the
implications of pricing strategies to finance, you further
strengthen your CFO's understanding of what marketing
does and why it's important.

Explain to your CFO that prices should be set from an
outside-in (customer and competition) perspective, not an in-
side-out (cost-plus) perspective. The critical determinants of
consumer behavior are *perceptions* of relative value for prices
charged. Your assumptions about how competitors will respond should also inform pricing decisions. That's why marketers should provide the critical input for pricing choices.
Cost-plus pricing, though widely used, makes no sense: Customers don't care about your company's costs. Nevertheless,
in determining prices, you can't ignore your company's cost
structure. After all, that structure must be able to support
your pricing strategy over the long term. Thus, you and your
CFO must collaborate to develop coherent pricing strategies
that work for customers and respect your firm's cost structure.

Budget Setting

Most companies develop a firm-wide budget once a year by
asking department and unit heads to submit their budget requirements for the coming fiscal year. These budgets are often

adjusted on a quarterly or other basis as the year unfolds. For example, if actual revenues fall short of expectations during a period covered by the budget, the finance department may cut expenses across the board to prevent cash flow from turning negative. CFOs typically use this method because it's easy and may seem fair. But across-the-board cuts don't necessarily make the best business sense. Why? Some activities and expenditures are more important than others for generating both immediate and future cash flow. A savvy CFO instead adjusts the company's budget based on an understanding of how increases or reductions in specific budgeted items will impact short-term and long-term cash flow.

For this reason, you need to explain the implications of marketing spending on cash flow when you present your department's budget needs during the annual budgeting process. And if your CFO proposes an across-the-board belt-tightening, present a compelling business case for why your marketing initiatives should be retained. Perhaps more than any other workplace challenge, winning budget battles requires top-notch presentation and negotiation skills. Defend your budget requirements with hard, cold facts about how slashing your funding will affect cash flow, profitability, growth, and other KPIs your company uses. Take whatever steps are necessary to strengthen your negotiation skills — including role-playing with a trusted colleague, taking a course on negotiation, or hiring a coach to help you.

Documentation of Financial Value Added

Explain to your CFO how your external outlook and your orientation toward your firm's future performance generate financial value for the organization. Taking time to explicate the impact of marketing activities on customer equity,[1] brand eq-

---

1. Larry Selden and Geoffrey Colvin, *Angel Customers and Demon Customers: Discover Which Is Which and Turbo-Charge Your Stock*, Portfolio, 2003; Roland Rust, Valarie Zeithaml, and Katherine Lemon, *Driving Customer Equity: How Customer Lifetime Value Is Reshaping Corporate Strategy*, Free Press, 2000.

uity,[2] price-earnings ratio, future earnings (cash flow), or any combination of these four key business concepts will go a long way toward showing your CFO that your work creates financial value for the firm.

Showing how marketing activities enhance profits and growth will earn you even greater appreciation on the part of your CFO. We examine these two forms of financial value more closely in the following.

MARKETING: THE WELLSPRING OF PROFIT

Profit is the most sacred word in business.[3] Indeed, profit is the lifeblood of any organization. If a business can't generate a profit — that is, bring in more money from selling its products or services than it costs to provide those offerings — the company will soon go out of business. Even nonprofit organizations must bring in more money than they spend in order to continue serving their constituents. (Such organizations don't call the difference between revenues and costs *profit;* they use the term *surplus* instead. To recognize all types of organizations, we call profit *cash flow.*)

The more you can show how your marketing efforts produce cash flow, the greater influence you'll have with the CFO. To demonstrate this link, you need to understand how your organization generates cash, demonstrate an entrepreneur's zeal for producing cash, and promote marketing's role as a cash generator throughout your organization. As you'll see in Chapter 5, you also need to select a set of metrics that enable you to show how each marketing activity translates (either directly or indirectly) into hard, cold cash for your company. But before we explore the notion of marketing metrics, let's take a closer look at the following guidelines:

---

2. Debbie MacInnis and C. W. Park, "How to Measure Brand Equity," www
.marketingprofs.com, 2004.

3. *Growth* rivals *profit* as the most sacred word, suggests Michael Treacy in
Double-Digit Growth, Penguin, 2003.

Show How Marketing Activities Generate Cash Now

Marketing generates cash by attracting and keeping customers. However, there are many ways to do this. Your choice of methods must depend on your company's business model — its approach to making money. Take ten different organizations, and you'll likely find that each one makes money through one or more different business models. Savvy marketing professionals find out which business model(s) their company uses and ensure that their activities support those models. Table 4.1 shows examples of business models, delineates marketing's role in supporting each model, and provides examples of companies that use each model.

Table 4.1
Business Models and Marketing

Business Model	Marketing's Role	Example
Pyramid: Provide a hierarchy of product or service choices to several customer groups simultaneously.	Identify needs of current and potential customer segments and suggest different levels of products or services that can serve three or more simultaneously.	American Express offers credit cards in platinum, gold, and silver—each providing different services and privileges.
Multicomponent: Sell one product in different forms to customers at different times with different price sensitivities.	Clarify and quantify customer price sensitivities on different purchase occasions. Factor price elasticity into other marketing-mix decisions.	Coca-Cola sells its beverage at different prices in restaurants, supermarkets, convenience stores, and vending machines.
Time: Diffuse a new product quickly in the marketplace to exploit interest.	Identify characteristics and motivations of early adopters who will pay a premium for the newest and the best and who will tell their friends.	Intel microchip technology regularly introduces innovations in speed and capacity.
Multiplier: Use one skill in many different forms, products, and contexts.	Apply or package a specific product or service for many different customer needs.	Disney ensures that its characters are used in movies, theme parks, and consumer products.

(continued)

Table 4.1 (*continued*)

Business Model	Marketing's Role	Example
Specialist: Cater to one target group willing to pay a premium for customized offerings.	Develop expertise to serve the needs of target group. Become recognized as the supplier who understands the customer. Design an à la carte menu.	EDS uses systems integration with specialization by industry.
Installed Base: Maximize sales of base product at tight margins and sell consumable related products at high margins.	Build sales of base product with an attractive quality or price to acquire users of compatible related products.	Hewlett-Packard makes more money selling the ink cartridges (related product) that go into its printers (base product) than it does selling the printers.
Blockbuster: Build R&D pipeline projects with the greatest business potential.	Increase feasibility and minimize risk of project investments. Increase speed to market. Position new products correctly in prospects' minds.	Genentech commands a substantial price premium by developing new drugs for the treatment of serious, life-threatening diseases such as cancer and heart disease.
Brand: Create consumer loyalty based on a desirable promise of value.	Create premium value based on unique and relevant emotional connections between the customer and the brand.	IBM, BMW, and Bose create a strong brand identity that attracts a loyal customer base that is willing to pay a premium price for the brand and that repurchases repeatedly over time.
New Product: Constantly innovate and introduce products with new features, latest technology, or improved quality	Recreate demand by making older products obsolete and by offering greater functionality in new models.	Sony has sold multiple units of its Walkman products to the same customer by offering newer technology, more features, and products designed for special occasions (such as lounging on the beach or jogging) and for specific markets (for example, "My First Sony" for children).
Digitalization: Achieve competitive advantages based on information technology.	Use information to drive improvements in production productivity, speed-to-market, inventory management, customer experiences, and loyalty.	Dell Computer uses the Internet to sell its products directly to consumers— bypassing distributors and warehousing and reducing costs accordingly.

Source: Adapted from *The Art of Profitability,* by Adrian Slywotzky, Warner Business Books, 2002.

As an expert in discerning and serving customer needs, you're in an ideal position to determine the best strategies for generating cash for your firm — that is, the most effective business models. However, in many organizations, top management does not involve marketing executives in setting such strategies. Left out of the discussions, the marketing department must guess at what top management wants. As a result, many marketers wrongly assume that top management wants them to focus on increasing market share. Yet expanding market share is just one of many possible strategies for generating cash.

To align your efforts behind your company's cash-generation strategies, you must first find out what those strategies are. You can do so by looking at the growth initiatives your CEO talks about in public presentations and in the firm's annual report. Stock analysts' reports are also a good source of information about a firm's business model. Most helpful is to just listen to how people in your organization talk about the business. Is growing market share mentioned often, or do you hear more about developing new markets? Does mention of cross-selling, or developing new products for which no competitors exist, seem to be on everyone's lips? Listening to the way business objectives are described and discussed provides considerable insight into how the enterprise hopes to succeed in the future. As a marketer, you need to link your own activities to these business objectives and the ways in which these objectives may be realized.

Once you've clarified which business model(s) your firm uses, you can further strengthen your relationship with your CFO by citing the initiatives and programs you're using to generate cash according to your firm's established model(s). In addition, accept that your marketing initiatives are only as good as the cash results they achieve. If your current approaches aren't generating cash — either in the short term or the long term — find a better track and make the change. You'll further demonstrate your entrepreneurial spirit and solidify your credibility in the CFO's mind.

Overcome Inaccurate Perceptions
of Marketing's Impact on Cash

Though your marketing efforts may be generating cash flow, your CFO may still not *perceive* you as a producer of cash. As we've seen, this perception often stems from the fact that marketing's outputs may not be as immediately visible as other functions' (such as sales') outputs. Learn how to respond to a CFO who views marketing as an expense that doesn't produce money. Work to convince him or her that "marketing is the root of all income."[4] Point out that "no marketing means no customers . . . no customers means no money . . . and no money means no business."

Understanding which of the many business models your organization uses enables you to demonstrate to a skeptical CFO how marketing produces cash now and how marketing can contribute additional cash in the future. As you saw in Table 4.1, your team can produce cash through many different activities. The more you can help your CFO see the connection between your marketing activities and the production of cash, the more likely he or she will be willing to approve the expenditures you need to generate that cash.

Marketing: A Growth Driver

For many companies, the word *growth* rivals *profit* as the most sacred word in business. But what is growth, exactly? If profit is the lifeblood of an organization, then growth is its heart. Both are critical: Profit creates short-term well-being, while growth sustains health over the long term. How? Growth reduces the cost of capital, and it boosts employee morale as workers get excited about being part of a successful enterprise. Higher morale in turn leads to greater productivity.

---

4. From a marketing tutorial for the National Park Service by Dr. Steve Hutchens of Creighton University, updated January 2002, at http://www.creighton .edu/~hutchens/nps_c_05.html.

Current and potential customers, too, like doing business with winners.[5] Clearly, without growth, organizations limp along and eventually die.

Because growth creates such critical advantages for a company, most CFOs take an intense interest in it — particularly in organic growth — which occurs through acquiring more customers and selling more product rather than through mergers and acquisitions. If growth slows, CFOs will want to know the reason: Is the loss of momentum due to aging business models? New, more nimble competitors? Breakthrough technology that has rendered the company's offerings obsolete? Cheap manufacturing labor overseas that creates lower cost alternatives to your company's products? Overall decline in the industry?

Though it may be tempting to blame a slowdown in growth on external factors, studies suggest that the problem often stems from poor strategic and tactical management decisions instead.[6] As marketing visionary Theodore Leavitt wrote over 40 years ago in his classic article "Marketing Myopia," "There is no such thing as a growth industry. There are only companies *organized* and *operated* to create and capitalize on growth opportunities."[7]

Take the personal computer industry as an illustration. Though the microprocessor industry overall has enjoyed astounding growth over the last 30 years, not all the initial players in that industry have benefited from its success. Some companies (Microsoft, Dell, Sun Microsystems) have been winners, and others (Xerox, Wang, Digital Equipment Corporation, Compaq) have been losers. Their fate has depended

5. Michael Treacy, *Double-Digit Growth: How Great Companies Achieve It*, Penguin, 2003.

6. In addition to *Double Digit Growth: How Great Companies Achieve It*, related information is included in *How to Grow When Markets Don't*, by Adrian Slywotzky and Richard Wise, Warner Business Books, 2002; *The Discipline of Market Leaders*, by Michael Treacy; and *Built to Last*, by Jim Collins and Jerry Porras, Harper-Business, 1994.

7. *Harvard Business Review*, July–August 1960.

on their leaders' understanding of the marketplace and customers' needs.[8]

As a marketer, you are well positioned to create growth opportunities and help your company capitalize on these opportunities. Why? Your unique *outside-in* perspective leads you to ask these crucial questions:

- What's happening in our marketplace?
- How are our current and potential customers' needs changing?
- What's causing these changes?
- Where are our opportunities to satisfy emerging needs?
- How can we fulfill those needs before anyone else does?

Once you've generated answers to these questions, you can fuel your organization's growth.

Despite growth's importance, many companies attempt to spur growth through traditional methods that have serious limitations. Senior executives often design their growth strategy based on their organization's existing assets — products and services, brands, distribution channels, core competencies. Then they ask the marketing staff to figure out "how to sell more of what we have now." Even if management includes the marketing team in defining strategy, it often expects that team to use incremental growth strategies. For example, marketers are asked to increase market share by introducing product line extensions, making minor updates to existing offerings, and strengthening existing brands and customer retention, often through loyalty incentives.

These methods can catalyze some growth in the short run, but they can't help a company *sustain* its growth. For one thing, price reductions intended to steal customers from competitors so as to expand market share only erode profits — therefore, this tactic is not sustainable.[9] And the relentless cre-

8. Ram Charan and Noel Tichy, *Every Business Is a Growth Business*, Random House, 1998.

9. *Double-Digit Growth: How Great Companies Achieve It.*

ation of new products and line extensions only adds expensive complexity to a company's operations and risks overwhelming and confusing consumers with a preponderance of choices.

In many companies, efforts to retain customers through rewards and incentives have come at the expense of investment in long-term projects and growth.[10] For example, soon after opening in 1986, Staples, the office supply retailer, tried various complicated incentive programs to increase its most profitable customers' loyalty. The programs proved so expensive and complex that they failed to generate the intended results. Now Staples uses a simpler program called Staples Business Rewards, which gives large customers up to a $15 rebate each month. Still, the company has yet to see any clear evidence that this program has improved customer loyalty.

The problem with customer retention strategies is that they're frequently difficult for an organization to control. Companies bombard consumers with a bewildering number of loyalty incentive programs, driving customers away. Even people who participate in such programs often switch to a rival company because they want variety or because another firm offers a better deal. Thus the strategy backfires. Your job as a marketing expert is to help the CFO see the limitations of customer retention and other traditional growth strategies and to demonstrate the advantages of more effective approaches to growth. Everyone's goal should be to generate *reliable and profitable* growth for your firm — not just growth at all costs. With your *outside-in* perspective, you can help your company exploit three major sources of profitable growth:[11]

10. Professor George Day, professor of marketing at the Wharton School of the University of Pennsylvania, in "Feeding the Growth Strategy," *Marketing Management,* November–December 2003.

11. Adapted from Chapter 4 — "Strategy from the Outside In" — in *Every Business Is a Growth Business* by Ram Charan and Noel Tichy, Random House, 1998, to build a case for the leadership of marketing in creating and driving growth opportunities.

1. Finding related markets or additional customer needs that your organization can serve.
2. Expanding or creating new market segments.
3. Identifying adjacent market segments.

Each of these three sources of long-term, profitable growth requires an understanding of customers' present and future needs and the ability to bring this understanding inside the organization — precisely your role as a marketer.

So the next time you find yourself in the elevator with the CFO, remember that CFOs live by numbers. Mention what you're doing to spur growth in top-line revenue or in bottom-line profit. Cite the number of new customers your company acquired over the last quarter or the share of their wallets in your category that you've gained. Then invite your CFO for coffee to learn more about his or her priorities and most pressing concerns. Through all these actions, you'll be delivering something of value to your CFO — and thereby laying the foundation for a positive bond.

But these steps aren't enough in themselves. To put the final seal on your friendship with the CFO, you must also communicate in a disciplined way with him or her about a wide range of marketing matters. The next section offers helpful guidelines.

LET'S TALK: COMMUNICATING REGULARLY WITH YOUR CFO

Without ongoing, effective communication with your CFO, you'll be hard pressed to Manage North — to sell marketing's importance to this major internal customer.

To get a sense of how marketing can build close ties with finance through ongoing communication, we interviewed a number of CFOs. The model CFO — from the marketing professional's perspective — is embodied in one interview subject we'll call *Bill*. This talented CFO works at a large, successful consumer-products organization that we'll call *TopCo*, which has operations around the world.

According to Bill, it's in his best interest to build a productive relationship with marketing through disciplined communication. And Bill knows that *all CFOs identify their primary responsibility as helping their organization grow.* So in light of TopCo's impressive record of double-digit annual growth — without an acquisition — for each of the past eight years, Bill has credibility when he says that a strong relationship between marketing and finance is critical to corporate success. He defines four keys to building a mutually beneficial alliance:

Key #1: Finance Should Take Responsibility for Revenue Accounting. If It Does Not, Marketing Must Show the CFO How Continually Analyzing Cash Flow Is in His or Her Best Interest

As we've seen, CFOs live by the numbers. But most organizations use more than one set of numbers to track their performance. Marketing can help finance fulfill its responsibility for one particularly important set of numbers — those that make up revenue accounting. To that end, Bill has organized TopCo's finance function into three groups: financial accounting, cost accounting, and revenue accounting.

In Bill's view, revenue accounting is the most essential tool for enabling the business to achieve its financial objectives. Why? Traditional cost accounting produces reports on how the organization *spends* money but does not show how the organization invests to generate an ROA or some other ratio. Financial accounting, for its part, is *public* accounting, which is strictly governed by generally accepted accounting practices (GAAP). These rules, common to all publicly owned companies and followed by most private companies, dictate that marketing inputs (expenditures) used to generate outputs (revenue) must be reported as expenses on an organization's income statement.

On most companies' income statement, marketing is shown as a line item in the expense section — often under sales and administrative expenses. Further, marketing inputs must be expensed within one year. Any marketing expenditures used to stimulate future demand for the company's offerings are never reported as capital expenses over several periods. Companies must follow this rule even though the impact of a given marketing outlay may continue for months or even years after the end of the reporting period in which the expense was recorded.

As Bill explains it, all finance professionals are experts in cost accounting and financial accounting. They may even be masters at evaluating potential investments, such as an acquisition and a capital expenditure. But few of them possess a broad business-strategy perspective, including an understanding of *why* and *how* the organization makes money. At TopCo, only the employees in the revenue accounting group possess this understanding.

Knowing that the typical finance professional is focused on costs, Bill asks all candidates who apply for a job in revenue accounting at his corporation how they would help the business grow and what they see as the most important sources of cash flow and profitability. Candidates who perceive the connection between marketing and cash flow make a strong impression on him.

Successful new hires in Bill's finance department understand that the organization must acquire new customers, identify and penetrate new customer segments, retain customers, introduce new products and new categories, and carry out other marketing activities to generate earnings and earnings growth. Bill's commitment to hiring marketing-savvy finance professionals ensures that the two functions understand one another and appreciate the value that each brings to the organization.

Key #2: Foster Regular Personal Contact between Marketing and Finance Staffs

Once on board, the finance professionals in TopCo's revenue accounting group must work face-to-face with marketers and others in cross-functional teams rather than spending all their time in their own offices. By collaborating cross-functionally, finance professionals demonstrate that they are not corporate police officers with an us-versus-them attitude. Rather, they are members of business or project teams that require financial management to help the company achieve its goals.

Similarly, all marketing staff at TopCo must take the initiative to meet frequently with finance staff. This means not only inviting finance employees to formal meetings but also gathering with them in informal settings, such as over coffee or lunch.

Through regular networking, marketing and finance professionals deepen their understanding of one another's challenges, concerns, and needs — and collaborate more effectively as they work toward the company's objectives.

Key #3: Finance Professionals Want Technical Expertise and Analytical Thinking from Marketing

Bill does not let TopCo's marketers carry out their jobs unchallenged. He refuses to give the green light to marketing proposals unless they're accompanied by convincing analytical thinking that supports the recommendations. For example, recently he declined to fund a new product launch in a new product category until he saw an analysis explaining why *this* launch would succeed when similar launches had produced disappointing results twice in the past. He faulted the proposal's advocates for not learning from experience and for conducting limited analysis of consumer markets.

The explosion of information and data-mining technology has made analytical rigor not only more possible but also more expected. For these reasons, we encourage you to master the technical tools you need to conduct reliable market research, to use the results of your research to generate new knowledge, and to translate that knowledge into effective action.

More than ever in this age of information, knowledge is power for marketers. Leading organizations win sales and market share because their marketing experts make decisions informed by hard information about customers.

Key #4: Marketing and Finance Must Develop and Implement a Marketing Performance Measurement System

According to Bill, TopCo's finance and marketing staffs have collaborated to create a marketing performance measurement system to guide investment decisions. His primary criterion for selecting metrics for the system is that they create a balanced picture of the company's short- and long-term performance. These metrics are largely behavioral rather than attitudinal — for example, "share of market for new and established products," "sales from products that did not exist last year," "sales of new products targeting new customer segments," and "spikes in sales of an established product due to a new promotional strategy." "We can tell right away whether a new advertising approach is a winner or loser," Bill maintains. Well-chosen metrics enable the finance and marketing staffs to conduct valuable discussions about performance problems and potential solutions.

Knowing that consumer brand preferences are important indicators of future performance, Bill also tracks performance on a few metrics related to brand health. All metrics, he says, must be understood by everyone and interpreted with an eye toward *future* performance, not used to defend past missteps.

Marketing performance measurement is a big subject, and we cover it in extensive detail in Chapter 5. The major point we want to make here, however, is that a marketing performance measurement system can serve as a helpful vehicle for communicating about your work with the CFO.

CFOS UNDER PRESSURE: A NOTE ABOUT SARBANES-OXLEY

The gulf that typically divides finance and marketing isn't just about poor or inadequate communication. Conflict between the two functions over how to account for expenditures further widens that gulf. In most firms, the marketing department spends a very large share of the company budget. The

CFO, for his or her part, is responsible for monitoring expenditures and accounting for their use. This difference in responsibilities often spawns tension between the marketing and finance functions.

And these days, CFOs have come under more pressure than ever to account accurately for expenditures. The reason? The Sarbanes-Oxley Act, signed into law by President Bush in 2002. A response to the wave of scandals that swept the corporate arena during the 1990s, Sarbanes-Oxley imposes new financial reporting standards and requirements on publicly traded companies. The intent of the law is to ensure that companies don't misrepresent their financial condition in order to attract investment dollars. While the act does not require privately owned companies to comply with its provisions, executives in all U.S. organizations can expect the government to scrutinize their financial controls more closely than before. For example, a privately held firm that does business with the government or with publicly traded firms may find that complying with Sarbanes-Oxley is a condition of continuing its business relationship with such clients.

Sarbanes-Oxley has important implications for marketing executives. Specifically, most enterprises will have to establish a much higher degree of visibility into the costs and results of marketing activities than they did in the past. They will have to do so through new systems, more formal internal controls, and auditable processes to track marketing's spending and forecasting. According to the industry research firm Gartner, "To do this, the marketing function must be transformed to comply with the new requirements."[12] Sarbanes-Oxley compliance requires major operational changes and investments in new systems and processes. Marketing is a particularly visible target because it manages significant budgets, often with weak oversight.

Section 404 of Sarbanes-Oxley is especially problematic for marketing departments. For one thing, it requires mar-

12. "Determine Your Approach to Marketing Resource Management," Kimberly Collins, Gartner Group, July 2005.

keting managers to assess and provide information on the effectiveness of internal control structures and procedures regarding financial reporting. Further, it mandates that every financial audit include an assessment by the auditors of management's representation of the company's internal control structures, including those used in marketing.

According to Michael Ferro, CEO of Click Commerce, "There is no room for error. Accuracy, timeliness, completeness, and transparency of financial reports are now essential requirements for every public company." For executives in publicly traded firms, the consequences of noncompliance can be painful: public humiliation, fines, and even prison. If noncompliance problems stem from the marketing department, your head, along with those of your colleagues, will doubtless roll.

Of course, the primary burden for compliance with Sarbanes-Oxley falls on the CEO and CFO, who must personally certify compliance and the accuracy of financial statements. To do so, CFOs must rely on managers throughout the organization — including marketing professionals.

To ensure Sarbanes-Oxley compliance, the finance department in one company produced a 15-question checklist for managers. The first question on the list is, "What controls ensure that orders are recorded properly in your department?" Respondents could choose from three possible answers:

1. Orders are keyed into an order-entry system in the field by the sales staff.
2. Orders are keyed into an order-entry system in the field by the sales staff. Orders are then reviewed and recorded by a member of the finance/accounting group.
3. Orders entered by a member of the finance/accounting group are reviewed by management. A complete audit trail of all activity is maintained in the order-entry system.

Answer number three is the one the government wants to see. How can you ensure that your marketing department is doing its part to help the company comply with Sarbanes-Oxley? Ask yourself questions such as the following:

- When a member of the marketing staff creates a large purchase order, who approves it?
- Is the expense in the budget?
- Does the finance or accounting department know about the expense? Does accounting match the purchase order against the invoice before it cuts a check?
- Are all documents related to the transaction — including e-mails and invoices — stored in a central archive?
- Do the electronic spreadsheets we use for forecasting, cutting purchase orders, and tracking expenses contain accurate data? Do we periodically validate the formulas used in the spreadsheets?

If you answer no to any of these questions, you're not doing all you can do to help your company with Sarbanes-Oxley compliance.

To further support compliance with Sarbanes-Oxley, also ask yourself these questions:

- Where are the material risks in the marketing department's activities?
- Do we have the appropriate control to mitigate these risks and to flag outliers as they occur?
- Do we apply our controls in a consistent and competent fashion?
- As the executive in charge, can I confidently attest to the accuracy and integrity of the marketing department's financial data?

Again, if you've answered no for any of these questions, you need to make some changes. Clearly, the new law requires much more rigor in companies' financial reporting. Before Sarbanes-Oxley, says Ken Kornbluh, CEO of Marketing-Pilot Software, it was enough to have good answers to questions like, "What did you know?" and "When did you know it?" Now every executive needs to be able to answer the question "How did you *not* know about it?"

Because much of the information conveyed between a company's marketing and finance functions directly affects the firm's financial picture, a tight link between the marketing information system and financial system is critical. Such a link enables managers in both functions to automate process controls, monitor performance, and create an audit trail. Sarbanes-Oxley is a wake-up call to every marketing executive to ensure that the processes for which they are responsible have security, integrity, and financial accountability.[13]

One final practical suggestion is to periodically conduct your own audit of the marketing department's processes — looking for places where links between marketing activities and financial results are unclear or missing. Start at the highest level, cash flow, and work backward to all the marketing activities that have had an impact on cash. If you can't make the linkages, ask why not. Any activity that has no direct or indirect impact on cash flow should be stopped. You'll learn more about this audit process in Chapter 5.

YOUR CFO SWOT ANALYSIS

1. Assess your communications with your company's CFO. How do you report the results of your activities to the CFO? What changes might help improve the quality of these communications? For example, should you establish a more formal reporting system or meet on a more regular basis?

2. How would your CFO rate your marketing expertise? What steps might you take to improve these perceptions of your value?

3. Evaluate your skills in these key business processes:

- Forecasting revenue
- Pricing

13. The discussion of Sarbanes-Oxley (including all quotations) relies heavily on Ken Kornbluh, "Sarbanes-Oxley: A Wake-Up Call for Marketing," *Market-*

- Budgeting
- Measuring performance
- Documenting financial value added

For any weak areas, what might you do to strengthen your skills?

4. Is your CFO interested in building a broader strategic understanding of the business — including customers and competitors — throughout your organization? If so, how might you support that effort?

5. How might you make the CFO your ally in securing the information and support from other parts of the organization — IT, sales, operations — that you need to deepen your understanding of customers?

6. Does your CFO understand marketing's role in identifying sources of cash flow through upstream marketing and harvesting cash through downstream marketing? If not, what might you do to help him or her gain that understanding?

7. What business model(s) does your organization use? How were the model(s) chosen? How well are they working? How does your marketing department support successful use of the model(s)? How might you improve the current business model(s)? If you think the model(s) should be changed, how might you make a compelling business case for the change?

8. Does your CFO see the marketing group as a driver of profits and growth? If not, what steps might you take to correct this misperception?

ing Magnified, the CMO Council, April 2004, and "The SOx 404 Checklist," Softrax Corporation, www.softrax.com.

5

Define Metrics for
What Matters

In the 1970s, the Polish government decided that it needed to make its furniture industry more competitive in the global economy. To achieve this goal, furniture factories were rewarded based on the total weight of the furniture products they produced. As a result, today, the citizens of Poland have the world's heaviest furniture.[1] The intent of the measurement system was not to produce heavy pieces of furniture but, rather, to increase production. Unfortunately, measurement does not always produce its intended outcomes. Metrics are important but only if they are relevant to what really matters.

There is no shortage of metrics in marketing. Marketers do a great job measuring both their activities and the effects of these activities on customers. Marketing strategies and interventions are well informed by these metrics. The problem is that CEOs and CFOs and the shareholders they serve are less concerned with metrics like customer awareness, customer satisfaction, and market share than they are about cash flow, shareholder value, market capitalization, return on assets (ROA), and return on investment (ROI). These metrics are generally not part of the marketing vocabulary, but they should be. They enable you to tell the story of how marketing contributes to your firm's performance. Use the wrong metrics to communicate North and you risk producing a lot of heavy furniture.

---

1. *New York Times*, March 4, 1999.

To establish a secure seat at the strategic planning table, it is essential that you translate marketing activities and their related metrics into financial results. Otherwise, how do you respond when your CFO asks, "What will happen if we cut the marketing budget 10 percent? or "What if we increase the marketing budget 10 percent?"

Translating marketing activities into financial results is not as difficult as it may seem. It is first about storytelling — that is, explicating the links between a specific marketing activity and expected financial results. For example, your story of brand advertising might be as simple as "Advertising today will allow us to charge a 20 percent premium for our brand over the next year." Sure, such links are based on many assumptions and are fraught with uncertainty. But assumptions and uncertainty are realities of life in every business function. By making the links between marketing activities and financial results explicit, you identify important assumptions and uncertainties and, where appropriate, test and validate them.

To translate marketing activities into financial results, you need to first develop the story of marketing's outcomes at a conceptual level, then identify metrics that enable you to gauge how well those outcomes are generating the financial benefits important to your firm. The financial outcome is the critical element in crafting a credible story about marketing's contribution to the bottom line.

We're not saying that marketing professionals don't use metrics. We *are* saying that many marketers select metrics that don't show their activities' impact on cash flow. For example, consider how most marketing executives assess how well an advertising campaign performed. They look at the cost to reach the target marketing in terms of cost per thousand (CPM). They measure readership (how many readers saw the headline, began to read the copy, and finished the copy). They evaluate awareness, or share of voice or cost per sales lead. All of these outcomes are important to know, but they don't tell management whether the ad campaign affected the company's cash flow. Even if the campaign reached its intended viewers or readers and improved their awareness of the product, these results have little relevance if they don't ultimately put cash in the company's coffers.

Customer satisfaction is another commonly used marketing metric that is often not translated into impact on cash flow. Through high product quality, exceptional service, and low prices, a company can satisfy virtually all of its customers. But it won't make any money if greater customer satisfaction doesn't lead to reduced churn rate, increased retention, higher customer lifetime value, or more cross-selling or up-selling. If high quality, excellent service, and low prices don't generate cash flow through these means, the company is giving away the store merely to make customers happy.

Market share is another example of a traditional metric that is used to evaluate marketing's performance but that isn't necessarily relevant to a firm's cash flow. Though market share may be one of the most widely used marketing measures, experts continue to debate its usefulness as an indicator of marketing effectiveness. After all, the company with the largest market share in an industry may not be the most profitable or have the best price-earnings ratio.

Return on investment, a measure of marketing profitability, may not be the best indicator to guide your decisions. "Marketers should avoid ROI as the key performance measure," says marketing professor Tim Ambler, "as it gives excessive importance to the 'I.' Modern goals such as profit, shareholder value, and discounted cash flow all express the returns as revenue less costs. ROI is therefore easier to achieve by reducing costs (and profits) than by increasing revenue. As a result, pursuing ROI leads to lower marketing spending and [therefore] sub-optimal . . . performance."[2] An additional problem with traditional, accounting-based measures of ROI is that *return* is defined over the short term. But cash flow over time, when appropriately discounted, is the

2. Tim Ambler, "The Long and Short View of Marketing Metrics," Marketing Science Institute conference "Measuring Marketing Productivity: Linking Marketing to Financial Returns," October 2002.

more appropriate measure of return and is the measure most widely recognized in the financial community.

In fact, many marketing metrics, including return on investment, may not actually help guide marketing to do its job more effectively. You must be careful to select metrics that help marketing improve cash flow and communicate results convincingly to upper management. Whether your metrics include customer satisfaction, brand identity, brand equity, advertising results, or some other measures of performance, don't end the conversation with your CEO or CFO by announcing, "And we've increased awareness!"

Drawing out these connections and selecting appropriate metrics requires some detective work and patience. For one thing, the data needed to evaluate performance on a particular metric may not be available, from either internal or external sources. Moreover, tracking data on marketing metrics costs money. And many marketing professionals have come under pressure to reduce expenses. Furthermore, most marketing organizations have no formal processes in place to systematically evaluate and improve the usefulness of their metrics.

Yet another challenge is that linking marketing actions to cash flow requires information systems that stream data together in a way that mirrors what has occurred in the marketplace. For instance, if your company can't determine precisely when a particular television commercial was aired, you won't likely be able to discern the commercial's impact on sales. And if sales data are reported at a high aggregate level, such as quarterly sales, the commercial's impact will get lost. Without the right information technology and IT teams, the connection between specific marketing efforts and their financial outcomes remains hidden. Companies spend enormous sums on IT systems to track inventory, to exercise accounting controls, and to manage other processes. Investing in IT systems that also clarify the connections between marketing actions and financial results is money well spent.

Lack of discipline in marketers' use of metrics presents another difficulty. Consider a marketing manager's forecast of a new product's sales. The manager bases his forecast on an early concept of the product, but the offering that is actually brought to market lacks key features and is more costly than the prototype that was tested. Or consider a test of a television commercial's effectiveness. If the commercial that is actually run differs from an earlier version that was tested — as is often the case — the results of the test are not very useful. When marketers offer forecasts based on tests that do not reflect actual events in the market, their credibility erodes.

Even when marketers use sophisticated mathematical tools to model the effects of marketing activities, they often do so only with hindsight. Historical analyses can be useful, but managing based on history is a recipe for disaster. Marketers must adjust their metrics and models when necessary to reflect *anticipated* changes in the market environment: Future competitive activity may be greater or lesser than in the past; final advertising copy may be stronger or weaker than the version tested or what was used in the previous quarter. Further complicating the issue, sales-force deployment may differ from one period to another. Such adjustments require discipline and a repeatable, systematic process.

One last difficulty you must recognize: no one marketing metric fits all businesses. There is no holy grail. Even what works for your lead competitor or other organizations in your industry may not actually work for marketing in your organization. So be skeptical of what is often referred to as "best practices." There is just no way to avoid doing the work to develop metrics that are most meaningful for your organization.

Thanks to these and other obstacles, marketing professionals face real difficulty in selecting and using metrics effectively. Thus, it's not surprising that their efforts often meet with skepticism. But that doesn't mean your goal of becoming a marketing champion will always remain just out of reach. There *is* a way to surmount the metrics challenge, what we call a *marketing metrics audit process* — or Marketing MAP. The remainder of this chapter lays out the steps in this process.

Your Marketing Metrics Audit Process (Marketing MAP)

Your marketing MAP enables you to link marketing activities and the results of those activities to your firm's cash flow. This process consists of six steps:

1. Identify Your Firm's Cash-Flow Drivers

As Figure 5.1 shows, each organization generates cash through a small number of possible drivers. There are *sources* of cash, that is, where the cash comes from (such as acquiring new customers or getting them to spend more on your company's offerings). And there are different *business models*: how the cash is actually generated (such as velocity — turning over inventory more quickly).

Note that there are only a few sources of cash. These include *customer acquisition and retention; share of wallet within a category* (the frequency of purchasing in absolute terms or,

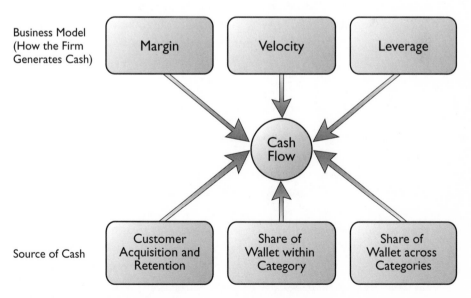

Figure 5.1 Step 1: Identify your company's cash-flow drivers.

more often, relative to the purchase of competing offerings);
and *share of wallet across categories* (sales of additional products
or services to existing customers).

Cash-flow drivers also derive from a company's business
model—its primary method for generating cash. Numerous
business models exist, as you saw in Chapter 4. But in most organizations, the business model is based predominantly on
margin (profit), *velocity,* or *leverage.* (You read definitions and
explanations of *velocity* and *leverage* in Chapter 2.) A company
that uses a margin-based business model measures margin as
net income (revenue minus costs) divided by sales revenue.
Velocity, or turnover of inventory, is measured by the amount
of finished goods or services sold within a given time period.
Leverage, or equity multiplier, is measured by the efficient
and effective use of the company's assets. Although all three of
these models are present in most firms, often one form dominates.

The first step in linking marketing activities to cash flow is
to identify your company's dominant cash-flow drivers: its
sources of cash *and* its primary business model. Understanding these, and routinely integrating them into your story about
how marketing contributes to the firm's performance, will go
a long way in establishing your credibility.

2. Identify the Marketing Activities and Metrics That Indirectly Affect Your Company's Cash-Flow Drivers

Your marketing department engages in a wide range of activities, and these activities produce many different outcomes.
Some of these outcomes are intermediate; that is, they don't
directly affect cash-flow drivers. Examples of intermediate outcomes may include brand awareness and sales leads. At this
step in the Marketing MAP, select those activities that indirectly influence your company's cash-flow drivers. Your list of
activities will be unique to your department because your
company's set of cash-flow drivers is unique.

Figure 5.2 depicts this notion of marketing activities and
intermediate marketing outcomes.

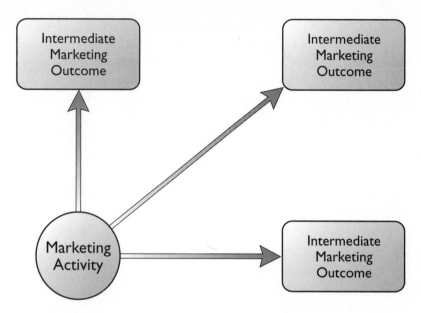

Figure 5.2 Step 2: Identify intermediate marketing outcomes.

When selecting activities that generate intermediate outcomes, consider your industry, your target customer segments, your organization's structure, your market position,
and your department's strategic goals.

For each marketing activity you identify, define an outcome metric — a measure that enables you to evaluate how
well the market activity generated the intended results. Such
metrics are likely to be those with which you are already
comfortable and use routinely. To illustrate, for a marketing
activity like execution of a specific television commercial, you
could define the outcome metric "brand preference." For a
marketing activity involving consumer promotions, you might
define the metric as "coupon redemption."

Note that your outcome metrics represent intermediate
results of particular marketing activities. For instance, for the
activity "participating in trade shows," you might define the
outcome metric "number of sales leads." Yet number of leads
is only an intermediate result. Leads don't necessarily turn
into sales (cash flow). Even if they do, some sales may only net

your company a demanding, unprofitable customer. In that latter case, the activity "participating in trade shows" actually has had a negative affect on cash flow. Likewise, for the marketing activity "creating a product web site," you may have defined the outcome metric "number of web-site hits." But if those hits don't result in sales, that activity has also failed to improve cash flow. Whenever you define an outcome metric that represents intermediate results not directly related to cash flow, you need to explicitly develop the links between the intermediate outcome and the sources and drivers of cash flow. This is where you develop your conceptual model — your story about how marketing works to influence cash flow. Step 3 shows you how.

3. Show How Each Outcome Metric Affects One or More Cash-Flow Drivers

For each intermediate outcome metric you've defined, articulate your theory of how successful performance on that metric (and its associated marketing activity) will affect one or more of your company's cash-flow drivers. For example, consider the three sources of cash. How might you influence customer acquisition and retention? How might you influence share of wallet within and across categories?

Also consider each of the three types of business models. You could influence margin by improving service quality to the extent that customers will pay a premium for your product or service. You could also influence margin by building brand preference (and therefore willingness to pay a premium) through advertising or loyalty programs. Brand preference might also make your brand less vulnerable to competitors' actions, such as price discounting. Some marketing actions are, in fact, defensive, so be sure to include effects like retaining share that would otherwise have been lost but for the marketing activity.

How might you influence velocity? You could do so with coupons or advertisements. You might increase distribution coverage or help your sales team close more sales. What about leverage? Is there an opportunity to extend a brand?

Figure 5.3 presents an example of how you could document your thinking about which intermediate outcome metrics affect which cash-flow drivers. To use such a worksheet, you would place a check mark in each box where you believe a particular intermediate marketing outcome metric affects a particular source of cash or your company's business model.

4. Test the Assumptions behind Your Cause-and-Effect Links

Clarifying the causal links between a marketing activity and cash flow is especially difficult when that activity produces an intermediate outcome that is not directly linked to cash flow. In such cases, you need to identify and test your assumptions

| | Cash-Flow Drivers | | | | | |
| | Source of Cash | | | Business Model | | |
	Customer Acquisition and Retention	Share of Wallet within Category	Share of Wallet across Category	Margin	Velocity	Leverage
Intermediate Marketing Outcome Metric						
Market Share		✓		✓		
Leads Generated	✓			✓	✓	
Purchase Intent	✓				✓	
Brand Preference (Equity; Loyalty)	✓	✓	✓	✓	✓	✓
Customer Satisfaction (Retention; Loyalty)	✓		✓	✓		
Coupon Redemption Rate		✓			✓	
Distribution Coverage	✓	✓			✓	

Note: This would be done for both short-term and long-term.

Figure 5.3 Step 3: Identify the links between intermediate metrics and cash-flow drivers.

about how the intermediate outcome ultimately will affect cash flow.

For example, if you're spending a significant portion of your marketing budget to improve customer satisfaction, and you're routinely measuring the results of such spending through customer-satisfaction surveys, what assumptions are you making about how greater customer satisfaction leads to more cash flow? Do you presume that more satisfied customers buy your more expensive products and thereby increase margin? That they buy more frequently from your company than from your competitors and thus improve share of wallet within category? That they buy more of the products offered by your firm and so improve the share of wallet across categories? Do you believe that satisfied customers tend to remain customers over time? If you dug deeply into purchasing data, would the data confirm the accuracy of your assumptions? Or would you discover, for example, that satisfied customers don't, in fact, buy more frequently from your company than from rival firms and have no greater probability of remaining customers than dissatisfied customers?

The more you can articulate your causal assumptions and gather data to confirm or disconfirm them, the more you can make a credible business case for which marketing activities will affect which cash-flow drivers — and how. Figure 5.4 depicts this concept.

Intermediate marketing outcomes are useful and even essential for marketing to perform its role in the firm. However, the use of intermediate outcome metrics can be misleading if you don't closely examine the assumptions behind them. This may be especially true among companies that employ sales representatives. The salespeople meet their revenue quotas (an outcome metric), so it appears that the sales force is generating value. The ROI in the sales force seems high. But if salespeople are going after quick, easy sales to meet their quotas, they may be hurting the company in the long run instead of helping it. Why? They could be targeting customers who buy low-margin products and who aren't likely to buy

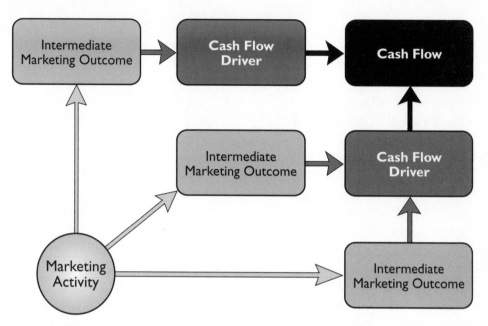

Figure 5.4 Step 4: Link marketing activities to Intermediate Outcomes and Cash Flow.

again — instead of going after relationship customers, who will pay more and buy more often. Unless you trace the link from the intermediate outcome metric (orders per sales call or revenue per call) to longer-term impacts on cash flow, you risk measuring the wrong dimensions of performance.

Activity, Efficiency, and Effectiveness: Measure the Right One

The challenge in Step 4 is to distinguish between metrics that help you gauge *activities,* such as how many sales calls were made or how many direct marketing mailers were dropped; *efficiency,* such as cost per thousand and cost per lead; and *effectiveness,* like redemption rate for coupons, brand preference, and distribution coverage. A cable television show, for example, may have an extraordinarily low cost per thousand (CPM), but if the viewers are not your company's target audience, why use this program? The lesson: Focus first on measures of effectiveness. Efficiency is meaningless if an activity is not effective, and continuing an activity that is not effective is silly, even if you can count how often you do it.

All too often marketers offer measures of activity or efficiency as substitutes for effectiveness. Reach and frequency are important but only if the right people are being reached and the message leads to sales. Cost per lead is also useful, but only if leads ultimately generate profitable sales. Product placement may be more efficient than a 30-second commercial in terms of gross rating points, but it may not be effective if consumers don't buy more of the product. A company may want to measure the number of new customers acquired. But if management does not consider the cost of serving and retaining new customers, which is often quite sizeable, the firm may end up acquiring expensive and therefore unprofitable customers. In this case, the activities designed to acquire customers are efficient but not effective. It makes no sense to compare alternative actions in terms of their efficiency unless you know that the actions are effective, that is, you can show that they generate cash flow.

Testing Your Assumptions

Testing your assumptions periodically even when you're certain about the link between an intermediate outcome metric and a driver can be useful. Harrah's Entertainment, like every other company in the gaming industry, long assumed that its best sources of cash flow were high-rollers — wealthy gamblers willing to drop $10,000 or more in an evening at the baccarat table. The company based its business model on attracting these customers with free flights, free hotel suites, free champagne, and more.

In 1994, Harrah's hired Brad Morgan as chief marketing officer. Formerly at Visa and P&G, Morgan began studying Harrah's customers. He found that people who spent between $100 and $499 per trip accounted for about 30 percent of the gamblers who visited Harrah's. Yet these same customers accounted for 80 percent of the company's revenue — and nearly 100 percent of its profits. These "avid experienced players" —

who mostly play slot machines, by the way — became Harrah's new target market.[3]

Here's another example of how you might test your assumptions regarding intermediate outcomes of marketing activities. Consider television advertising. For a given television commercial, you can obtain several intermediate results — such as reach, frequency, purchase intention, and brand preference. Let's also assume that you've drawn a link between these intermediate results and share of wallet within a category. That is, you believe that your company will generate more cash by increasing the frequency of purchase of your product relative to your competitor's products in the same category. (In other words, you believe that you will gain market share.) Let's also assume that your company has a margin-based business model.

How might you test your assumptions about the links between your intermediate outcomes and cash-flow drivers? Suppose you assume only that the more people who see your commercial (reach), the more customers will buy the product (at a given price). This is a testable proposition: Does greater reach actually result in more purchases by consumers? Inherent in the assumption that reach drives cash flow is the belief that the commercial's content has no impact. Yet you know that content is important — reach with the right content is really what drives cash flow, not reach alone. Thus, you'll need some way to measure the influence of the commercial content.

Intermediate measures obtained in copy testing allow you to project the influence of your ad's content to all consumers who see the commercial. But this assumes that you've ascertained a link between the specific copy test results and sales. If you want to accurately forecast sales resulting from the commercial, you need to be certain that your copy test bears a strong relationship to in-market sales. It's not just copy testing but the specific measure that comes out of the test. Does a

3. Christina Binkley, "Lucky Numbers: Casino Chain Mines Data on Its Gamblers," *The Wall Street Journal*, May 4, 2000, p. 1.

measure of purchase intention obtained really predict in-market sales? Does a brand preference metric provide infor-mation about future market share? And are some of these in-termediate metrics better than others in terms of prediction? The search for better intermediate metrics with stronger links to cash flow provides a solid foundation for continuous im-provement over time.

A Note about Data

All business-function executives gather data to test their as-sumptions about how their activities will affect cash flow and other aspects of their company's performance. By revising their assumptions as necessary, they formulate strategic rec-ommendations for their unit. But many business leaders wrongly believe that the strategic recommendations of execu-tives in operations, IT, R&D, and finance are grounded in much more solid data than recommendations provided by marketing executives. A finance or IT leader, for example, has solid figures. Marketing has only a promise and wishes, hopes, and dreams. Other departments have science. Market-ing has alchemy.

Yet what the other departments seldom discuss in detail in their reports and recommendations are the assumptions underlying their use of data — and there are plenty of them. These executives make guesses about developments as wide ranging as the cost of crude oil in six months, the probable re-sults of clinical trials, and changes in the federal interest rate. Gary John Previts, a professor of accountancy at Case West-ern Reserve University's Weatherhead School of Manage-ment observes: "Some would say the income behind return on investment is an estimate and not a fact, because income re-quires judgment. Depreciation is a guess and accrual-based measures are somewhat guessy."[4]

The issues are not that marketing makes assumptions, confronts uncertainty, and has to deal with soft data while

---

4. Robyn Goldwyn Blumenthal, "'Tis the Gift to Be Simple," *CFO Magazine*, January 1, 1998, pp. 61–63.

other functions do not. Rather the issues are, What are the assumptions and how do they stand up to scrutiny? How much uncertainty can we tolerate, and how much is reducing that uncertainty worth? How can we best use the data we have while gathering more valid and reliable data in the future? How can we be sure that there *is* a link from marketing activity to cash flow?

Nonmarketing executives often make assumptions that don't reflect reality. The head of operations assumes the firm will grow a steady 5 percent in the future and uses that assumption to craft strategies for the production line. Marketers, by contrast, know that markets don't grow in a linear, steady fashion. Thus, they're more aware of the uncertainties the firm faces than any other function. This awareness is part of the value they contribute and it should be turned into a virtue — but not at the expense of appearing soft.

Turning Uncertainty into a Virtue

Marketers study competition more than any department in the company. They study customers. And they know that uncertainty is inherent in both. Rather than being embarrassed by this situation, marketers must make a virtue of their understanding of uncertainty. By pointing out uncertainty, they are modeling risk management for other executives. As a marketing professional, you have a responsibility to alert your CEO, CFO, and other members of the executive team to uncertainties in your company's business and to lay out the assumptions you're making about your activities' impact. You study customers and markets, and you have a good idea of what will likely happen as the result of an action. One way to frame marketing-strategy discussions is to suggest what will happen if your organization does *not* engage in a certain marketing activity. For example, "If we cut the advertising budget two million dollars this quarter, here's what will happen — in the short and long term."

Kmart discovered the perils of underinvesting in advertising a few years ago. The chain decided to cut its Sunday circular advertising in half in September and October 2001 following cuts of 7.5 percent in ad pages in the first quarter and another 15 percent in the second. Kmart's objective was to cut costs and to switch customers from promotions to everyday low prices. While midweek traffic did perk up slightly, Kmart lost many weekend shoppers who relied on Sunday circulars. Sunday traffic dropped by double digits, and in the third quarter, Kmart lost $224 million, while same-store sales sank 1.5 percent.

"There is no doubt we made a mistake in cutting too much advertising too fast," said chairman and CEO Chuck Conaway at the time. "It also didn't help that we decreased our promotion when the competition increased theirs. Clearly we've learned where the threshold of pain is in advertising."[5] Kmart might have avoided all of this pain if the links between specific marketing activities, such as Sunday circular advertising and promotions, had been more clearly articulated and tested over time. It would not have been difficult to test the link between store traffic and Sunday circular advertising in a small market before making a decision that had national consequences.

5. Quantify Cash Flow Over Time

After testing your assumptions, estimate your marketing activities' impact on cash flow over time. Of course, under current accounting rules, companies must expense marketing costs. They cannot defer those costs to future periods when some of the results of an activity will occur. In addition, under generally accepted accounting practices, a company cannot take credit for revenue that has not yet been realized.

But these accounting conventions should not cause you to throw up your hands in despair. You can still make a compelling case for current marketing expenditures by linking them to cash flow over time. The brand you create today has the potential to generate a premium price and cash flow many

---

5. Debbie Howell, "Kmart Cuts Circulars," *DSN Retailing Today*, December 10, 2001, p. 1.

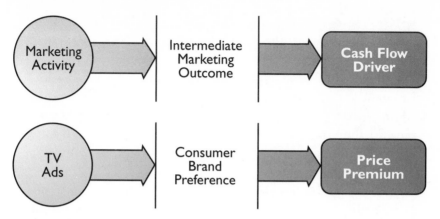

Figure 5.5 Step 5: Link marketing outcomes to future financial performance.

years down the road. Identify this long-term cash flow and quantify it in a defensible manner for your executive team — even as you recognize the underlying assumptions and uncertainties in your forecasts. Figure 5.5 depicts this concept.

6. Identify Future Opportunities for Your Firm

Marketers also create future opportunities for their firm, and these opportunities have value. For example, when your marketing function creates a brand, it also lays the foundation for opportunities to extend that brand in the future. Procter & Gamble, for instance, has extended Tide into all kinds of categories. Procter & Gamble was able to exploit these product-extension opportunities because it invested in creating its powerful Tide brand. Similarly, when Merrill Lynch invests in building a relationship with a customer, it creates opportunities to sell additional products and services to that same customer in the future.

So as you're applying the Marketing MAP, also identify promising opportunities you are creating for your firm to exploit in the future. What is the value of those opportunities? That may be hard to calculate, but finance people do it all the time — by putting a dollar figure on an option.

Tips for Selecting and Using Marketing Metrics

Now that you've walked through the Marketing MAP, take a moment to digest what you've just read. Clearly, defining marketing metrics for your work in your organization takes some careful thought. The following tips for selecting and using metrics provide additional support as you create your Marketing MAP.

- Define metrics that have clear links to company- and unit-level strategic objectives. An effective marketing metric represents outcomes of activities that support these goals.
- Keep it simple, especially when reporting unit performance to senior management. During such reporting sessions, identify the three or four key marketing metrics that are *most* clearly linked to the corporate strategy and cash flow.
- Select a mix of metrics that reflect both effectiveness and efficiency. For example, while number of leads (efficiency) is important, the share of leads that ends in a sale (effectiveness) is an even more vital metric.
- Define leading (forward-looking) metrics (such as brand preference) and lagging (backward-looking) metrics (such as sales and number of new customers acquired). Convert leading indicators into forecasts of demand and then translate those forecasts into future cash flow. And be sure that your forecasts incorporate known or anticipated changes in the market, in competitive activity, and your firm's own marketing activities.
- Keep your eye on the competition and overall market. Define metrics — such as market share and profitability — that help you gauge how your organization is performing compared to the competition.
- Involve stakeholders — such as your CFO — in defining your marketing metrics. Establishing new performance metrics or revising existing ones constitutes a major cultural change and requires broad-based buy-in.

- Recruit objective judges from finance or another function outside of marketing to audit your measures and help establish credibility for data and underlying assumptions. This process should also help settle turf battles. In addition, it provides a basis for objectivity, credibility, and continuous improvement.
- Set realistic expectations for which marketing programs can be measured meaningfully.
- Define the relevant metrics first; then consider how you'll gather the data needed to evaluate performance on those metrics. Also consider which technology you might need to gather the data.
- Use actual performance data on your metrics to create a culture of continuous improvement.
- Make decisions based on data, rather than your intuition or others' energetically voiced arguments. Without data, decisions get made by those who have the most political clout.
- Be careful what you measure. You want measures that move you in the right direction.
- Use your metrics to communicate — North, South, East, and West.

See the following box for an example of how savvy selection and use of marketing metrics can pay big dividends for a company.

◆◆◆◆◆

Marketing at a Mortgage Bank: A Case in Point

One of the United States' largest retail mortgage originators has nearly 1,500 loan officers (LOs) operating nationwide. The role of marketing is to support LOs' efforts to sell mortgages across the country.

Cash flow at the mortgage bank is a function of margins (the spread between the cost of capital and the mortgage interest rate) and velocity (the volume of mortgages sold). The firm targets two relationship-focused customer segments. These include *advice seekers* (24 percent of the market) and *people with more money than time* (13 percent). Together, these two customer segments represent over one-third (37 percent) of the total mortgage market. Moreover, profit margins are highest in these segments. That's because end customers are willing to pay a bit extra for the service of an LO who they feel cares about them and who ensures that the high-stakes transaction unfolds smoothly.

The more loans an LO writes, the more money the bank makes. To build their own businesses, LOs want to sell; they don't want to spend time on marketing. They want to close deals; they don't want to develop communications that may or may not yield new business. The effort required to build a mortgage loan business leaves little time for creating communications to keep in touch with existing and prospective customers.

So the mortgage bank realized that it could increase its own cash flow (as well as help LOs build their businesses) by assisting LOs in identifying high-margin customers and completing transactions more quickly. Toward this end, the bank's senior vice president (SVP) of marketing created the *Media Center* system, which provided automated marketing services for LOs. If the bank could do the marketing for the LOs, he reasoned, the LOs would be more productive, and both they and the company would benefit. The SVP also contended that the system could help the mortgage bank recruit and retain loan officers because the service was unique to the company's LOs. Most of the bank's competitors offered signing bonuses to attract talented LOs, but, unlike the automated marketing services, the effectiveness of bonuses (the SVP reasoned) were short lived and didn't help lenders build long-term connections with their best producers.

Understanding the company's business strategy as defined by the CEO, the SVP identified three cash-flow drivers:

1. LO acquisition.
2. LO productivity (velocity).
3. LO retention.

The new Media Center was designed to advance each of these drivers. However, the marketing group had never systematically tracked its impact on these drivers, and top management challenged the group to justify its investment in the new system. Until it received this call for action, marketing had focused so intently on its ever-growing list of activities that it hadn't concerned itself with key metrics associated with the firm's business success. The marketing team had long relished the creative aspect of its work and produced brilliant programs to wow loan officers and, in turn, top management. Its members had extensive experience in designing compelling communications programs, including newsletters, post cards, LO web sites, and gift mailings. The senior marketing team also delivered LO orientation and training programs across the country.

Recognizing that customers in the mortgage bank's targeted market segments are generated largely by realtor referrals, the marketing group created a Realtor-in-a-Box program that provided automated marketing services for realtors making it likely that realtors would give referrals to the bank's LOs.

The Realtor-in-a-Box program generated impressive results in the form of growth in LO participation. And the marketing staff took great satisfaction in reporting these results to top management. They also enthusiastically shared the written testimonials and stories they received from many LOs.

Yet top management became increasingly uncertain of the marketing group's business impact. Executives wanted proof that innovative marketing programs were generating measurable financial results. That meant linking marketing activities and metrics to cash-flow drivers. The marketing group conducted the following Marketing MAP process.

Marketing's Impact on LO Acquisition

Surveys of LOs had shown that a leading reason for joining the bank was the Media Center. LOs saw the automated marketing system as a way to gain an advantage in the competitive marketplace because the system freed them to focus on closing deals.

However, the marketing group had to express this competitive advantage in financial terms. For example, how much less did the mortgage bank pay to recruit new LOs, compared to what rival companies paid? The marketing team quantified the advantage in two ways: First, it determined that rival companies paid an average signing bonus of $10,000 per LO. Second, it calculated the Media Center's cost savings in executive recruiter fees, which came to roughly one-third of LOs' average annual compensation.

Marketing's Impact on LO Productivity

To continue the assessment, the SVP asked the question, "Were the LOs who used the Media Center more productive than LOs who didn't? That is, did they sell more mortgages?" Fortunately, the data existed for these two groups to support the analysis, which confirmed that the answer was a resounding yes. In fact, LOs using the Media Center closed, on average, one loan per month, or 12 per year, more than nonmembers. By taking the average profit of an average loan the marketing group was able to express its impact on LO productivity.

The higher productivity of Media Center members generated another benefit as well: increased end-customer satisfaction (a marketing metric), as revealed in customer surveys. But increased end-customer satisfaction alone did not express the impact in financial terms. Marketing had to link this intermediate marketing metric to a financial metric. Using the survey data, marketing showed that this increased satisfaction in turn led to increases in referrals and repeat end customers. The team was then able to easily translate the additional referrals and repeat customers into profits. Even Wall Street, the marketing group knew, takes notice when a mortgage company's LO production (or velocity) is higher than the industry average, thus helping to boost the stock price.

Marketing's Impact on LO Retention

The retention rate for LOs who were Media Center members was 25 percent higher than that of nonmembers. Clearly, marketing had exerted a significant impact on this key metric. Once again, however, the marketing team still needed to articulate the impact of the higher retention rate (an intermediate result) in financial terms.

To that end, the SVP expressed the Media Center's cash-flow value as 25 percent of loans written over the course of the year by members, multiplied by a 10 percent margin on each loan. That's the revenue contribution from increased LO retention. He then applied the retention rate over several years to derive the lifetime value of an LO. Of course, this analysis assumed that the Media Center *caused* retention rates to improve. An alternative theory could hold that more ambitious LOs were drawn to the Media Center, and were more likely than less ambitious LOs to stay with the company. If this were the case, top management might reasonably have discounted some of the financial impact the marketing group had calculated. Nevertheless, the SVP's analysis went a long way to establish one significant element of the financial value that the marketing team had generated.

Putting It All Together

By totaling up all the incremental cash flow generated by marketing's impact on LO acquisition, productivity, and retention, the bank's marketing team demonstrated the financial value it had created. To calculate their net financial impact, the staff subtracted all the costs of producing the new cash flow (for example, staff, materials, technology, overhead, and so forth) from the extra cash flow.

The bottom line result of this marketing initiative: The CEO and others now understand how marketing contributes financial value to the business. Marketing is now recognized as a significant contributor to business impact, not just the creator of a growing list of flashy communications programs.

◆◆◆◆◆

As the story of marketing at the mortgage bank reveals, defining and using the right marketing metrics can help you provide quantifiable proof of the value that your activities deliver. By showing marketing's connection to measurable financial results, you can also make a compelling business case for your initiatives to your CEO, CFO, and other Northern constituencies. The Marketing MAP thus constitutes a powerful tool in this sector of the marketing landscape.

It's going to take numbers with financial significance to demonstrate how marketing makes business impact. Take it from Fred Reichheld, the loyalty guru with the management consulting firm, Bain & Co, and proponent of a metric he calls the "net promoter score as a strong indicator of future growth." Reichheld said, "Accounting has become the universal language of business. [But] accountants can't tell the difference between good and bad profits. Cash flow comes out of customer wallets, but that is not entirely obvious the way most companies measure their performance and motivate their troops." Reichheld believes, as we have been saying throughout this book, that marketing has lost its connection to business strategy. He says, "It seems strategy got pulled away. What got left was advertising and promotion, not how it all fit together to create a winning experience for the customers and shareholders."[6] When you identify the business-critical metrics that marketing influences, you stand a good chance to win back marketing's connection to good cash flow.

6. Michael Krauss, "Create Customer Promoters, Avoid Detractors," *Marketing News*, April 1, 2006, pp. 10–11.

PART THREE

Manage East

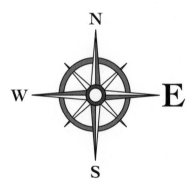

6

Bust Silos and Build Bridges

In Chapters 3 through 5, you discovered strategies for Managing North — that is, making marketing matter to your CEO and CFO and using performance metrics to demonstrate marketing's power to generate value for your organization. In this chapter as well as in Chapters 7 and 8, we'll shift our gaze from North to East — to the peer functions (such as sales and R&D) with which you must interact productively in order to fulfill marketing's promise.

This chapter focuses on the functional silos in general — interdepartmental tensions, conflicts, and miscommunications — that prevent marketers from collaborating effectively with peer managers throughout the company. Silos keep your organization from providing customers with the best possible experiences and offerings. Like audiences attending a play, your customers don't care about backstage squabbles over scenery, lighting, and lines: They've come for the show. And they want a seamless experience.

Because you and your team have the deepest understanding of your company's customers, you must take the initiative in dismantling interdepartmental silos that threaten the quality of your customers' experiences with the firm. You'll then need to replace those silos with bridges that create a seamless experience — and the impression of a united front — for customers.

In this chapter, we examine the nature of silos and the reasons they arise. And we offer guidelines for how you might replace silos with cross-functional bridges. In Chapter 7, we sharpen our focus further on building positive relationships with the sales staff. Sales is a particularly vital Eastern constituency in your company because most executives associate short-term cash flow with sales more than with any other department. And in Chapter 8, we explore ways to collaborate effectively with R&D, another key Eastern partner, to delight your customers. The R&D group is an important constituency because many executives strongly associate it with the source of innovation for long-term cash flow.

A CLOSER LOOK AT SILOS

Silos are the invisible but often destructive barriers that can arise between functions in a company. They may take the form of unwillingness to communicate, to share information, and to collaborate as well as a tendency to compete over resources. Though silos can hamper a company's operations, they arise for understandable reasons. Business functions — marketing, sales, finance, operations, R&D, human resources — each have distinct objectives. And these different goals can lead to an us-versus-them mind-set on the part of managers and employees from the various functions.

As a business grows or changes, silos may also take shape for political, economic, or structural reasons. For example, a company acquires another enterprise, and managers at the acquired entity try to differentiate their responsibilities in the hopes of protecting their jobs — a common political maneuver. Or managers in a company suffering budget cuts may hunker down inside their departments and take a me-versus-them mentality to ensure that they get a piece of the dwindling pie. Or a firm expands globally, and its satellite offices set up structures, systems, and processes that isolate it from headquarters.

Silos aren't necessarily always destructive. Indeed, sometimes they create efficiency. For instance, when Henry Ford was innovating mass production, it made sense to have one worker on the line screwing nuts onto vehicles' rear left wheels, while others performed similar specialized activities.

Specializing work in this way enabled Ford to produce vehicles quickly and efficiently, and the resulting silos remained hidden from customers' eyes.

But in many companies, silos create difficulties that become visible to customers and thus sour their experiences with and perceptions of the firm. This is particularly true when employees in different functions are unwittingly working at cross-purposes owing to conflicting goals or compensation systems. For example, in a retail store, salespeople who earn a salary may adopt a relaxed manner with customers, helping them to find what they need but avoiding aggressive selling. Meanwhile, customer-service reps who earn bonuses for cross-selling to customers while processing their phone orders may adopt an aggressive stance with callers. Customers who visit the store *and* order from the company by phone may have totally different experiences and grow confused and frustrated by what they see as mixed messages coming from the enterprise.

Lack of shared information about a customer's status can also spawn negative perceptions of a firm. Consider Sally's plight: A married woman with a home-based business, Sally wanted to link her personal checking account to both her husband's account and her business's account to make electronic transferal of funds across the accounts easier. She went to the bank and filled out the required forms. But a month later, when she logged onto the bank's web site to transfer funds from one account to the other, the online service wouldn't allow the transaction. Sally phoned the bank and was told that the accounts "weren't shown as linked in our system" and that she would have to fill out the forms yet again. The bank had recently been acquired and had outsourced its customer service function. Owing to the resulting chaos, the phone reps didn't have the information they needed to handle complaints such as Sally's. Her frustration rising, she decided to switch banks.

Companies that provide services rather than products can be particularly damaged by functional silos. Consider a hotel. Management must smoothly coordinate a huge range of processes — all performed by different teams — in order to ensure that each guest has a satisfying experience in his or her dealings with the hotel. These processes include guest check in and check out, room preparation, room service, restaurant service, business center services, and so on. If even one of those processes experiences a glitch, a guest may well consider the entire stay unsatisfactory. Think about times you've traveled for business or pleasure. If your room's high-speed Internet connection doesn't work, you'll likely feel highly frustrated, no matter how nice the hotel is otherwise. If your nonsmoking room stinks of ashes, you probably won't care how efficiently the front desk handled your check in.

Process glitches often stem from poor communication across functions. For instance, if the housekeeping staff can't directly inform the maintenance staff that the toilet in room 336 is broken, but must go through a manager instead, the repair takes longer to complete, and the hotel risks annoying the customer. The box titled "The Ritz-Carlton: Silo-Buster Extraordinaire" shows how one major hotel chain avoids the destructive impact of silos in this competitive service industry.

◆◆◆◆◆

The Ritz-Carlton: Silo-Buster Extraordinaire

The Ritz-Carlton hotel chain does an impressive job of eradicating silos so that guests have a consistently positive experience. Every morning, the entire staff of each hotel meets to address service issues. Participants include gardeners, housekeeping staff, the restaurant wait persons, the front-desk staff, and so forth. If a guest's luggage wasn't delivered to her room in a timely basis, the staff member who received the complaint lets other employees know about it. That evening, as the guest takes his or her seat in the dining room, the waiter might say, "We understand you had a delay in getting your luggage. Please accept a complementary dessert as our way of apologizing for the inconvenience."

Through ongoing communication, the Ritz coordinates service across the hotel and demonstrates its awareness of and appreciation for guests' concerns. This kind of careful coordination among functions can go a long way toward overcoming a negative experience—so customers keep coming back for more.

Of course, the Ritz-Carlton has enormous resources at its disposal and has built its brand on the notion of the highest-end service possible. Not all organizations can say the same. However, that doesn't mean this example isn't relevant for your company. No matter how large or small your firm is, how deep its pockets, or how sterling its services or products, you can still find opportunities to bust silos. Indeed, you must—if you hope to help your company present a seamless, high-value experience to your customers, whoever they may be.

◆◆◆◆◆

The recent explosion of customer touch points in many companies has made silos more dangerous than ever. *Touch points* are the many ways in which a customer interacts with a company. In a hotel, these points include the front desk, the housekeeping staff, the concierge, the restaurant workers — everyone whom a guest may encounter (face -to-face or otherwise) before, during, and after staying at the hotel. In a retail business, touch points may include sales rep visits or phone calls, marketing communications, call center services, the company's web site and physical store, and postsales service technicians.

With the proliferation of touch points, the risk of miscommunication between functions — and resulting confusion and annoyance for customers — has increased. Consider the Royal Bank of Canada. In the early 1990s, the bank invested heavily in making its services as convenient as possible for customers. Executives assumed that more convenience would attract new customers and increase existing customers' loyalty. The company built new branches, extended its hours of operation, installed more ATMs, added online access, and began offering insurance, investment, and other new services. But a survey revealed that people don't choose a bank based on its convenience. Instead, they want "a bank that demonstrably cares about them, values their business, and recognizes them as the same individuals no matter what part of the bank they do business with."[1] It's difficult to explain to a customer who has a home-equity line of credit why the bank needs him or her to fill out yet another application for a retirement account — a document that asks for much of the same information provided in the first form he or she filled out.

SILOS AND YOU

So what does all this talk about silos have to do with you? Unfortunately, the silos between a company's marketing function and its other functions can prove particularly damaging. Take marketing and R&D. Experts from both functions are smart and well trained and could learn a lot from each other. But in many companies, management asks R&D to operate in a vacuum. Research and developments's goal is to come up with new products or services without considering their cost or market demand. Management rationalizes this approach with something like, "We don't want to put any constraints on creativity." Unlike the marketing staff, the people working in an R&D group may never talk with customers. Instead, they create wonderful products in their laboratory. These offerings might deliver impressive-sounding benefits — but the benefits may be irrelevant to customers, as we saw in the Royal Bank of Canada's initial drive to enhance convenience. Or the products may cost so much to manufacture that customers wouldn't be willing to pay the premium price the company would need to charge to make a profit on the offerings.

At the 2005 Frankfurt Auto Show, the CEO of Volkswagen AG, said, "The biggest failure in Volkswagen is too little customer focus." Volkswagen managers and engineers paid too much attention to technology and features that customers didn't want to pay for. He said that even though features make sense to engineers, they don't necessarily belong on cars: "The

---

1. Jay Gulati and James B. Oldroyd, "The Quest for Customer Focus," *Harvard Business Review*, April 2005, p. 3.

first question is, how does the feature help the customer? And will the customer pay for it?"[2]

Here's another example of silos between marketing and other functions — in this case, operations. A company's operations team typically wants to run the firm's factory as cost-effectively as possible. To meet that goal, the operations manager advocates long production runs to spread manufacturing costs over many units. Meanwhile, the marketing group — after analyzing rival firms' order-delivery times and product quality — determines that the company must deliver customized orders within two business days to remain competitive. The two functions' goals conflict with one another: If operations uses long production runs to manufacture one item before changing over to manufacture another item, the company can't very well crank out custom-built products quickly enough to fulfill the two-day delivery goal.

Sometimes a company's marketing department contributes to silo building. For example, we've heard some R&D people say that when their company's marketing practitioners go off to survey customers' preferences, opinions, or perceptions, the information they bring back is useless. To illustrate, what does "The customer wants a more reliable product" mean for R&D in practical terms? What, precisely, should the R&D staff do with this finding as they develop products?

Busting Silos: Five Tactics

Silo busting isn't easy. It requires major changes in a company's culture and processes, and it means that employees throughout the organization must begin doing their work in new ways and defining their priorities differently. Often, a silo-busting initiative succeeds only when top management visibly and vocally supports it — and when changes in compensation systems reward cross-functional collaboration. If your company's management team is leading a silo-busting

---

2. Joseph B. White and Stephen Power, "VW Chief Confronts Corporate Culture," *The Wall Street Journal*, September 19, 2005, p. B2.

effort in your firm, do all you can to support the effort. For example, as we explain more in the following sections, you can actively offer to join cross-functional teams and spend more time learning what your colleagues in other parts of the organization do.

But in many companies, top management is reluctant to initiate and lead a silo-busting program. The typical CEO, for example, is more worried about making stockholders and his or her board of directors happy than fussing over the company's internal problems. If this describes the situation in your firm, eradicating silos will prove particularly difficult. However, you can still help chip away at your company's silos, particularly those that have the most significance for marketing's influence. The effort will pay big dividends — not only for your company but also for you. When you bust silos, you connect your activities to those of other parts of your organization, enabling your firm to provide a unified, seamless experience for customers. *Customers* buy more from the enterprise. And *you* win a company-wide reputation as a cash-flow leader. Your reward? Greater clout throughout the firm, and a more powerful impact on important decisions.

The following sections present five particularly potent silo-busting tactics.

Focus Your Colleagues' Attention on the Customer

To help break down silos, focus managers throughout your organization on one question: How can we satisfy our customers better? Answering that question requires an understanding of what customers want from your company and how silos are preventing your company from fulfilling those wants. As a marketing professional, you can articulate these answers in terms that other managers can understand:

- "Customers want to be known by our company — whether they choose to interact with us face-to-face in our stores, by phone, through e-mail, through the U.S. Postal Ser-

vice, or in all of these ways. They don't want to have to provide the same information to the different parts of our company because those parts aren't communicating with one another."

• "Customers want us to fill their orders quickly and
accurately. They don't want to wait endlessly for their order
because, in order to control costs, we've committed to long
production runs."

• "If customers experience a problem with an order, or
with our products or services, they want us to solve the problem promptly, pleasantly, and permanently. They're not interested in hearing about how our staffing shortage or our latest
reorganization is the reason we sent them the wrong product,
charged them the wrong price, delivered their order late, or
shipped them a defective item."

• "Customers want to tell us about their problem once —
not over and over again as we hand them off from one department to another because our IT systems aren't talking to each
other."

Once you've articulated what customers want from
your firm and how silos are preventing your company from
fulfilling those wants, explain to the management team and
your peer managers how these failures are hurting your
firm's financial performance — particularly cash flow, sales,
and growth. Use compelling numbers that paint a graphic picture that everyone can understand viscerally. For example,
"We lost two major, longstanding customers last quarter to
BestCo — our biggest competitor — because of repeated mistakes in their orders. These customers' defection translates
into two hundred and fifty thousand dollars that's now fatten-
ing BestCo's bank account instead of ours."

Also consider drawing on respected research to make
your point. For instance, "I'm holding in my hand the latest research findings from Marketplace Analysts. This report contains some disturbing news. It shows that a customer who has
to phone a company more than once to get his problem solved

is *ten times more likely to defect* to another firm than a customer who gets his problem solved in one phone call. And a customer who's forced to call several times will tell fifteen friends about his annoying experience — while the customer whose problem is solved on the first call tells only five friends about the positive experience. So every time we fail to solve a customer's problem on the first call because sales and customer service aren't talking to each other, we're activating a very damaging word-of-mouth cycle."

Even presented with compelling statistics and anecdotes showing the destructive impact of silos on your firm, your executive team and peer managers may respond only slowly to the notion of eradicating silos and focusing on the customer. That's okay, and it's to be expected. Cultural change on the order of what we're talking about here takes time and patience.

However, once executives and managers are convinced of the benefits of focusing on customers, the impact can prove dramatic. Take Harrah's Entertainment. The company began collecting customer information in a dedicated way in 1997 when it instituted its Total Gold frequent-gambler card. The cards gathered minutiae on gamblers' habits in exchange for letting guests know how to attain free drinks, hotel rooms, show tickets, and other rewards. The idea was that gamblers would bet more if they knew what they needed to do to get a freebie.

But it didn't work out that way. Freebie levels differed from one Harrah's casino to the next, confusing customers. And casino managers (still suffering from a silo mind-set) did not want to share their customer data with their counterparts at other properties. Harrah's executives were drowning in data they didn't know how to use. "I went through a period of frustration," says Phil Satre, Harrah's chairman and chief executive. "I said, 'Why isn't any of this stuff working?'"

In desperation, he talked to Sergio Zyman, then Coca-Cola's marketing chief. Zyman recommended that Satre hire a chief operating officer (COO) with a marketing background. With authority over all 22 Harrah's properties and over the company's operating vice presidents, the new COO could make marketing the driving force in the entertainment giant. Satre thought of Gary Loveman, a Harvard Business School marketing professor who had consulted to Harrah's about marketing and training. He offered the COO job, and Loveman took it.

As his first strategic move, Loveman replaced all of Harrah's existing marketing staff with marketers who had data-crunching skills and knew how to work with IT. "[The original staff] were never going to get our program where it needed to go," he says. And they were "never going to build the decision tools or be able to plot out the mathematics of this program the way we needed. So we brought in the kind of people we have now, who have the horsepower to do this kind of work . . . . We created a marketing council. I chaired it as the senior operator and the senior marketer, and I brought together three of the four senior corporate marketing people and the four senior field marketing people as well as our outside agencies, our PR agencies, and our senior technology person, because so much of our marketing runs through technology systems . . . . It's an effort to make sure that all our marketing work is a collaboration between corporate and the field and that everybody owns these decisions."[3]

Harrah's new marketing staff members turn the data the company generates into usable information and conduct experiments to produce even more data. For example, the company discovered that customers who received $60 in free chips gambled more than customers who received a free room, two steak dinners, and $30 in free chips. Profits from the new promotion nearly doubled to $60 per person per trip.

Today, through sophisticated customer-satisfaction surveys, Harrah's can measure the revenue it will gain by moving a customer to a higher satisfaction level. "They can do any

3. From a Conference Board Marketing Conference presentation "Marketing and IT Teaming to Grow Revenue and Profit," by David Norton, SVP of Relationship Marketing, and Tim Stanley, CIO of Harrah's Entertainment, October 2003, and an interview with Gary Loveman, CEO, in the *McKinsey Quarterly* 2003, Number 2.

business initiative and target specific customers and feed back how it changed their satisfaction levels and their spending," says Mark Jeffery, who teaches executive education at the Kellogg School of Management at Northwestern University. "That gives them a huge competitive advantage." Jeffery studied best practices in IT portfolio management. Of the 130 *Fortune* 1000 companies he evaluated, Harrah's ranked first. "Everything I teach in executive education, these guys are doing. They blew me away," he says.[4]

Leverage Technology

In addition to focusing everyone on the customer, you can use technology to build bridges between marketing and other parts of your company. Software (and now the web) can enable the easy transfer of customer information among your company's many different customer touch points — including the back office, where production and finances are handled.

However, owing to legacy systems, leveraging such technology can prove difficult. If your company is like most, it contains scores of separate customer databases created and maintained by different groups. For example, accounting will have one database to track financial numbers, and marketing may have a different database to track customers. Of course, if you want to tie customers to the financial impact on a company, these two databases need to communicate with each other. Some firms have tried to integrate their many databases by implementing *middleware* — software that links the various databases together. The problem is that the databases were never originally set up to talk to each other, so this tactic often turns into an IT nightmare. The IT staff must try to learn the

4. Christina Binkley, "Lucky Numbers: Casino Chain Mines Data on Its Gamblers and Strikes Pay Dirt," *The Wall Street Journal*, May 4, 2000, p. 1; Carol Pogash, "From Harvard Yard to Vegas Strip, Forbes.com, http://www.forbes.com/asap/2002/1007/048; Kathleen Melymuyka, "Betting on IT value: Harrah's has a sophisticated process for tracking the true payback of IT projects," *Computerworld*, May 3, 2004, p. 33.

structure of all the databases and then design or buy software that will make all the connections work. As in many situations in business, the prospect for disruption that such integration can cause often scares executives away from supporting the initiative.

A far easier technology solution is to employ a customer relationship management (CRM) system. These systems consist of integrated databases and software. Often, CRM suppliers are willing to do the heavy lifting of integrating with your legacy systems. CRM systems are built from the ground up, but their main advantage is that the entire system's starting point is the customer and the effort to make buying and interacting with your company a seamless and satisfying experience.

However, the urge to protect turf can create resistance to using a CRM system. For example, salespeople may assume that if they input all their knowledge of customers into the system, it will be available to everybody, and the company will no longer need them. Though understandable on one level, this concern misses an important point: A salesperson's value resides not in the customer data he carries in his or her head or PDA (personal digital assistant)—but in the relationships and personal connections the rep cultivates with customers.

Software that automates salespeople's contacts and schedules for visiting or phoning customers can support such relationship building. For example, a salesperson can go online first thing in the morning and obtain messages from customers who are having problems. Marketers can further reinforce this technology's value by sharing what they know about the customer—such as knowledge about a particular customer segment and ways to appeal to that segment. For instance, perhaps the firm is about to introduce a new portfolio of products that the salesperson could mention to customers from the relevant segment when he contacts them.

Customer relationship management technology is expensive, and if it's not used properly, it can waste a great deal of a company's time and money. If you want to get the most out of your system, start by understanding that information is power and that various parts of the organization might be threatened by turning over their information to a software solution. This isn't an easy barrier to overcome, but it's an essential first step.

You can also take a lesson from the history of innovation adoption and make sure people can see how using a CRM system is compatible with the ways they've been working in the past. It is well known, for example, that people are less likely to adopt a new way of doing things when they see it as incompatible with their prior behaviors. For this reason, you cannot simply buy some CRM software and expect people to start using it. Instead, plan on some training time and consider ways to encourage people to use the system.

Of course, adopting CRM doesn't automatically mean you'll gain its promised benefits. That's because, like all software, CRM comes with lots of different features and capabilities. Often, these prove so overwhelming that people avoid using the software. Here are some suggestions for getting people to derive some quick benefits from this tool.

First, focus your initial CRM efforts on reducing pain. Where in your company are you losing the most money or seeing the worst inefficiency? Start there. For example, you might be extremely inefficient with order entry, or you're losing lots of money because the sales force isn't getting timely marketing materials. Or perhaps people who respond to your e-mail campaigns are never showing up as sales force leads. Bite off these smaller pain points first. When you show improvement, you can move on to the myriad other features most good CRM systems have.

Once you've focused on the main pain points, you'll quickly realize that a CRM system captures a lot of data. Make sure to devote time to analyzing this data. Indeed, this is the ideal opportunity for you to help others in your organization extract the full value of a CRM system. Use the data to demonstrate how customers are making purchase decisions, which points in the organization they are touching, what problems they are running into, and other insights. The more you understand, the more opportunities you will find to initiate other valuable marketing efforts that are intimately tied to cash flow, such as up-selling and cross-selling.

Spotlight Common Goals

Another effective way to replace silos with bridges between marketing and your company's functions is to foster mutual understanding of one another's concerns and encourage information sharing. To apply this practice, you must model such behavior yourself. For example, as often as you can, have lunch or meet informally with your counterparts in R&D, sales, IT, manufacturing, and other functions. Find out what these colleagues' most pressing challenges are. Share similar information with them. These exchanges will help all participants expand their view of the company and may generate insights about how you might help each other.

Regular networking with your peers — whether through lunches, informal hallway chats, or meetings — can also help you become familiar with one another's skills and expertise. Once you're more aware of what each of you brings to the company, you can draw on one another's abilities to solve cross-functional problems.

As you spend time with colleagues, don't limit your conversations to just business. Also discuss outside interests and hobbies. In particular, look for interests you might have in common with a peer — whether it's long-distance running, community outreach work, cooking, antique car restoration, or some other passion. When people discover shared interests, they more easily form a bond of mutual liking. And when people like one another, they tend to have more influence with each other and a greater willingness to resolve differences and collaborate — essential ingredients for busting silos.

Whenever you gather with peers from other functions, also look for signs of silos. For instance, suppose you're having lunch one day with the head of your company's retail stores, and she mentions how online sales of the retail store's products are cannibalizing her profits. In this case, you might begin breaking down this silo by helping to devise an acceptable way for each store to offer different products.

Finally, further solidify your bridges to peer managers by asking for their opinions whenever you have an idea for an important new marketing initiative or program. Explain your idea to them, and get their thoughts about how the project might affect them and what cross-functional implementation challenges the initiative might raise. By inviting peers' input early on, you boost your chances of winning their support for your idea. And you learn more about how activities initiated in the marketing department can have repercussions — both good and bad — in other parts of the company.

Through all these means, you become what's known as a *silo spanner* — a person who helps managers throughout the company understand one another's perspectives, look beyond functional differences to shared concerns and challenges, and work together more productively. Silo spanners often become the go-to people from whom other managers seek advice and ideas. They thus exert enormous influence in their organizations. See the box titled "Marissa Mayer: Silo Spanner" for a particularly apt example.

◆◆◆◆◆

Marissa Mayer: Silo Spanner

Marissa Mayer's success at Google derives from her ability to travel easily between different worlds, write the editors of *Business Week*. "When she first joined [Google], the company had something of a high-school cliquishness, albeit in reverse. At lunch, the coolest kids—in this forum, the smartest geeks—sat together. On the periphery, sales and marketing folks gathered." Mayer, who is now Google's director of consumer web products, could hold her own in either realm. "She's a geek, but her clothes match," quips one former employee.

Mayer continues to bridge the gap between MBAs and PhDs, according to *Business Week*. "She helps decide when employees' pet projects are refined enough to be presented to the company's founders.

Such decisions are often made through an established process, with Mayer giving ideas a hearing during her open office hours or during brainstorming sessions. Yet she is also good at drawing out programmers informally, during a chance meeting in the cafeteria or hallway."[5]

◆◆◆◆◆

Seek Out Cross-Functional Teams

Participating in and leading cross-functional teams can also help you bust silos. Cross-functional teams contain at least three members from diverse functions — sales, marketing, and finance, for example; or marketing, operations, and IT — all of whom are working together toward a common goal. A cross-functional team is typically responsible for all or some segment of a process intended to deliver a product or service to an external or internal customer. For example, people from marketing and product development can comprise a cross-functional team focused on developing products that marketing has determined customers really want. Because the team's work requires input from several functions, collaboration is essential. When led properly, cross-functional teams enable a company to accomplish important objectives with flexibility and speed, coupled with multidisciplinary knowledge.[6]

Yet we've discovered that marketing's participation in such interdepartmental collaboration is sketchy. In our survey of MarketingProfs readers in organizations with 1,000 or more employees, we asked, "To what extent do you work collaboratively with the functions listed below?" The choices ranged from "not at all" to "a lot." Figure 6.1 shows the results.

Seventy-seven percent of the respondents who work in business-to-business (B-to-B) organizations say they work a lot with sales, while only 52 percent of the respondents who work in business-to-consumer (B-to-C) organizations do so.

5. Ben Elgin, "Managing Google's Idea Factory," *Business Week*, October 3, 2005, p. 88.

6. "Crossfunctional Teams," http://best.me.berkeley.edu/-pps/teams.html.

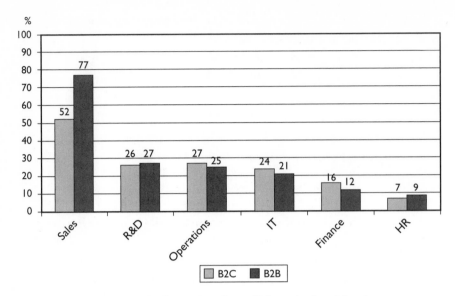

Figure 6.1 Extent marketing works collaboratively with other functions (% saying "A Lot" for each function). *Source:* Survey of MarketingProfs readers in organizations with 1,000 or more employees, 2005; question reads: "To what extent do you work collaboratively with the functions listed below?" Choices are "not at all," "not very much," "somewhat," "a lot," and "not applicable."

The different percentages are likely due to the tendency for B-to-B firms to rely more heavily on sales as compared to advertising.

However, as the figure indicates, collaboration between marketing and other functions — R&D, operations, IT, finance, and human resources (HR) — is much rarer. Only 27 percent of the B-to-B respondents work extensively with R&D, and only 26 percent of the consumer marketing respondents do. The responses are almost the same for collaboration with operations and IT, with significantly less collaboration between marketing and the finance and HR groups.

What explains these dismal numbers? The likely culprit is underestimation of marketing's value on the part of managers in these other functions. Consider Figure 6.2, which shows responses to our survey question, "In the view of those individuals or groups listed below, how valuable to your company is marketing?" The responses suggest that only about one-third of the sales managers and sales reps in B-to-B companies regard marketing as very valuable, and even fewer salespeople in B-to-C companies do. As Figure 6.2 indicates, these marketing executives believe that perceptions of marketing's value are even worse among operations, IT, HR, and R&D staffs. Whatever the reason for these managers' underestimations of marketing's value, such perceptions reduce marketers' opportunities to participate in cross-functional teams: Sponsors of such teams simply don't think to ask marketing professionals to contribute.

How might you combat these perceptions? Do whatever it takes to open doors to cross-functional opportunities. When people work together toward shared goals, they come to appreciate each other's knowledge, contributions, and perspec-

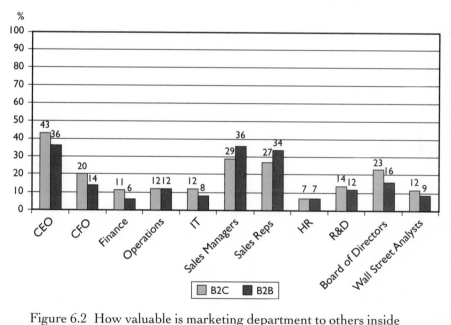

Figure 6.2 How valuable is marketing department to others inside the organization? (% of marketers saying "Very Valuable" to each individual/group). *Source:* Survey of MarketingProfs readers in organizations with 1,000 or more employees, 2005; question reads: "In the view of those individuals or groups listed below, how valuable to your company is marketing?" Choices are "not valuable at all," "not very valuable," "somewhat valuable," "valuable," and "very valuable."

tives. Cross-functional teamwork requires participants to agree on a purpose as well as the team's goals, problems, and decisions. In the most effective cross-functional teams, the group goal overrides the parochial goals of any one member's department.

Of course, the diversity inherent in cross-functional teams is a double-edged sword. A wide range of work styles, skills, and knowledge is essential for solving problems creatively. Yet this same diversity can intensify conflict within the team — one reason that some people steer clear of cross-functional work. Team members from different functional backgrounds inevitably have different perspectives on many issues; it's the reason they were chosen for the team. And those contrasting perspectives can lead to disagreement about how to resolve a problem, how to carry out a process, or how to deal with some other aspect of the team's work.

To see what such conflict can look like, let's revisit our operations versus marketing scenario — in which the operations manager wants the most efficient production system possible, while the marketing expert wants the right mix of products available at the right time, even if that means short production runs. Now suppose that these two individuals are working together in a cross-functional team. Their diametrically opposed goals will doubtless bring them into conflict as the team's work proceeds. In such a situation, the two participants can ease the conflict by understanding one another's perspectives. For example, our marketing practitioner must understand that if the factory is inefficient, manufacturing costs rise — and margins suffer or prices go up. The operations manager has to understand that if the product isn't available, customers will go elsewhere, costing the company sales. Both parties may have to compromise in order to meet the company's higher-level goals of making money and satisfying customers.

If cross-functional team members have difficulty making the compromises necessary to resolve conflict, the team leader or project manager must step in. If you're leading a cross-functional team, you'll soon learn that managing conflict is something of an art.

Encourage Job Shadowing

You can further break down silos by spending time in other parts of your company, observing how your peer managers do their jobs, seeing the kinds of problems and successes they experience, and even performing some of their duties. Encourage your colleagues from other functions to do the same in your department as well. By engaging in mutual job shadowing, you deepen your understanding of one another's view of the company and expose additional ideas for collaborating on common problems. You also gain further opportunities to stress the importance of satisfying customers' needs.

Some companies make job shadowing a required practice. For instance, Intuit — the company that makes the renowned Quicken accounting application — required its software programmers to spend time working at the help desk. The programmers (who typically operate within a rock-solid silo) heard users' concerns and were more likely to program the software to solve these problems.

Employees who work for companies that encourage job shadowing behave very differently from those who don't. As one respondent to our survey, a marketer in a mental health care provider, told us, "We are fully integrated into each area of operation. We attend other departments' staff meetings; we inform them about marketing projects that are currently going on and what we are planning to do next. We don't have much involvement with the finance area; however, with a new CEO, I believe this practice will change. IT and marketing work very closely with each other. IT is the 'science' behind the web page, and marketing represents the 'art.' Together, we are making good progress on how we look on the Internet."

By breaking down silos and collaborating with one another, managers from different functions stop hoarding their power and knowledge and start sharing it. This may make some managers feel that their power is being diffused or taken away from them. However, it actually increases the *organization's* overall power — its ability to better serve its customers and thus enhance its financial performance. And this is an outcome that everybody can appreciate, no matter where in the organization they work.

With the importance of bridge-building in mind, let's now turn to Chapter 7 — where we propose ideas for collaborating more effectively with the sales, the function tied most clearly to cash-flow harvesting. In many companies, the relationship between marketing and sales is notorious for its contentiousness and its turf battles. For this reason, your efforts to bust silos between these historically conflicted teams will pay particularly big dividends.

7

Scratch Sales's Back

Marketing and sales share a crucial objective: generating cash flow. That's why marketers — more than any other professionals in a company — stand the best chance of aligning their efforts with sales and creating results that both teams want. The reward? Marketers become champions, in the eyes of both the sales group and the company's top leadership. And the sales team fulfills its purpose — generating as much short-term revenue as possible — in record time and with record success.

As you know, sales professionals work alone out in the field to bring home the fruit. You may point them to the right tree — the place where the field is most fertile and where they will likely make a sale. And you probably arm them with the best equipment, such as product differentiation to combat price resistance, brand awareness and values to warm up cold calls, and lead management to identify and nurture prospects through the buying cycle. But ultimately, it takes adroit effort on the part of salespeople to reap a bountiful harvest. If these folks fail to pick fruit, your organization will starve; if they don't sell today, your marketing for tomorrow will be irrelevant.

Whether sales reports to marketing (as part of the promotion mix) in your organization, or marketing reports to sales (to support the communications effort), the two functions share the goal of identifying sources of cash flow and finding ways to harvest the cash. Yet as we've said throughout this book, your connection to cash flow may not be apparent to

others. To correct this situation, you must include sales in
your campaign to Manage East. You need to align your efforts
with those of sales, the function seen as exerting the most impact on cash flow. This chapter shows you how.

In the pages that follow, you'll learn how to help salespeople do their work more efficiently and make savvier use
of their time, budgets, and energy. And you'll discover ideas
for helping sales operate more effectively in an increasingly
competitive marketplace. When you apply these guidelines,
everyone wins: you, your peers in sales, and your company.

The good news is that, in all organizations, both sales and
marketing (unlike other functions) see the world from the
outside-in. And you both know that the only source of cash
flow is customers. You each have a strong motivation to build
powerful customer-focused teams. Yet you've probably discovered first-hand that marketing and sales speak different
languages — and perhaps you've concluded that marketing
is from Mars and sales is from Saturn. For example, in a marketer's view, a qualified lead is a contact who fits the target
market. For sales, a qualified lead is a prospect who is ready
to purchase now. But don't buy into the implication that differences in language mean that a positive collaboration is outside the realm of possibility. Reach out and build a bridge. You
have everything to gain and nothing to lose.

HELP SALES BOOST VELOCITY

The road to bridge-building with sales begins with understanding your company's business model; that is, how the firm
makes money. As you saw in Chapter 5, business models can
be based on margin, velocity (inventory turnover), or leverage. In most companies, one business model dominates. For
example, some companies are low-priced sellers, such as Dell
or Wal-Mart, who make money by maximizing velocity at low
margin. Other companies, such as Bose or Volvo, rely on high
margin, the difference between the costs to produce a product
or service and the price consumers are willing to pay for the
offering. Companies using this business model develop prod-

ucts or services that are highly differentiated and targeted to niche markets. Still other companies, such as Disney or IBM, rely on leverage: generating more sales with the same investment, perhaps through cross-selling multiple products and services to a customer during a sales call. In most companies, top management selects the business model and communicates it down through the ranks.

Typically, neither sales nor marketing managers have input into the selection of the business model. However, both groups share a strong motivation to increase velocity — to accelerate the selling of the company's products or services, regardless of how those offerings are priced or what they cost to produce and distribute.

The more you can help the sales force perform this job — selling your firm's offerings as quickly as possible — the stronger cash-flow partner you'll be. The first step to building this partnership is to understand how you can help salespeople get more of what motivates them: money. Once salespeople see you helping them make more money, they will welcome you as a vital part of the sales team.

Most companies use specific types of compensation programs to motivate salespeople to sell. Senior management sets performance expectations for the entire sales team. Using these targets, the sales manager assigns accounts or territories and sets sales quotas for individual reps. When you understand the sales compensation structure, you can more easily see the importance of helping reps close more sales — and thus make more money. Remember: Sales reps must make their quota, or they are gone. Consequently, sales reps are intensely focused on the short term. Marketers, in contrast, rarely feel such life-or-death pressure to show immediate results.[1]

In addition to understanding how salespeople are compensated, you need to know how they're managed. When sales is managed by a vice president of sales or a vice president of sales and marketing who has been promoted from the sales or-

---

1. Bill Babcock, Bill Koss, and Bill Rozier, "Truce! Ending the War between Sales and Marketing," MarketingProfs.com, January 31, 2006.

ganization, it's likely marketing will take a back seat to sales. As the final arbiter of conflict, a vice president of sales and marketing will probably take the position that all cash flow is a result of sales efforts and not the fruit of marketing's foresight. Under these conditions, it's all the more important for someone in marketing to know firsthand how sales reps do their job. If you're this individual, you can be thought of as a silo spanner — as described in Chapter 6

If you're a silo spanner, perhaps you worked in sales before joining the marketing team. It's preferable that whoever the silo spanner is, he or she has come up through sales in *your* organization, or at least in an organization in the same industry. Or maybe you've accompanied sales reps on visits to customers. Knowing from experience what interacting with customers is like strengthens your understanding of the market as well as the needs of individual customers. You can empathize with salespeople's often difficult jobs and challenge them to overcome prospects' objections — while still having their respect and appreciation. At the very least, they'll know you care about them and their work — a key element in building a bridge between your two functions.

At Farmers Insurance, executives take this to the extreme. Every new marketing hire is required to spend time in the field selling insurance and studying sales processes firsthand. In turn, salespeople are expected to rotate through the marketing department to learn what information from the field would be helpful to marketing and what types of consumer data they can get from marketing.[2]

To help salespeople sell more of your company's offerings more quickly, you must aid them in identifying new cash-flow sources. These sources take numerous forms, including the following:

- New customers
- Repeat purchases from existing customers

2. Constantine von Hoffman, "Culture Crash," *CMO Magazine*, July 2005, pp. 38–40.

- Share of wallet within category (selling a wider range of offerings from a particular product line to existing customers)
- Share of wallet across categories (selling offerings from different product lines to existing customers)

Unlike business models, cash-flow sources are usually determined by marketing and sales. The best way to become a marketing champion is to partner with sales to grow these sources. Sources of cash flow are food for salespeople. Feed them frequently and well — using these five strategies:

- Define qualified leads
- Manage the lead pipeline
- Quantify the financial value of the pipeline
- Help salespeople overcome price resistance
- Make the sales funnel flow faster

Let's examine each of these closely.

DEFINE QUALIFIED LEADS

To do their job, salespeople need leads, or prospects, who are ready to buy. Marketers — especially in B-to-B marketing — are often responsible for generating a steady source of qualified leads to give to sales. But what is a *qualified lead*, exactly? It's vital that you and your counterparts in sales agree on the meaning of this term. Otherwise, you may end up blaming one another when supposed leads don't become actual customers. Poor-quality leads waste a sales rep's time. How often have you heard sales complain that the leads generated by marketing aren't good quality? And how often have you accused sales of being unable to close a deal? Clarifying terminology can help you mitigate this conflict.

It matters less *how* you define *lead* than that you and sales agree on and stick to a definition. And definitions can vary from company to company. For example, in one firm, a lead may be nothing more than a potential customer who demonstrates the characteristics of your company's target market. In another organization, it may be a business customer that has already put the firm on its short list for a lucrative deal.

To help clarify your company's definition of *lead*, ask yourself and your sales partners the following questions:

- How did the prospect learn about our offerings?
- Is the individual contact a decision maker? A user? A check writer?
- Where is the prospect in the decision-making process? For example, have we identified the person's company as part of our target market, but they are unaware that they need our offerings? Are they aware of symptoms of a problem they're having? Are they aware of a problem that needs a solution? Have they evaluated our offerings? Have they compared our products to competitors' offerings?
- Is the prospect using our competitors' offerings? Or are they new to the product category we're selling?
- Can the prospect become a customer based on what you know about them? That is, what is the probability of closing the sale?

You may have defined a *lead* and identified the decision maker, but have you also identified all the people associated with an account that influence a decision or that write the check? Especially for products and services with long sales cycles, it's critical to know all the people who are involved, however remotely, in the decision. This is where branding activities, which communicate your offerings' value and attributes, are most important. Why? A salesperson from your firm may never actually meet all those involved in the potential buyer's decision, especially top executives who are signing off on the decision.

Clearly, tensions may arise between marketing and sales regarding when to act on a lead. Even though you want to maximize the number of leads you pass on to sales, consider giving sales the option to accept or reject leads. This way the burden is entirely on sales to close, that is, you have taken away the option for them to judge a lead's quality as poor. In addition, if you are working alongside salespeople throughout the buying cycle (see the following discussion on lead management), you may also want leads to be highly qualified. Neither sales nor marketing wants to devote resources to prospects with a low closing probability.

Regardless of the quality and quantity of the leads you give to sales, you can expect no more than an average of 20 percent of those prospects to become new customers.[3] This is the typical experience of most companies. However, there can be a large variation on this average, across industries and across organizations. Together with the sales manager, establish a goal for the number and share of customers who come from marketing's leads.

Another point about generating high-quality leads: As a marketer, you're probably convinced that you need to invest heavily in brand-building to condition the marketplace to buy. However, you may find it difficult to demonstrate the direct impact of such investments on the quality of the leads generated. For that reason, many companies' sales teams oppose spending limited resources on branding and view such investments as wasteful. This means you'll need to convince sales of the need for branding investments. How? Argue that such resources are being used to warm up sales calls. Sales people dislike nothing more than making cold calls. By strengthening your brand, you increase the likelihood that your sales partners will receive a warmer welcome while visiting prospective customers. Leads who are aware of your brand are more likely to feel that they know and trust your company's sales reps. They're also more likely to return reps' phone calls and to invite them to give presentations on your company's products or services. Of course, salespeople must also be trained to walk the walk of your brand and evangelize the positive associations that the brand exudes. To persuade them to do so,

---

3. Benchmark Study of Sales and Marketing Alignment conducted by MarketingProfs, March 2005.

show them how investments in brand-building make their jobs easier.

MANAGE THE LEAD PIPELINE

As you generate leads, don't assume that your work is done the minute you hand off a lead's contact information to sales. Stay involved with sales during the rest of the process — from the salesperson's first contacts with the lead to the prospective buyer's evaluation of the proposed deal and final decision. For example, by working with sales throughout the sales cycle, you provide valuable advice that helps sweeten the salesperson's odds of closing a sale, determining that a lead isn't going to buy, or winning back a prospect who has changed his or her mind about buying or is wavering. And help sales not only with the leads generated by marketing but also with leads generated by other resources. We call this process *managing the lead pipeline.*

To manage the lead pipeline with sales, you need to understand what experts call the *buyer's journey:*[4] the steps a potential customer goes through before deciding to purchase. These steps include becoming aware of a *negative present* — pain caused by a problem. Potential customers also consider making a change, such as buying and using your product or service, which will move them to a "positive (pain-free) future." The steps in the buyer's journey unfold in a specific sequence and constitute a prospective new customer's decision process, with the total time ranging from an hour or less to as long as several years, based on such variables as product complexity and cost.

Of course, you and sales want to reduce *leakage,* or prospects lost from the lead pipeline, by moving prospects through all the stages of the buying cycle — from awareness,

---

4. Hugh MacFarlane, *The Leaky Funnel,* Bookman Media, 2003; Jim Lenskold and Hugh MacFarlane, MarketingProfs, 2006; Jeff Thull, *The Prime Solution,* Dearborn Trade Publishing, 2005, pp. 148–150.

consideration, and research to evaluation and the decision to buy. When prospects *leak* — that is, they cut off the conversation or fail to respond to prompts, indicating no further interest — you will want to discern the reasons for the leakage so you can discourage loss of other prospects. But at the same time, you will want to accelerate *inevitable* leakage. Why? The only thing worse than losing a potential customer is knowing that you've invested extensive time and resources to woo a prospect who, as it turns out, was never going to buy anyway. With leads, you need to know when to cut your losses of time and resources and move on to more promising possibilities. If a prospective customer is likely to leak, you will want that leakage to occur as soon as possible. By understanding patterns in the marketplace, you help salespeople identify likely leakers and accelerate the leakage. Thus, you help sales avoid wasting time.

QUANTIFY THE LEAD PIPELINE'S FINANCIAL VALUE

You can help sales determine the size of the lead pipeline and the revenue it promises to generate, discounted in current dollars. This information is vital to salespeople because it sheds light on their potential income. It's also crucial to the organization as a whole because it represents potential cash flowing into the enterprise. While sales may be too close to specific accounts to make objective judgments about the likelihood of closing a deal, you may be better able to project business based on past experience. To convert leads into a revenue forecast, take into account the probability of winning the business based on the experience gained from similar accounts.

In addition to producing a revenue forecast, your objective evaluation of the pipeline's financial potential helps salespeople decide where to invest additional time and effort. Tracking activity involves measuring the possible revenues from new prospects if they buy, identifying leaks (and their reasons for dropping out), noting stalled prospects, highlighting prospects who are progressing toward a close, and documenting recent closed business.

As part of the work to quantify the lead pipeline's financial value, marketing must evaluate the profitability of its contribution. That is, you must answer the question, "In what ways does marketing increase the value of the lead pipeline?" In other words, how does marketing increase the likelihood of closing deals, and what is the financial value of such deals?

Yet most marketers don't address these questions. Why? Many are too busy thinking about how to *condition* the market—identify the target market, shape the value proposition and product differentiation, and create awareness to generate leads for sales. While this work is valuable in creating leads that have been warmed, it's not where the cash-flow "rubber" meets the "road." The sales funnel is really where this cash-flow action resides. In fact, a big source of contention between marketing and sales is that marketing often spends much of its resources to set up the market to produce sales leads, rather than to move prospects toward a purchase decision. Meanwhile, sales is focused exclusively on closing deals. If marketing devotes more resources to moving potential buyers along the journey to a purchase, sales would certainly understand and appreciate the value of marketing.

To reorient your attention on increasing the probability of closing leads and estimating the financial value of the lead pipeline, consider these guidelines:

1. Plan marketing communications for each phase of the sales cycle, from awareness through consideration to purchase. Don't focus marketing efforts just at the top of the funnel, but rather at critical decisions throughout the path to purchase.

2. Document marketing's contribution at each critical phase in the funnel. Assess the value of the leads at the top of the funnel. For example, "Are we getting the *right* prospects? And how can we improve our lead generation?"

3. Pinpoint marketing resources where prospects are leaving. Determine what marketing does to reduce the rate of funnel "leakage," and test methods for continuous improvement.
4. Quantify the financial value of marketing activities that reduce "leakage" and that help increase the probability of closing deals.

Through these tactics, you demonstrate how marketing increases the financial value of the sales pipeline.

Marketing can also contribute to management of the lead pipeline in two additional areas: helping sales people overcome price resistance and making the sales funnel flow faster. Let's look at each of these in turn.

OVERCOME PRICE RESISTANCE

In most organizations, sales and marketing inherit a pricing structure developed by top management.[5] The two functions may offer input and provide pricing information from the marketplace, but in most companies they don't make final pricing decisions. Our own survey found that just 27 percent of B-to-C marketers and 18 percent of B-to-B marketers are responsible for pricing decisions in their organizations.

Yet salespeople often cite price resistance as the primary cause of losing a deal. "Drop our price," they say, "and we'll get more business." Marketing professionals know that competing on price alone is not the right way to win business because consumers don't base their purchase decisions solely on

---

5. According to the Strategic Pricing Group, a leading consultancy, pricing often lies at the intersection of marketing, finance, and sales, with the ultimate decision made by top management. Marketing recommends a moderate price based on customer research, finance recommends a high price to recoup R&D investments, and sales lobbies for a low price point to persuade prospects to switch from competitors' offering. See their newsletter article titled "How to Regain Your Marketplace Power by Investing in Pricing Strategy, Structure and Systems," by Elliot Yama, Peter Walsh, and John Hogan, *SPG Insights*, Spring 2005.

price. If that were the case, the lowest-priced product in every category would achieve 100 percent market share. Apple's iPod, for example, dominates the MP3 player market, yet it is more expensive than most competitive offerings.

Instead, the best way to get prospects to say yes is to help them perceive the value of your offering. The more value they perceive, the more likely they are to buy it — at the price your company has stipulated. At Bass Pro Shops, for example, customers buy the same utility knife that Wal-Mart sells for $57.95 for a much heftier $69.99.[6] How does Bass Pro pull this off? It provides customers with a uniquely appealing shopping experience. With annual sales of $1.6 billion in 25 stores nationwide and an average customer visit of three hours, the company is clearly competing on something other than price. In an age of discounters and online sellers, Bass Pro's 300,000-square-foot store in Springfield, Missouri, is a top tourist attraction that pulls in more than 4 million visitors a year. Outdoor enthusiasts say that a visit to the store is more fun than going to Disneyland. According to former president Jim Hagale, "If you take a product — even something that can be turned into a commodity — and wrap it in a memorable experience, you're adding value [for the customer]."

In today's marketplace — whether it's a B-to-B or B-to-C sale — success is not *only* about price. Nor is success only about your product. Instead, it's about the benefits — functional, economic, or emotional — that the customer experiences as he or she evaluates, buys, and uses your products and services. These benefits constitute the *value* your offering delivers. And by understanding that value, you and the sales team can work together to define it in the minds of potential customers.

To help salespeople overcome a prospect's price resistance, apply the 5 Cs of value-based marketing:[7]

6. "Luring 'Em In," *Business 2.0,* March 2005, p. 44.
7. "Using Pricing as an Engine for Profitable Growth," an Executive Briefing by John Hogan of the Strategic Pricing Group, June 29, 2004, at UCLA.

1. **Comprehend** the key value drivers for customers (the pain or problem they want to eradicate).
2. **Create** value for customers (relieve the pain or provide a solution to the problem).
3. **Communicate** the value you've created (in pain relief or reduced cost).
4. **Convince** customers that they must pay for value (no free lunch).
5. **Capture** value with effective price tactics (make the cost palatable).

The Honeywell Building Controls pursuit of the education market is a good illustration of value-based marketing. This company's strategy might best be described as "making money by giving the product away." A number of years ago, Honeywell Building Controls, which makes thermostats and heating equipment, discovered that schools represented a market segment with a strong need for its energy retrofit products. But schools have no money for capital expenditures of the sort typically required for these products. So Honeywell's value proposition for this customer segment was, "You'll save money if you retrofit." Here was a market where there was a need, but the sales force was selling nothing because schools had no budget for these products.

Knowing that the schools would save energy costs if they adopted the new equipment, Honeywell offered to finance sales of the products and let the schools pay the loans back from the resulting savings in energy costs. In fact, the company went so far as to guarantee a level of savings. If the schools didn't achieve that level, Honeywell would write the school districts a check for that amount. By forgoing any payment upfront, Honeywell came to dominate the market. Through these creative ideas, Honeywell's marketing staff identified a way to overcome consumers' price resistance. The sales force, as you might have guessed, loved it.

The Honeywell example illustrates the point that marketing can help sales identify ways to create and identify the value a company's products or services will deliver for consumers. Armed with this understanding, salespeople can make a compelling case for consumers to buy their products at the listed price.

Accelerate Sales Funnel Flow

As we've discussed, the driving objective of salespeople is to sell your firm's offerings as quickly as possible. While they are in constant pursuit of closing business fast, many of them perceive marketers as being in no particular rush to ring the cash register. When working with sales, realize that *time* is their most valuable and scarce resource. When you speed up the sales cycle, you become their hero. So, think about *how you can make the sales funnel flow faster*. If you leverage salespeople's time to help them maximize velocity, you will become a marketing champion in their eyes.

Salespeople make decisions daily about whom to call, what to pitch, and how to communicate. Do they call on higher-volume or low-volume customers, new or existing customers, headquarters or field managers? (Any of these could be the right decision, depending on the company's business strategy.) Do they sell new or existing products, high- or low-volume offerings, or easy- or hard-to-sell products? And do they hunt or farm, sell or service, get assistance from others or do it all personally? You can help sales answer these questions in ways that increase the sales funnel flow.

Moreover, at each stage of the sales funnel, you can find opportunities to move prospects through faster. Salespeople know that prospects control the purchase timetable. The prospect advances through stages toward a decision to buy by gathering information — a lot in the case of a complex sale, and a little in the case of an impulse buy. A prospect won't be forced through this process by a salesperson. "Done right," according to Bill Babcock, a CEO of a direct marketing agency, "[lead] cultivation shortens the [purchase] timeframe by delivering the information prospects need to make their decision. . . [We] all know that people who are not ready to make a purchase don't want to talk to a salesperson. . . . Marketing can perpetuate a conversation where a sales force can't even establish one."[8]

To accelerate prospects' movement through the sales funnel, you can draw on two models. First, consider the widely used hierarchy of communication effects model, whereby your communications programs focus on one or more of five objectives — each aligned with a different phase of the buyer's journey. The five objectives are: Attention (to a particular problem or source of pain), Awareness (that potential solutions are out there), Knowledge (of your product's benefits), Attitude (understanding that your product is the optimal one), and Action (the purchase). As we've seen, before consumers can become customers, they must pass through each of these cycles — from recognizing your message as worthy of their attention to requesting information about your offer or actually making a purchase.[9]

Each of these five stages has inherent challenges that can slow down the buying process. Getting the prospect's Attention, for example, can be very difficult in a market where there are many offerings and a cacophony of advertising messages. However, the most challenging phases in most product categories are Knowledge and Attitude. During the Knowledge phase, your objective is to help the consumer understand the specific appeal and benefits of your offering. The consumer is conducting research, either proactively or reactively. Here's where, in almost all product categories these days, your web site plays a critical role in moving prospects to the Attitude phase. During this phase, prospects recognize that your product may provide solutions to their problems, but they may have doubts about whether yours is the *best* solution.

As Michael Webb, sales coach, advises, marketers should "identify the stages prospects go through in solving their problems, identify where they get stuck in their journey and why, and . . . devise questioning tactics that help prospects

8. Babcock et al., "Truce!," 2006.

9. Allen Weiss, "The Hierarchy of Communication Effects," MarketingProfs .com, 2001.

progress through those stages, especially where they get stuck."[10]

The box titled "Moving Prospects Quickly through the Sales Cycle" lays out one process you can use to help sales on this front — using follow-up on trade-show leads as an example.

◆◆◆◆

Moving Prospects Quickly through the Sales Cycle

Suppose you generate sales leads from an exhibit at an industry trade show. How might you help move those prospects to the next phases of the sales cycle? Your first step is to find out whether the prospect is ready for follow-up by a salesperson—using these tactics:

- Ask the qualification questions on your show contact form.
- Use follow-up communications to qualify. This is especially important if your questions are comprehensive. If possible, use e-mail for these communications.

Collaborate with the sales team to decide on the qualification criteria you use. There are four general categories, although your organization may have different ones from those shown below:

- **Budget:** Is the purchase budgeted in the prospect's organization? If so, what size budget does the prospect have available?
- **Authority:** Does the respondent have the authority to make the purchase decision?
- **Need:** How important is the product or solution to the company? In other words, how deep is their pain?
- **Time Frame:** What is the prospect's readiness to buy? When will the purchase likely be made?

Not all leads are ready to see a salesperson, so sort through your leads to determine the readiness of each. Score each lead based on readiness, perhaps by using the following system:

10. Michael J. Webb, "Three Strategies (and How to Use Them) to Make Your Sales Funnel Flow Faster," MarketingProfs.com, December 6, 2005.

A: The prospect is ready to see a sales rep.

B: The prospect still needs nurturing, but the contact is to be made by the sales team.

C: The inquiry still needs nurturing, to be done by marketing.

D: The inquiry is not worth nurturing. Put the inquiry into the marketing database for ongoing communications or throw it away.

If the prospect is not ready to be contacted by sales, initiate a *nurturing process*—a series of ongoing communications that move the prospect to the point where he or she is ready to buy. Outgoing communication can improve your lead qualification by up to 500 percent—a handsome return on the resources invested.

It would be impossible for any sales force to manage this entire process—no matter how large the force. They are too focused on what has to happen now so they can make a sale today. Yet if marketing doesn't do this work today, no one can make a sale tomorrow.

Source: Ruth Stevens, Trade Show Marketing Template, MarketingProfs, 2006.

◆◆◆◆◆

Another buying-cycle model that B-to-B marketers, in particular, may find useful is the marketing funnel. According to Michael Perla, a sales effectiveness consultant, the marketing funnel works as a parallel process to the sales funnel. He says, "There is a large opening at the beginning (large awareness pool) and a winnowing or funneling down at the end (customer list). . . . The marketing funnel in the B2B world starts with branding, and then builds awareness and interest, targeted prospecting, lead management, sales funnel support and, finally, customer lifecycle marketing."[11]

The marketing funnel starts with branding in order to build awareness and favorable associations. Next, it moves to targeted prospecting, whereby you determine the most likely consumers of your offering. Then it advances to lead management, whereby you qualify leads and see that sales follows up on them, or you help sales to follow up. The model's next step

11. Michael Perla, "Have You Filled Your Marketing Funnel?" MarketingProfs.com, October 4, 2005.

is sales funnel support, whereby you design communications that align your company's solution to customers' specific problems. Finally, the model ends with ongoing management of relationships with existing customers.

In the sales-funnel support stage, just before acquisition of a new customer, marketing plays a vital role. The more the prospect trusts the salesperson and the company's offering, the faster the sales funnel will flow. To gain this trust, you can explain to sales how or why customers with similar profiles have decided to buy your company's solution. In addition, you can provide sales with the tools to address prospects' questions quickly and directly. See the box titled "A Case in Point: GE Access Distribution" for an example.[12]

A Case in Point: GE Access Distribution

GE Access Distribution, a subsidiary of General Electric, is a distributor of complex computer products, solutions, and services. To more aggressively help its resellers and internal sale staff sell solutions—with customers increasingly buying groups of products, services, and software—the marketing company developed a set of web-based sales support tools, collectively called the *Online Solution Selling Resource Library*. The Library's components include the following:

- A customer overview presentation slide deck
- White papers explaining the technology's value proposition in Microsoft Word that can be edited and customized
- Web pages illustrating solutions
- A prospecting guide to help resellers understand the market and issues or needs of specific consumer segments and decision makers
- Prospecting e-mails
- An ROI value generator to help the salesperson describe the value of the solution in quantitative terms
- Question scripts designed to raise a prospect's awareness of pain so as to build a sense of urgency in the buyer organization

12. Louise Revers and Judy Hodges, "CMO Advisory Research: Best Practices in Aligning Marketing and Sales," IDC, May 2004.

In 2004, IDC named GE Access the winner of its CMO Best Practices Award. As judges at IDC explained, "[GE Access] has achieved a means of delivering *fast, efficient, and integrated marketing information* that adds real value to the sales process." The marketing information system embodied in GE Access's Library has made the sales funnel flow faster.

◆◆◆◆

Turning to the last phase in the marketing funnel, once a prospect has become a customer, marketing can play an important role in determining whether an ongoing relationship is likely or even desirable. Salespeople may or may not be responsible for identifying and retaining profitable customers. However, you can determine which customers are likely to leave regardless of what the company does to try to keep them and which customers are likely to become loyal. With the emphasis that many companies have put on customer loyalty, it's vital that sales know which customers are looking for a relationship and which customers are more transient, interested only in one-night stands.

As researchers Reinartz and Kumar have written, "Different customers need to be treated in different ways." The names these authors use for customers who are highly profitable but differ in their loyalty are *butterflies* and *true friends*. Butterflies are profitable but disloyal. Once you've identified customers as butterflies, "milk them for as much as you can for the short time they are buying from you." In contrast, true friends are both profitable and loyal; they're "steady purchasers, buying regularly, but not intensively over time." To keep them, avoid pestering them with too-frequent communications; they'll only start ignoring you. Instead, reward their loyalty with exclusive access to special events and high-quality, limited-supply products.[13] By knowing who is likely to be a butterfly and who a true friend, you can help salespeople understand which of their current customers they

13. Werner Reinartz and V. Kumar, "The Mismanagement of Customer Loyalty," *Harvard Business Review*, July 2002.

should devote time to in the hope of moving them through the sales funnel once again.

A key to making the sales funnel flow faster is the amount of time sales reps spend talking with prospects and customers. The following story about Hewlett-Packard reveals the value that can arise when marketing frees up salespeople to spend more time with the right customers.

Soon after arriving at Hewlett-Packard as CEO, Mark Hurd began hearing complaints about H-P's sale force from top corporate customers — the company's "true friends." These customers lamented that it was impossible to see a sales rep. Meanwhile, internal sales managers complained that they could not get sales reps to make personal sales calls. H-P isn't alone in this problem: In many companies, sales reps are buried in administrative responsibilities, which rob them of valuable time for doing what they do best — selling. Upon investigating, Hurd found that H-P sales reps indeed spent less than 30 percent of their time in front of customers.

After just one year after recognizing the problem, customer "face time" at H-P increased on average to 40 percent of a sales rep's time — still not ideal, but at least headed in the right direction.[14] The lesson for marketers? Take on as much planning, evaluating, and reporting as you can, to free up salespeople to spend more time with customers. Help sales prepare for customer presentations, ensuring that all marketing materials are ready for immediate use by sales. Develop presentations and collaterals that sales can customize as needed for specific prospects. Also consider using "percent of sales reps' time spent face-to-face with customers" as a metric for tracking the allocation of this valuable resource. You and your colleagues in sales know that the most valuable use of a sales rep's time is to invest it in meeting with prospects and customers. Increasing performance on this key metric is likely to augment cash flow somewhere, sometime.

There's no doubt about it: You can serve as a powerful ally

14. Pui-Wing Tam, "Hurd's Big Challenge at HP: Overhauling Corporate Sales," *The Wall Street Journal,* April 3, 2006.

for the sales team. And most salespeople know this. Imagine a sales rep responsible for a territory that management decides will no longer receive marketing resources. Even the most marketing-averse salesperson would immediately protest the decision. After all, in most organizations, salespeople are rewarded based on individual performance. If marketing resources are diverted from one region to another, regardless of what the loser has thought about marketing support in the past, the noise of protest would be significant.

To learn about how these strategies have helped IBM build bridges between marketing and sales, read the following interview with Alex Gogh, Vice President of Marketing, Global Public Sector.

◆◆◆◆

An Interview with a Sales-Savvy Marketing Champion at IBM

The following excerpt—from an interview with Alex Gogh, Vice President of Marketing for IBM's public-sector division—provides a glimpse into the mind of a particularly sales-savvy marketing champion.

ROY YOUNG: We hear a lot about the contentiousness between marketing and sales. But if marketing is to become a cash-flow function, it must take the initiative in building a positive relationship with sales.

ALEX GOGH: I do think that a good relationship is all about marketing's synergy with sales. At IBM, we try to figure out how we can best align marketing to ensure that sales occur. The two functions need to work hand in glove. We want marketing to wake up every day and say, "Am I making it easier to sell?" If you can instill that in the DNA of your organization, you're saying, "I'm going to plug marketing into the whole sales process—whether it's identifying opportunities, closing deals, or providing post-sales support."

The public-sector market is the largest sector in the world in the IT industry—it's roughly a $230 billion market. So it's critical that we enable all our channels to achieve unparalleled velocity, information access, and flow through the sales pipeline.

YOUNG: What has made this relationship work so effectively at IBM?

GOGH: We instill in our marketers that it's their job to make it easier for our salespeople to sell. I'm sure you've seen marketing organizations that believe they just shape the brand. Well, we shape IBM's brand, but we also transcend that to clarify what our brand means for the guys selling our wares. Those individuals *are* the brand, day in and day out, for our customers.

To do that, we speak salespeople's language. We don't say, "We're going to give you a brand management lesson." We say, "Here's what a customer of the U.S. federal government expects you to have." We give them in-depth industry knowledge—which is a brand attribute of IBM, something that the customer values highly. And we help them know how to deal with the federal government. By successfully aligning marketing and sales in this way, we raise IBM's brand equity together.

But we don't stop there. We make sure that marketing and sales stay aligned throughout the sales cycle. Too many marketers say to sales, "I've got a thousand leads for you," but they don't help sales move those leads through the pipeline.

YOUNG: Can you say more about how marketing helps sales manage the pipeline?

GOGH: We constantly take the pulse of how the pipeline is progressing, by program or product—how leads are moving from identification to qualification to proposal to closure. And our marketers know that salespeople need different types of collateral and information at each stage in the sales cycle—whether it's recent wins, proposals, or latest references. For marketers, there's no substitute for experiencing the entire sales process to test their assumptions about what's going on in the market. The most powerful marketing organizations constantly deliver on the entire end-to-end process of the company's sales cycle. Marketers need to hear and see how customers' behavior changes at different steps in the sales cycle—something that salespeople experience every day.

YOUNG: I've also heard a lot about how marketing and sales battle over data—that many salespeople are rather protective of their data. What is your experience with that?

GOGH: We're fortunate in that we have CRM systems that everyone has appropriate access to, and it's part of salespeople's job to show us the pipeline. It's a bit of cultural discipline that we've established. Any battling over data seems to be more about information related to organizational memory, such as knowledge about informal relationships.

YOUNG: At IBM, does marketing quantify the financial value of the pipeline and forecast sales?

GOGH: Sales is responsible for forecasting. We watch it and make adjustments accordingly, as well as provide insight to sales. We try to provide the macro view of the market and help sales anticipate what's shaping up for upcoming quarters.

YOUNG: What about helping salespeople spend more time in front of customers?

GOGH: We do look at that metric—time in front of customers—constantly. You always want to make sure your salespeople have more time with customers than they do with internal processes. And at each stage of the sales cycle, marketing can help salespeople be more productive in their use of time.

Source: Telephone interview with Roy Young, May 8, 2006.

Of course, sales isn't your only Eastern contingency with whom you must build bridges in order to shape perceptions of marketing's value. If you are to connect marketing to cash flow not just in the short term but also in the long term, you also need to forge connections with another key Eastern constituency: R&D. Chapter 8 shows you how.

YOUR SALES PARTNERSHIP SWOT ANALYSIS

1. In what ways do you currently help sales boost velocity—turnover of inventory—in your company? How effective have these efforts been? What changes might you make to ensure that your velocity-boosting moves generate better results?

2. What criteria does your company use to define a qualified sales lead? How do you currently help sales manage the lead pipeline? What steps might you take to be more helpful to sales on this front?

3. What are you currently doing to help quantify the potential financial value represented in the sales pipeline? How might you improve the effectiveness of these efforts?

4. Through what means do you now help sales overcome price resistance? How might these efforts be further improved?

5. What are you currently doing to make the sales funnel flow faster? Consider the hierarchy of communication effects model, as well as the marketing funnel model. In what ways might you apply each of these models to further accelerate the flow through the sales funnel?

8

Dream with the R&D Team

Many marketers overlook a far less evident ally than sales: the research and development (R&D) team. When you build bridges with R&D — another vital aspect of Managing East — you help develop the products and services that will generate cash flow in the *future*. Think of your collaboration with sales as harvesting cash now and your work with R&D as planting seeds that will lead to future harvests.

In this chapter, we introduce practical recommendations for removing the silos that separate marketing and R&D in so many organizations. In Chapter 6, you found some general-level silo-busting suggestions, such as job shadowing and net-working with your colleagues in R&D and sales. In the pages that follow, we get more specific in our recommendations — offering tactics geared especially to improving your relation-ship with R&D. Even if your company has a silo-oriented culture, you can still take the initiative to build bridges between marketing and R&D. Your reward? Executives and managers throughout the organization will gain a whole new appreciation for marketing's role in ensuring future cash flow and growth for your company.

Marketing and R&D: A Crucial Partnership

The techniques you use to build a bridge to sales won't work with R&D because the two functions play sharply different roles in the company and have different connections with marketing. Sales and marketing naturally align because both are externally focused, customer-facing functions. By contrast, many R&D departments are inwardly focused — as revealed by their intense interest in products' features over the benefits that those features create for customers. Moreover, in many companies, marketing and sales share a formalized relationship as one department reports to the other. If marketing reports to sales, its practitioners' job description often includes generating leads for sales. And both functions strive to generate cash flow in the short run.

Things work quite differently between marketing and R&D. For one thing, R&D's job is to generate long-term cash flow by developing first-to-market, high-margin products that differ radically from existing offerings and that persuade consumers to change their buying behavior. In addition to breakthrough products, R&D generates ideas for product extensions — variations on existing product lines that can further boost revenues. Whereas sales depends on marketing to go to market (sharpen consumers' awareness of current offerings and loyalty to the company), the R&D experts can benefit from marketers' assistance in identifying and developing new and revised products that will score successes in the marketplace.

However, stereotypes about the supposed differences between R&D and marketing — shown in Table 8.1 — can make even the best-intended efforts at collaboration between these functions difficult. Of course, many stereotypes contain a grain of truth. That is, someone, somewhere, and at some time acted in ways that encouraged others to draw conclusions about his or her abilities and motivations. For instance, in some companies, members of the R&D team indeed care far more about developing cool product features than about answering the question, How well do those features deliver benefits that consumers value? And in those same organizations, the marketing staff may in fact fail to provide rigorous evidence to support their advocated courses of action.

Despite the very real differences that exist between mar-

Table 8.1
Stereotypes about R&D and Marketing

R&D	Marketing
Techcentric	Big picture
Complex solutions	Go to market fast
Scientists	Artists
Detail oriented	Detail ignorant
Features focus	Sales focus
Problem oriented	Scattered
Inventions without a market	Opinions without justification
No concern for price, costs, or profit	Concerned only about sales volume and market share
Customer? What's that?	Scientific rigor? What's that?
Poor communicators	Expensive advertisers
Ivory-tower dwellers	Does a job that anyone can do

keting and R&D, these two groups can still be natural allies. Indeed, the differences between these functions can serve as sources of strength — as each team brings a unique perspective to bear on the company's efforts to succeed. The key is to build bridges across destructive differences while leveraging the strengths that such differences provide. Taking a moment to identify what marketing and R&D share in common can help. For example, practitioners from both functions make their company's future welfare a top priority (even if many executive teams force marketers to focus on the short term). And the key to any firm's future welfare — not just survival but healthy growth — is product and service innovation, in which marketing and R&D play crucial roles. According to the Product Development Management Association, new products bring in as much as one-third to all of an organization's revenues.[1] Consider these additional statistics about the importance of innovation: Half of *successful* new products achieve a 33 percent ROI or better, have a payback period of two years or less, and achieve a market share of 35 percent or better.[2] And according to one *Fortune* survey, the single strongest predictor of investment value in a public company is its degree of innovativeness.[3] On the other hand, innovation isn't easy — as we'll see in the following. It's risky business, and only you can help boost R&D's chances of delivering blockbuster successes — through innovative new offerings and extensions of existing ones.

The Innovation Engine

What drives corporate innovation? Many senior executives identify changing customer needs as the engine. To satisfy their rapidly shifting requirements and preferences, consumers hunger for new products and services. As author Robert Cooper notes: "Marketplaces are also (in addition to technology) in turmoil, with market needs and wants and customer preferences changing regularly. The company that seems omnipotent only a few years ago suddenly falls from favor with the consumer . . . Consumers have become like kids in a candy shop—[they] see what's possible, and [they] want it."

Source: R. G. Cooper, *Winning at New Products*, Basic Books, 2001.

Clearly, marketing and R&D teams must join forces — silos be damned — to fuel their company's innovation efforts. After all, that's where the future money is. But how, precisely, can you dream with the R&D team about the breakthrough

1. A. Griffin, "Drivers of New Product Development Success," Product Development Management Association, 1997.

2. R. G. Cooper and E. J. Kleinschmidt, "Performance Topologies of New Product Projects," *Industrial Marketing Management* 24, 1995, pp. 439–456.

3. R. G. Cooper, *Winning at New Products*, Basic Books, 2001.

and refined offerings your firm needs to create? Start by being a good partner. As you know, the best partnerships are mutually beneficial — each party receives something valuable from the other. And through the parties' collaboration, they generate more value than either could have done on their own. But in building a partnership with R&D, you have no control over what R&D does for you — you control only what you can do for R&D. The benefit to you is a tie to sources of future cash flow. With that in mind, what steps can you take to provide something of value specifically to R&D? We provide potent strategies in the following.

CONDUCT AN INNOVATION REVIEW

To gain insights into how best to support R&D, review your company's behavior regarding innovation — past, present, and intended future — even if you have to do so covertly. Gather information to answer the following questions:[4]

1. What is the historical level of R&D spending in the company? Has it been increasing, decreasing, or remaining steady? How do your firm's patterns of R&D investment compare to those of your competitors?

2. What proportion of the company's current sales comes from new products introduced in the past five years? What proportion comes from sales of remaining products?

3. What will the firm's portfolio of products look like over the next five years? What proportion of your sales growth will come from new products, growth in sales of existing products, and increased market share of current products?

4. How well is your company faring in the new-product game? What proportion of its new offerings succeeds in the marketplace? What proportion fails? What is

4. Robert Cooper, *Winning at New Products*, 3rd edition, Basic Books, 2001, pp. 9–19.

the attrition rate of new products? Do winners receive the lion's share of our resources? Or do losers receive it?

5. What types of new offerings has the organization introduced: new-to-the-world products or services, new product lines, extensions of existing product lines, improvements and revisions to existing products, repositionings, cost reductions? How would you classify the company's new offerings overall in terms of degree of innovativeness: moderately innovative? highly innovative? not very innovative at all?

In answering these questions, you'll probably discover that innovation is a hit-or-miss game: Some of your company's new offerings score successes in the marketplace; others fail miserably. Still others generate lukewarm results. Losers consume most of your firm's resources just as often as winners do. According to some experts, more than 90 percent of the 30,000 new consumer products launched each year fail.[5]

There's no doubt about it: Innovating is a risky, uncertain business. And risk is the bane of any R&D team. If you can reduce the risk inherent in R&D's job, you'll provide unprecedented value for this important partner — while sweetening the odds of creating cash-generating marketplace successes for your firm. Here's how.

REDUCE R&D'S RISK

Your company's R&D team has two jobs: to figure out which projects will succeed in the market (doing the right projects) and to develop the selected projects correctly (doing the right projects right). You can help R&D excel at both jobs — and thereby mitigate the risk inherent in R&D's work — by applying the following six strategies:[6]

5. *The Wall Street Journal*, November 29, 2005.

6. R. G. Cooper, *Winning at New Products*, Basic Books, 2001, pp. 83–112.

Suggest Products That Offer Unique Value to Consumers

Consumers perceive new offerings as valuable when those products or services meet some or all of the following criteria: They have unique features, meet consumers' needs better than alternative offerings do, demonstrate good quality, reduce consumers' costs, and seem novel. Some experts have also maintained that offerings that enable consumers to accomplish a particular task more easily, quickly, cheaply, or conveniently stand a good chance of succeeding in the marketplace.

You can help R&D select projects for development that meet such criteria by providing comparative analyses of competing products as well as by sharing your knowledge of consumers' needs and costs. When innovations meet these criteria, success can be spectacular — as Federal Express discovered firsthand after it began flawlessly performing the "when-it-absolutely-has-to-get-there-overnight" job for consumers.

Encourage a Customer-Focused Development Process

Sharing your understanding of consumers' needs and preferences with your colleagues in R&D can encourage them to keep customers in mind while developing new products and services. Ongoing customer contact through market research is the crucial means by which you generate valuable knowledge of consumers.

But to gather and present market-research data that will be meaningful and useful to R&D, you must demonstrate the scientific rigor and familiarity with the language of research that R&D experts appreciate. For example, establish a sound statistical foundation for your research, gathering input on methodology if necessary from technical staff on topics such as statistical significance and research design. Pay close attention to your sampling: Do respondents to a survey represent an adequate cross section of the consumer population you're interested in? Should you augment surveys with focus groups or one-on-one interviews? Could interviews with ex-

isting customers shed additional light on potential new customers' needs and interests?

Consider conducting field research — observing consumers as they shop for and use products in your target market. Marketers at Procter & Gamble, for instance, undertake
anthropological expeditions using ethnographic methods to
see how consumers are actually using the company's products
(such as Febreze fabric freshener) in their homes. They use
their findings to generate ideas for entirely new offerings and
revisions to existing ones. See the box titled "Shell Oil: Surprise Visits to the Gas Pumps" for an additional example of
how field research can generate valuable results.

◆◆◆◆◆

Shell Oil: Surprise Visits to the Gas Pumps

At Shell Oil, marketing surveys revealed that drivers wanted to refuel at
reasonable cost, while being sheltered from rain, wind, and snow. They
wanted to pay and exit the gas station quickly, and they wanted clean
pumps and bathrooms. Yet senior executives didn't believe that fixing
these basics would make a difference in their business. The marketing
group suggested that executives take surprise visits to gas stations to see
for themselves what consumers wanted and how they felt about their
refueling experiences.

This firsthand observation convinced the executives that retro-
fitting the stations was a good idea after all, and they approved the necessary spending. A year after the overhaul, Shell Oil reported double-
digit growth in gasoline sales and in return on capital (which had sunk to
zero before the change initiative). Both figures far exceeded targets.

Source: Patrick Barwise and Sean Meehan, "Making Differentiation Make a Difference," *Strategy & Business,* September 30, 2004.

◆◆◆◆◆

And don't forget to gather input from expert consumers in
the product category at hand — for example, chefs if your
company's developing cookware, physicians if you're working on a new medical device, and musicians if you're consid-

ering high-end audio equipment. Insights from these experts can spark additional ideas for new products and services. Talking with staff members from other units in your company — sales, customer service, operations, and so forth — and consulting with trade-show participants can yield further valuable information about consumers' needs.

Help R&D Do Its Homework

With any new product or service under consideration, R&D has extensive homework to do before beginning development on the project. You can help your R&D colleagues complete their homework by conducting market research to identify who the target customer is, how the product should be positioned, what consumers would be willing to pay for the new offering, and what features should be designed into the product so as to deliver the benefits that consumers want. By clarifying these matters ahead of time, you help ensure that products and services are designed for marketplace success. See the box titled "Bank of America: Helping R&D with Its Homework" for an example of how this careful preparation worked in one major service industry.

◆◆◆◆◆

Bank of America: Helping R&D with Its Homework

"We expect no less than 80% of our future growth in retail banking from the Hispanic market," declared Bank of America CEO Ken Lewis. The chief executive meant business. Mexican immigrants in the United States wire more than $9 billion each year home to relatives, many of them paying up to 10 percent of the wired amount in fees. Moreover, immigrants are the fastest-growing group of *unbanked* lower-income consumers, according to the report "Banking on Technology: Expanding Financial Markets and Economic Opportunity," published by the Brookings Institution in June 2002. Spotting an opportunity, domestic and foreign banks alike—including Wells Fargo, U.S. Bancorp, and Banco del Ahorro Nacional y Servicios Financieros (a government-backed Mexican bank)—have begun competing to serve this market.

Bank of America did its homework before developing innovative services for this target market—determining that low and predictable cost, flexible use, and assistance with establishing credit records would all appeal to immigrants. The resulting offering? The SafeSend program, introduced in 2002. SafeSend lets holders of checking accounts or credit cards set up separate accounts for transferring funds. Users have personal codes that give them access to the program through ATMs, phones, or the Internet—all for a flat fee. By leveraging financial services technology, Bank of America was able to offer the program at a lower cost than similar services provided by other banks. To further ensure the program's success, the Bank also began accepting matricula consular cards (identification issued by the Mexican government) as a form of identification for customers interested in opening accounts.

Thanks to Bank of America's careful research before developing the SafeSend program, the innovation stands the best possible chance of succeeding in the marketplace. Indeed, SafeSend has already demonstrated its ability to attract consumers and secure their loyalty: Thirty-seven percent of Hispanics who have signed up for SafeSend have ended up opening other accounts with Bank of America.

Source: Shawn Tully, "BofA Is Betting Its Future on the Hispanic Market," *Fortune,* April 14, 2003. www.winwinpartner.com.

◆◆◆◆◆

Ensure a Well-Executed Launch

Of course, all the market research in the world won't help a new product or service make a splash in the marketplace if the offering isn't launched properly. The heart of a well-executed launch? A solid marketing plan — one that you start building early in the development of a new offering, not as the product is coming off assembly lines at the factory. The sooner you start crafting your marketing plan, the more likely the details of your plan will support the objectives of the development effort.

The best marketing plans outline effective go-to-market strategies and communication programs. They take into account consumers' emotional attachment to products and reflect deep understanding of how much people are willing to pay for specific benefits provided by an offering. Messages about a new product or service — whether delivered through radio spots, magazine ads, broadcast e-mails, or some other channel — lead with the need. That is, they acknowledge the need that consumers want the product or service to fill, and they explicate how the offering fills that need better than alternative offerings do. Marketing messages also don't waste time: They pack their punch immediately because their creators know that consumers have short attention spans. See the box titled "The Splenda Success Story" for an example of how one company applied these principles to ensure a well-executed launch of a new product.

◆◆◆◆

The Splenda Success Story

Splenda, the trademarked name for a food sweetener called sucralose, has scored a smashing success in the marketplace, thanks to the savvy marketing strategies developed by McNeil Nutritionals, a division of Johnson & Johnson. Discovered in 1976 by English ingredient maker Tate and Lyle, sucralose is a sugar molecule that tastes far sweeter than sugar yet isn't absorbed by the body as a carbohydrate. It can also be used in cooking. After sucralose was approved by the FDA in 1998, McNeil created the Splenda brand.

Under the leadership of Debra Sandler, worldwide group president, the company managed to take the new brand from utter unknown to the number-one seller in less than five years—one of the most impressive feats in consumer-marketing history. The secrets of McNeil's success? Build buzz by rolling out the product gradually, persuade niche food and beverage makers to use Splenda and then target high-profile brands, and view sugar (not just other low-calorie sweeteners) as the competition.

For example, marketing experts at McNeil decided to initially make Splenda available to a small but important consumer base: diabetics. In 1999, the company began selling Splenda on the web site of a Johnson & Johnson division that makes glucose monitors. Members of the diabetic community rapidly spread the word about the new product's benefits—resulting in sales of more than 1 million units in just two years.

At the same time, marketers at McNeil began partnering with the medically seasoned Johnson & Johnson sales staff to teach doctors and nutritionists about Splenda's advantages over sugar and existing artificial sweeteners. The company also seized advantage of the low-carb diet craze that swept the American population around this time. For instance, it approached Atkins Nutritionals and persuaded the firm to use Splenda in its new line of snack bars. Robert Atkins himself even promoted the product in his book and on TV.

As another key component in McNeil's marketing plan, the company moved to get Splenda into everyday consumer products. For instance, it convinced Cadbury Schweppes that using Splenda instead of aspartame (an artificial sweetener branded as Nutrisweet and Equal) in its Diet Rite cola would enable Schweppes to differentiate itself from Coke and Pepsi—as well as reinforce its own "Better for you" marketing message. The reformulated Diet Rite has seen sales climb steadily since 2000.

Thanks to the solidity of McNeil's marketing plan for Splenda, sales of the product surpassed those of Equal as the number-one artificial sweetener in 2003. And some research firms maintain that the product has contributed to the 11 percent drop in sugar sales that occurred between 1999 and 2004.

Source: Elizabeth Esfahani, "Finding the Sweet Spot," *Business 2.0,* November 2005.

Leverage Your Firm's Core Competencies

As another way to reduce R&D's risk, you can point out ways to develop offerings that take advantage of what your company does best already. As some experts maintain, *step-out projects* — those that require entirely new competencies — tend to fail. By leveraging your firm's established talents, you and the R&D team go into the competitive arena powerfully equipped to trounce rivals.

Consider LG, the $38 billion electronics and appliance global powerhouse based in Seoul, Korea.[7] A core compe-

7. Elizabeth Esfahani, "Thinking Locally, Succeeding Globally," *Business 2.0,* December 2005, p. 96.

tency crucial to LG's success has been the company's ability to customize its products carefully to local needs and preferences. For instance, its kimchi refrigerators — a must-have in many Korean homes — feature a dedicated compartment whose sole purpose is to isolate strong-smelling kimchi (spicy, pickled, and salted vegetables) from other foods. LG deepens its understanding of local markets' idiosyncrasies through in-country R&D, manufacturing, and marketing facilities where specialists collaborate to identify the product designs and features that will best enable LG to serve local tastes. In India, which boasts a 1 billion-plus population comprising numerous religions and languages, LG operates as if it's competing in dozens of small, regional markets.

But how do you identify the core competencies that best lend themselves to breakthrough products and services? In all too many companies, executives overemphasize technology-related strengths — such as engineering, manufacturing, and operations. Sure, these strengths are important. But organizations that focus solely on such abilities overlook important marketing-related competencies, such as a company's existing customer base, sales force, and distribution channels. Additional valuable marketing competencies include customer service resources, advertising and promotion talent, and market intelligence. Unlike technology-related strengths, marketing competencies can help companies design offerings that are geared specifically to consumers' changing needs. See the box titled "Starbucks Sound: Adapting Music to Customer Demographics" for an apt illustration.

◆◆◆◆◆

Starbucks Sound:
Adapting Music to Customer Demographics

Starbucks has adapted its Starbucks Sound offering—a collection of music CDs sold in coffee shops—to its customers' changing demographics. Executives realized that its customer base had changed in recent years. For instance, in 2000, roughly 3 percent of the company's customers were between 18 and 24 years old. Sixteen percent of them were people of color, and 78 percent had college degrees. Average yearly income was $81,000. But by 2005, the percentage of Starbucks customers between 18 and 24 years old had jumped to 13 percent. People of color now constituted 37 percent of the company's customers—up dramatically from 16 percent. And average annual income had dropped to $55,000. Starbucks' response? Start offering music CDs featuring the works of artists such as Beck and Coldplay in addition to Bob Dylan and Carole King.

Source: Steven Gray and Ethan Smith, *The Wall Street Journal,* July 19, 2005.

Target Promising Markets

You can further help reduce R&D's risk by identifying the highest-potential markets for which to develop products and services.[8] High-potential markets are large—and getting larger. Customers in these markets have a strong need for products, and the competition is relatively light. In contrast, low-potential markets are characterized by lukewarm growth and intense competition, where rival companies boast a well-trained and effective sales force, an agile distribution system, and strong support services such as IT and Customer Service. Help R&D develop products targeted at more attractive markets, and you greatly enhance the team's likelihood of success.

This is precisely what the marketing team at innovation leader 3M did.[9] At 3M, scientists and engineers lacked the knowledge and skills required to get their breakthrough innovations to promising new markets. Marketing and R&D began collaborating in new ways to address this weakness. For example, most of 3M's scientists were reassigned to work in major business units, where marketing teams could help find a market for a product in development and thus increase the chances that new offerings would ultimately prove commercially viable. Larry Wendling, the head of 3M's central lab, was also assigned eight full-time marketers charged with help-

8. Michael Porter's classic "five forces" model, as described in *Competitive Advantage: Creating and Sustaining Superior Performance*, Free Press, 1985.

9. *Business 2.0,* November 2005.

ing scientists to think futuristically about products and to mingle with potential customers early in the development process. As Wendling notes, "When I tell my colleagues outside of 3M that I have marketers working for me, they salivate."

In addition to changing the way its marketers and R&D experts worked together, 3M redefined scientists' job responsibilities. For instance, researchers who were not reassigned to business units now had to focus their efforts on products intended to serve markets projected to grow 10 percent or more each year. In addition, early in the development process, researchers were required to identify the commercially viable products their work could yield.

All of these changes yielded impressive results. To illustrate, under the new regime, one chemist who had tinkered for years with nanotechnology-based materials developed a film of reflective material that boosted brightness and clarity in liquid crystal display (LCD) screens used in cell phones, laptop computers, and televisions — a highly marketable offering. As Bill Schultz, a top scientist with 3M since 1968, explains, "Finding a business unit that knows its market makes us more confident. Nothing is more frustrating than doing good tech development and not having your product commercialized . . ."

CRAFT COMPELLING PRODUCT STORIES

Clearly, you can do a lot to support R&D's efforts so that the company develops the right products, the right way. If you're overwhelmed by the many different partnering strategies described perviously, one way to make the material more manageable is to envision your role as that of screenwriter for your company's new products and services. The screenplay that you write serves as a valuable road map for your own and R&D's efforts. Early in the innovation discovery and development phase, you can begin crafting a clear, compelling narrative that has all the qualities and virtues of a great movie. Ensure that your product narrative accomplishes the following.

Set the Stage

Identify your company's strengths and weaknesses as well as important opportunities and threats presented by external changes in consumer preferences, technology, and other business forces. Take stock of your firm's competition — what it looks like now and how it might change in the future. Determine whether the potential markets you're considering serving are promising enough to be worthwhile — and will remain so in the future.

Develop the Characters

Find out what your current and potential new customers want and need. Segment them based on their needs and the benefits they're seeking from alternative offerings. Identify the customer segment(s) that your company can serve better than rivals can — based on its core competencies and unique advantages and strengths.

Establish the Plot and Conflict

Determine what features your offerings must have in order to deliver the benefits that consumers need, value, and are willing to pay for. Clarify precisely how a product's or a service's features deliver those benefits. Identify key risks and uncertainties surrounding the plan for delivering those benefits.

Resolve the Conflict

Develop a marketing plan that includes strategies for communicating your product's unique value to customers and explains exactly how the product provides the benefits consumers want. Explain in your plan how you'll address the risks and uncertainties you've identified. Provide details not only on relevant product features but also pricing, promotions, and place (distribution) — the traditional *4 Ps* of marketing.

The box titled "Telling Stories about Products" demonstrates the financial value that a compelling product narrative can generate.

Telling Stories about Products

When marketers tell compelling stories about products—by providing products with intriguing names or advertising them through engaging narratives—consumers often prove willing to pay handsomely for the offering. Consider this example from Godin's book *All Marketers Are Liars*:

"Costa Rican Tilapia. That's what the sign said at the fancy fish market in Manhattan. It was more than $10 a pound, and it sure sounded exotic." It turns out that Costa Rican tilapia are grown in backyard ponds by women who raise 500 at a time and who charge about 75¢ for each. "When you see the sign in New York, though," explains Godin, "you imagine spear fishermen or spring-fed crystal clear rivers. You certainly don't think you're buying a home-farmed commodity. Somewhere between cheap protein near the equator and my home in New York, the price and the value of the fish skyrocketed. Not because of the cost of shipping. Because of the story. Tilapia sounds exotic. Costa Rica *is* exotic. Put them together and amateur chefs are ready to line up and pay a premium."

Godin continues: "Chowhounds like me want to buy something that sounds exotic. Fishmongers want to find new supplies of fish and also want to charge enough to cover their risk. And my friend in Costa Rica certainly deserves the higher prices she'll get if her fish becomes popular in the United States. Everybody is telling a story so that I'll be able to lie to myself when I cook dinner tonight."

Source: Seth Grodin. "AllMarketersAreLiars.com," May 9, 2005.

Building bridges with R&D takes initiative, creativity, and discipline. And the process becomes even more difficult if you work in an organization marked by solid, established silos and negative stereotypes about how marketers and R&D professionals differ. Yet even within the most uncooperative culture, you can still forge bonds with the R&D team and mitigate the risks that the team faces every day in its work — by executing the strategies described previously. When you share your knowledge of the market with your colleagues in R&D, you help them not only identify the right innovations but also develop new offerings in the right ways so they succeed in the marketplace. Result? You plant seeds for future cash flow — a key contribution of a true marketing champion.

Of course, Managing East — including busting silos between marketing and sales and R&D — is especially challenging because you don't directly control these other key players in your organization. For this reason, you must also Manage South, that is, leverage the resources you *do* control to establish a bright future for marketing in your organization — and for yourself in the marketing profession. To that end, we invite you to shift your gaze from East to South in the following two chapters.

YOUR R&D PARTNERSHIP SWOT ANALYSIS

1. In what ways do you and other marketing practitioners in your company currently collaborate with your firm's R&D team on new product selection, design, and development? How well have these ways of collaborating served your company so far?

2. How would you describe your company's innovation track record? What percentage of new products and services succeeds in the marketplace? Fails? How much does your company rely on innovative offerings to generate revenues? How much does the firm invest in new products and services?

3. What stereotypes about the differences between R&D and marketing professionals are active in your company? How do these stereotypes affect the innovation process? Which stereotypes have some founding in reality? What steps might you take to eradicate such stereotypes?

4. Consider the risks inherent in your company's R&D ef-

fort. Which type of risk does your R&D team most often fall victim to — identifying the wrong products and services to develop or designing appropriately selected products poorly? What have been the consequences of these problems for your company?

5. Consider the six strategies described in this chapter for reducing the risks inherent in R&D's work: identifying products that offer unique value to consumers, encouraging a customer-focused development process, helping R&D do its homework, ensuring a well-executed launch, leveraging your firm's core competencies, and targeting promising markets. Which of these strategies do you currently use? What is keeping you from using strategies that you're not currently employing? What steps might you take to incorporate more of these strategies into your collaboration with R&D?

6. How skilled are you at crafting a clear, compelling narrative for your company's innovative products and services? Does each narrative set the stage, develop the characters, establish the plot and conflict, and resolve the conflict? If not, how might you strengthen your screenwriting skills to create narratives that expertly guide your company's innovation designs and activities?

PART FOUR

Manage South

9

Build a Brand for Marketing

Congratulations! You've just completed two long journeys — to the North and to the East. In the Managing North section of this book, you learned how to strengthen your influence with your company's higher ups — including your CEO and CFO — and develop metrics that enable you to demonstrate the value you deliver for your firm. In the Managing East chapters, you discovered ways to bust the silos that prevent you from collaborating effectively with leaders in other departments — particularly sales and R&D.

Though Managing North and Managing East are important, you'll need to do more in order to become a true marketing champion. Following our compass model, you must shift your gaze South. In our model, Managing South means building the right brand for marketing in your organization — one that says, loudly and clearly, "Marketing is all about cash flow, now and in the future." And it means delivering on that brand promise within your company. Managing South differs markedly from Managing North and East in that it entails leveraging resources — inside *and* outside your company — over which you exercise direct control. While you have no formal authority over your superiors and cross-functional peers, you *do* have control over resources such as the people you hire, the vendors and agencies that your group uses, the information and data you gather, and the ways in which your team or unit communicates and presents itself to the rest of the company. By employing such resources strategically, you can powerfully shape perceptions of marketing in your firm *and* deliver the value that your resulting marketing brand promises.

We've structured the two chapters in this Managing South section with these twin objectives in mind. In Chapter 9, we help you take stock of current perceptions of marketing in your organization and identify ways to strengthen the association between marketing and cash flow in your colleagues' minds. But building a marketing brand that screams cash flow isn't enough. You must then ensure that your department behaves in ways consistent with that brand — including assembling the right teams, developing the right relationships with external partners, and communicating a consistent, on-brand message to others in your firm. We explore these aspects of Managing South in Chapter 10.

We've got a lot of ground to cover — some familiar and some not so familiar. So set your compass for South, and let's get started.

PERCEPTION BECOMES REALITY

How do people throughout your organization perceive the marketing department? That is, what is marketing's brand in your company? If your superiors, peers, and direct reports don't associate marketing with cash flow, then you stand little chance of becoming a marketing champion. Put another way, you won't likely acquire the credibility and influence you need to win support for your ideas and generate measurable value for your firm. As we've seen, in many organizations, nonmarketing executives, managers, and employees don't view marketing as associated with cash flow. Rather, in their minds, this function is typically linked with connotations such as big spenders, creative, sensitive types, or other equally unflattering and inaccurate images.

But that doesn't mean you can't change those perceptions. Indeed, you must change them if your organization is to extract maximum value from its marketing function. The process of changing perceptions is similar to creating a brand for a product or service: You assess current perceptions of what the offering stands for, compare those perceptions with the connotations you'd *like* consumers to have in order for your offering to succeed, and adjust your marketing strategies to close any perceptual gaps. And as you know, a powerful brand can often be captured in just one or a few words. For example, as we've seen, when most people hear the name *Volvo,* the word *safety* comes immediately to mind. That's the Volvo brand. Likewise, *Nike* swiftly triggers the phrase *Just do it!* in many consumers' minds. Notice, too, that these brands demonstrate three defining characteristics: They're unique, relevant, and enduring.

Like products and services, organizational departments and functions have brands — strong associations that arise in people's minds when they think of accounting, marketing, R&D, or any other function. These associations can be positive or negative, depending on a corporation's culture and the efforts a department has made to shape companywide perceptions of what it stands for. You probably experience these associations yourself when considering various other departments in your firm. For instance, perhaps for you the accounting group has connotations such as *bean counters, green-eye-shade-wearing number crunchers,* or *sharp-eyed watchdogs.* Or maybe you think of IT as a group of *geeks, high-tech geniuses,* or *charming nerds.*

Departmental brands can also be more or less appropriate. To illustrate, the professionals who work in R&D probably don't want their colleagues in other parts of the organization to view them as merely conducting chemical experiments. Though they in fact may perform chemical experiments as part of their role, they'd likely much rather have others see them as experts who create profitable new product breakthroughs. Likewise, salespeople don't want to be thought of as only people who follow up on leads. They'd rather be seen as professionals who close lucrative deals.

Obviously, such associations strongly affect what people expect from one another and how they interact. For instance, if people in your organization view marketers as merely creative, sensitive types or brochure designers, they'll be far less likely to seriously consider your ideas than if they saw you as a cash-flow generator. For these reasons, it's vital to ensure that others in your organization view marketing in a positive, significant light — and to transform any negative perceptions into a positive brand that highlights marketing's connection to cash flow. After all, many other parts of your organization are associated with cash flow — either explicitly (think sales) or implicitly (such as R&D). You can build a similarly strong brand for marketing. But to do so, you must first take stock of current perceptions of your function.

TWO LITTLE WORDS

So let's get back to our original question: How *do* people throughout your organization view marketing? To find out, conduct an informal poll. Visit as many superiors, peers, and employees in your company as possible and ask them, "What are the one or two words that come to mind when you think of the marketing department?" Depending on the individuals you select, you may get different degrees of frankness in the responses you hear. Some people may couch their response in positive terms — such as *advertising genius* or *good communicators*. Others may provide more frankly negative terms, for example, *big budgets* or *oversensitive artists*. Of course, your relationship with a particular respondent and his or her standing in the company, relative to yours, will also influence the nature of the answers you receive. Document all the responses you get.

In addition to conducting an informal poll, to gain a deeper understanding of internal perceptions of marketing, you can also take a more formal approach. For example, survey numerous departments, gathering anonymous responses so that people feel free to share honest opinions. Explain that your purpose is to help marketing better meet the needs of its internal constituencies. Below is one possible list of questions to include in your survey. Ask staff to rate the marketing staff or function in your organization on each item shown below, on a scale of 1 to 7, where 7 means "strongly agree" and 1 means "strongly disagree." Ask respondents to report their functional area only if the number of employees is large enough so that respondents will trust that their identity will remain anonymous.

Creating Equity in the Marketplace

_____ Keeps the organization focused on customers

_____ Makes decisions based on analysis and testing

_____ Produces results in earnings for the business in the short term

_____ Produces results that grow revenues in the long term

_____ Drives speed to market

_____ Develops breakthrough ideas for selling products/ services

_____ Produces winning new product/service concepts

_____ Creates effective communications with customers and prospects

_____ Establishes strong relationships with vendors and supply chain partners

_____ Applies the best marketing tools and techniques

Creating Equity in the Organization

_____ Works effectively across organizational boundaries

_____ Is trustworthy and credible

_____ Applies hard evidence to communicate or sell ideas

_____ Uses soft evidence to communicate or sell ideas

_____ Uses effective work processes

_____ Develops meaningful measures to determine its effectiveness

_____ Helps me in my work

_____ Works productively

_____ Provides input to customer-related issues throughout the organization

_____ Uses information effectively to make decisions and communicate to others

Creating Future Equity

_____ Takes risks for future returns

_____ Identifies changes in the market and consequences for the organization

_____ Evolves in anticipation of changes and plans
accordingly
_____ Leads new product development teams effectively
_____ Provides valuable input for new product development
teams
_____ Initiates new ideas for future growth strategies
_____ Communicates future scenarios throughout the
organization
_____ Evaluates long-term profit potential of different
customer segments
_____ Grooms and mentors key staff for the future
_____ Learns from successes and failures of the organization
and other organizations

A thorough analysis of the data from the survey provides useful insight into perceptions of marketing's strengths and weaknesses. You should certainly distribute a summary version of the survey results throughout your organization, indicating some elements of an action plan to strengthen relationships.

Also conduct your own assessment of your marketing staff. Below are possible questions to ask yourself:

1. How much time each week on average does each member of your staff spend now with staff in other functional areas? How does this compare to last year?
2. What functional areas have strong connections to marketing? What functional areas have weak connections to marketing? Why? What can be done to improve the weak connections? How can you use the strong connections more effectively?
3. What needs to be done to improve the relationship between marketing and sales? Consider top-management oversight, willingness to share customer information, divergent assessment of the competition and the changing marketplace, servicing of key accounts, and new customer acquisition versus customer retention.

Regardless of the content in the responses you gather — either through an informal poll or a more formal marketing brand survey — look below the surface layers to the real substance of what you're hearing. If you see no mention of cash flow in the answers, then your mission is clear: You've got to change organization-wide perceptions of your function, that is, you must build a strong brand for marketing that associates this vital function with cash flow. Another sign that your brand needs strengthening is that people throughout your organization describe marketing's contribution in terms of inputs (what marketing does in the firm) rather than outputs (what marketing produces for the firm). Examples of input answers to an informal survey may include the following:

- **Creative Work:** Writing copy, designing brochures, creating ads
- **Account Management:** Building and maintaining customer relationships
- **Project Management:** Ensuring that marketing materials meet their identified objectives and are delivered on time and within budget
- **Team Leadership:** Managing a multidisciplinary team of professionals
- **Web Expertise:** Implementing innovative marketing strategies through online marketing activities
- **Media Buying:** Investigating and purchasing media to meet marketing objectives
- **Research:** Performing primary research and obtaining secondary research to support marketing goals and make informed decisions

All of these inputs are valuable. But they won't help you build a strong brand for marketing if others in your firm don't understand how each type of input eventually generates output — cash — for the company.

On the other hand, you may identify signs of at least a fragile perception that marketing is associated with cash flow.

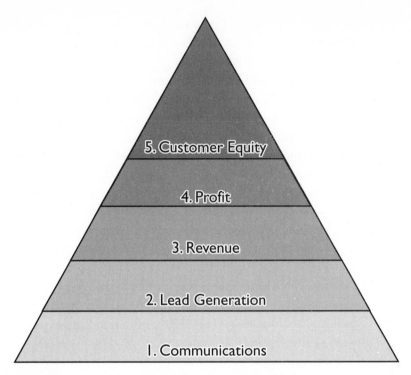

Figure 9.1 Hierarchy of cash-flow responsibilities.

Indeed, as you saw in Chapter 1, marketing has five possible levels of responsibility related to cash flow. We call this series of levels the cash-flow hierarchy and depict it again in Figure 9.1. As the figure suggests, enhancing customer equity — including attracting and retaining profitable customers — is the level most closely associated with cash-flow responsibility because it takes into account short-term cash flow (through customer acquisition) *and* long-term cash flow (through customer retention). It's also clearly about managing an important asset — your firm's customers.

As you may recall from Chapter 1, "Communications" in this figure refers to marketers' ability to get the word out about their company's offerings. "Lead Generation" means identifying people or organizations who are likely to buy the firm's products or services in the near future. "Revenue" refers to top executives' perception of marketing as a function that generates sales. "Profits" refers to cash left over *after* costs are subtracted from revenues. "Customer Equity"—the highest role for marketing in any organization—has both short-term and long-term links to cash, because the management of customers as an asset is the focus. Marketers who fill this role are responsible for customer acquisition, customer profitability, and customer retention.

As we've also seen, different organizations use marketing in different ways. By analyzing the responses from your informal poll as well as clarifying your own thoughts about your primary responsibilities in your firm, you can determine where *your* marketing function sits in this hierarchy. For example, suppose the top-most priority for marketing in your organization is to generate sales leads, with secondary responsibilities including communications. In this case, marketing sits relatively low in the hierarchy. Nevertheless, you can still strengthen the link between marketing and cash flow in your colleagues' minds. How? Show how generating and managing sales leads ultimately produces more cash for the organization.

As you saw in Chapter 5, demonstrating this series of connections may require tracing the intermediate links between the metrics "number of sales leads" and "cash flow." For example, you may need to point out that effectively managing leads increases the percentage of prospects who become actual customers, which generates more sales, which in turn enhances revenues and ultimately improves profits and cash flow. Skillful lead management also means culling out *leaks* early—prospects who were never going to buy anyway. This translates into cash by saving your company the time and money it would have wasted by nurturing connections with a dead-end prospect.

In your company, it may not be possible to move marketing up a rung or two in the cash-flow hierarchy. Marketing's primary responsibility may be dictated by company culture, history, senior management, or industry. But no matter where marketing sits in that hierarchy, you can still strengthen its connotations of cash flow in the minds of your superiors and peers.

RESHAPING PERCEPTIONS OF MARKETING

Whether others in your organization see no link at all or a tenuous link between marketing and cash flow, you can help them grasp the link *or* strengthen their appreciation for the link through several means. Many of these means have been discussed in previous chapters.

Speak the Language of Business

As you saw in Chapter 2, you can use the language of business and cite cash-flow-related metrics while discussing marketing activities and accomplishments with higher-ups, such as your CEO, CFO, or supervisor. To illustrate, suppose you believe that your company's web site should be improved in order to make it easier for customers to buy products while visiting the site. Of course, these improvements will cost money, so you anticipate getting some resistance from those who approve such expenditures. In this case, you'll want to steer clear of arguing that improving the web site will burnish the company's brand image. That's marketing-speak — useful in your own circles of fellow marketing professionals but of less interest to your Northern constituencies.

To present your idea in terms they can understand and appreciate, you'd instead argue your case using language such as the following: "Because our web site is confusing to visitors, fifteen percent of the people who come to the site depart without buying anything. That translates into between one hundred thousand and three hundred thousand dollars in lost sales every quarter." Talk in terms of lost sales, and you'll quickly get the attention of your CEO, CFO, or supervisor.

Break Down Cross-Functional Silos

As you saw in Chapters 6–8, you can also build a strong brand for marketing by breaking down the silos preventing you from collaborating effectively with your peers in sales, R&D, and other departments that have a more obvious link to cash flow.

When you work collaboratively with colleagues in other departments, you enable them to generate more cash flow. As a result, they begin viewing you as a generator of cash.

For instance, let's say the R&D team has developed a product or service that's chock-full of beguiling features — a new software application, a kitchen appliance, a healthcare plan. The offering has something for everyone, and the company fully expects to expand its market share after launching this supposed blockbuster. But *you* know that trying to be all things to all people often backfires: The marketplace is littered with feature-laden products or services that have proved so confusing to consumers that they appeal to no one. Moreover, such offerings frequently don't generate a profit. They provide features that consumers don't need or value and for which they don't want to pay a premium.

Here's where you come in: You target several different market segments to which the product might appeal and develop appropriate marketing campaigns tailored to each of those segments. Sales soar, and market share grows — bringing scads of new cash into the company's coffers. You've scored a success for your firm, and you've helped your colleagues in R&D look good. Chances are, they and others who become aware of your coup will begin viewing you in a whole new light.

Support Your Company's Business Model

Another way to strengthen marketing's link to cash flow in the minds of your superiors and colleagues is to conduct marketing activities in ways that support your company's agreed-upon business model. If you recall, a firm's business model reflects the primary means by which it generates cash. And as you've seen, there are three types of business models:

- Margin (generating high profits on sales)
- Velocity (selling products and services rapidly)
- Leverage (extracting money from existing assets and those owned by other entities)

Companies can use all three of these models, though in any particular firm, one of the three will most likely dominate.

By supporting your company's business model, you make it instantly clear that marketing has strong links to cash flow. To illustrate, suppose your company primarily uses the velocity business model. To support this model, you'd want to formulate strategies for accelerating turnover of your company's inventory — its products or services. Such strategies might contain elements including affordable pricing, basic product design, and accessible purchasing processes, such as an easy-to-use shopping cart on your company's web site. The common theme underlying all your marketing strategies? Efficiency.

Or suppose your firm relies primarily on the margin business model. If so, your marketing strategies would look very different from those in the previous scenario. Rather than aiming for efficiency (basic products delivered easily to customers at low cost), you'd want to focus on helping your company develop innovative products, tailored to customers' individual needs, and delivered through high-touch service. Your goal? To persuade customers to pay a premium price for what they perceive as high-value offerings — a price that significantly exceeds the costs of providing the product or service. To accomplish this goal, you'd need to develop a deep understanding of individual customer's unique needs and requirements — possibly through innovative market research tactics. And you'd have to gauge potential customers' perceptions of different price points. For example, at what price points might customers stop feeling they were paying for extra quality and begin feeling that they were overpaying for your offerings? You'd probably also want to assess how often customers would be comfortable hearing from your company and what types of contact they prefer — such as phone calls, on-site visits, e-mails, special web offers, and so forth.

Regardless of the business model that predominates in your company, you can help your superiors and colleagues see your connection to cash flow by actively supporting that model.

Focus Your Energy on What You *Can* Control

Yet another way to strengthen marketing's brand in your enterprise is to take stock of what you can and can't change — and focus your efforts on factors under your control. For instance, as discussed previously, you may not be able to change marketing's position in the cash-flow hierarchy, given your company's culture or the role that's been defined for your department. But as you saw earlier, that doesn't mean you can't clearly explicate the connections between marketing's primary responsibility in the firm — such as communications or sales leads — and the eventual generation of cash.

Another factor that may lie outside your control involves interpersonal difficulty. For example, perhaps you don't get along well with your CEO or supervisor: You and he are like oil and water whenever you interact. Or maybe the CEO or your boss is dead set on viewing marketing as a necessary evil, and there's no way you're ever going to change his or her opinion. In situations like these, it's best to focus your brand-building efforts on elements you *can* control. Take stock of these: Perhaps you get along beautifully with the head of sales or R&D. Or maybe you've heard the CFO express positive views of marketing. Regardless of who these individuals are, start your brand-building campaign with them rather than wasting time and energy on colleagues or superiors whom you have little or no hope of converting.

Be Seen as a Cash-Flow Leader

As we stated in Chapter 1, to be a true marketing champion, you must do more than help others see how marketing is connected to cash. You must also be perceived as *a cash-flow leader:* someone to whom others in the organization look to generate the dollars needed for fulfilling the firm's mission.

How do you determine whether you're a cash-flow leader? If you read any business books on leadership (and there are lots of them), leadership comprises many dimensions. When it comes to cash flow, however, we need just a few indicators to assess your leadership prowess. For example, perhaps you have decision-making authority over changes in the marketing budget. In addition, you might have a leadership role in identifying new business opportunities as well as determining product and market investment choices. Note that leadership can have a passive quality. For instance, you might identify new business opportunities on an incidental or opportunistic basis, or perhaps others consult you only occasionally about new business opportunities. What we're talking about goes far beyond these more passive types of leadership. True cash-flow leaders take a strong position that the rest of their organization follows.

Do such marketers and marketing organizations exist? To find out, we conducted a brief survey of 214 marketing professionals in companies that had at least $10 million in annual revenues. This sample included medium-size businesses ($10 to $100 million), large business ($100 million to $1 billion) and very large business (greater than $1 billion). We asked our respondents three questions concerning their leadership role with respect to the dimensions discussed in the preceding (that is, discretion in budget changes, identification of new business opportunities, and determination of product and market decisions). We also asked them the extent to which they were connected to cash flow. As evidence of this connection, we looked for signs that their performance was measured according to specific profitability or cash-flow objectives.

We then organized the responses into four cells (by using standard measurement and statistical techniques), consistent with the Cash-Flow Driver Index we introduced in Chapter 1. Here is what we found:

- **60 Marketing Champions** (high on Cash Flow and high on Leadership)
- **14 Rainmakers** (high on Cash Flow but low on Leadership)
- **97 Politicians** (low on Cash Flow but high on Leadership)
- **68 Minions** (low on Cash Flow and low on Leadership)

So marketing champions *do* exist — heartening news for anyone seeking to change perceptions of marketing in their organization and optimize the value that marketing delivers. There also seem to be a lot of Politicians out there. To be sure, these individuals play a strong leadership role: They collaborate with colleagues in other parts of the organization, make suggestions about how the company might invest its resources, and help set direction. However, they are not marketing champions because they have not convincingly made the connections between what they do and how it relates to cash flow. That is, they work only on specific and well-defined tasks (managing marketing research, creating collateral sales materials, scheduling media for advertising). Or they're responsible for tasks with revenue objectives, but not for dealing with the cost side. Thus they're not accountable for profitability. For this reason, Politicians often "talk a good game," but they're not necessarily "delivering the goods" in terms of cash. Thus, they risk becoming marginalized eventually.

A small percentage of our sample falls into the Rainmaker category. These marketers have the opposite problem of Politicians. They are tightly linked to cash flow (the good news) but aren't perceived as cash-flow leaders. While this situation describes many sales professionals, it's an unfortunate position for a marketing practitioner or organization. Why? Rainmakers are tactical: They bring in the cash, but they don't shape the company's direction. Thus, they tend to be followers.

Last, we have those marketing professionals and functions in the most trouble. Minions (and there are a lot of them out there) run the greatest risk of being marginalized in any organization. They are not cash flow leaders, and their activities are not perceived as having any connection to cash flow.

So which quadrant would you and your marketing function fit in this model: Are you a Marketing Champion? Rainmaker? Politician? Minion? By building the right brand for marketing in your organization — and delivering on that brand promise — you boost your chances of migrating into that all-important Marketing Champion quadrant.

No matter how marketing is perceived in your organization or where you sit in the firm's organizational chart, you can still Manage South. That is, you can leverage the resources under your control to burnish marketing's image in the minds of at least some of your colleagues and superiors. But building a strong brand for marketing in your firm isn't enough. As with any brand, you also need to deliver on the promise that your brand communicates. Put another way, you must behave in ways that are consistent with the brand promise, that reinforce the promise, and that meet the expectations regarding your brand that you've created in your constituents' minds. After all, you can imagine what would happen to Volvo if, after making consumers believe that its cars were safe, the vehicles turned out to be death traps.

In Chapter 10, we turn to this notion of delivering on the brand promise you establish for marketing in your organization. We examine additional resources under your control — such as the processes you've established (including market segmentation), the vendors and agencies you select, the data and information you gather, the staff you hire, and your communication prowess. And we show you how to use these resources to further strengthen and elevate your marketing brand and execute marketing strategies that generate the cash flow promised by your brand. With these goals in mind, let's now explore this second aspect of Managing South.

YOUR BRAND-BUILDING SWOT ANALYSIS

1. By what means might you assess current perceptions of marketing's purpose and value in your organization? For example, will you conduct an informal poll of your superiors and colleagues? Will you ask people throughout your company to take an online marketing brand audit?

2. If you've conducted an informal poll or asked people to take an online marketing brand audit, what do the results suggest about how marketing is perceived overall in your firm?

How strong is the link between marketing and cash flow in the minds of your organizational peers and superiors? To what extent do people understand how marketing activities contribute value to the organization in terms of cash flow?

3. Based on others' perceptions of marketing in your company, where does your function sit in the cash-flow hierarchy? Consider the following levels, in increasingly order of cash-flow responsibility: communications, sales leads, revenues, profits, and customer equity.

4. If marketing sits relatively low in the cash-flow hierarchy of responsibilities, do you believe its position can be elevated? Why or why not? If your answer is yes, what are the one or two highest-leverage actions you can take to elevate marketing's position in the hierarchy? Consider actions such as speaking the language of business, supporting your company's dominant business model, using a series of metrics to highlight the series of links between marketing activities and cash flow, and employing other techniques you've discovered in earlier chapters of this book.

5. If your organization's culture or other factors mean that marketing's position in the cash-flow hierarchy must remain as is, how might you nevertheless strengthen the link between marketing's primary responsibility *as it stands now* and the generation of cash flow? Again, consider how you might use business language, metrics, and so forth.

6. Who in your organization is most likely to be amenable to viewing marketing as playing a key role in identifying future sources of cash flow and harvesting that cash flow (if they don't already hold this viewpoint)? Why? How might you target your marketing-brand-building efforts to each of these individuals in order to get the results you desire?

7. What do you see as the two or three largest obstacles to building a strong brand for marketing in your firm? What weak spots in these obstacles might you exploit in order to overcome these challenges and strengthen marketing's brand in the company?

8. Based on our descriptions of the four quadrants in the

Cash-Flow Driver Index — Marketing Champions, Rainmakers, Politicians, and Minions — where would you place yourself and your marketing organization in this model? Why? What steps might you take to move yourself into the Marketing Champions quadrant?

10

Deliver on Marketing's Brand Promise

Using the suggestions in Chapter 9, you've taken stock of how marketing is perceived in your organization — that is, you've assessed marketing's brand. Moreover, you've pegged your marketing department's position on the cash-flow hierarchy and in the Cash-Flow Driver Index. Perhaps the news isn't good: In the minds of your firm's higher-ups and your colleagues, marketing has little or no connection to cash flow or to cash-flow leadership. Instead, people view the purpose of your function as primarily designing marketing communications or, perhaps, generating sales leads. Worse, maybe they even disparage marketers as wasteful spenders of limited resources on advertising, or as left-brain, unpredictable creative types. Or they believe that marketing doesn't require specialized skills — that anyone can do it.

You know that marketing activities generate both short- and long-term cash for your company. So how do you help others throughout your enterprise see those links? That is, how do you strengthen marketing's brand inside the organization? In Chapter 9, you reviewed some brand-building techniques that had been discussed in detail in earlier chapters — such as speaking the language of business with the executive team and with your colleagues; forging mutually beneficial bonds with peer managers in sales, R&D, and other departments; and identifying marketing activities and strategies that support your company's dominant business model. Such techniques can help you strengthen the link between

marketing and cash flow no matter where your function sits in
the cash-flow hierarchy. They can also enable you to elevate
marketing's position in the hierarchy, for example, by raising
perceptions of marketing's core purpose from, say, generating
sales leads to enhancing customer equity.

But as we explained in Chapter 9, true marketing champions don't stop at establishing a strong, positive brand that
firmly links marketing to cash flow in their organization. They
also *deliver* on that brand's promise — by fulfilling the expectations of marketing that they've created in their internal constituents' minds. Yet in order to satisfy those expectations —
to generate cash through effective marketing activities and
initiatives and to be seen as a cash-flow leader — you need to
win support for those activities and initiatives from people
throughout your firm. To garner that support, you must build
a solid track record of accomplishments as well as present a
convincing case for your ideas to diverse constituents in your
organization.

Delivering on the brand you've worked hard to create
requires thoughtful management of the numerous resources
directly under your control — including your persuasive
powers, the information and data you gather, and the vendors
and agencies you work with. In this chapter — the final section
in Managing South — we show you how to leverage such resources so that marketing's role as an engine of cash flow becomes undisputed in your company.

LEVERAGE THE POWER OF PERSUASION

We've talked a lot about internal communication in previous
chapters in this book. For example, in Chapter 2, we argued
that, to be associated with cash flow, marketing professionals
must learn to speak the language of business when communicating with members of the executive team and with peer
managers throughout their organization. In that chapter, we
introduced five business terms that every marketing practitioner should understand and know how to use. We also
stressed the importance of clarifying the meaning of market-

ing terms and using those terms consistently. And we argued that establishing repeatable, transparent marketing processes can further encourage you to use business and marketing terminology consistently.

In this chapter, we examine the notion of internal communication from another, equally important angle: persuasion. As a seasoned marketing professional, you're a persuasive communicator. You know how to deliver messages that speak to consumers' most pressing needs and concerns and that enable them to perceive the unique value provided by your company's products and services. Your communications *within* your organization must meet the same standards of excellence and effectiveness if you hope to win support for the marketing initiatives you know will generate cash for your company. Just as you must present a clear, compelling case to consumers for why they should buy your company's offerings, you must make a convincing case to executives and colleagues for why they should buy your ideas. Only then will you receive the approvals, funding, assistance, and other forms of support you'll need to get your ideas off the ground and soaring.

Marketing champions enhance their perceived value in their firm by communicating effectively with internal audiences. Put another way, they enable those audiences to understand their ideas and to agree that the proposed initiatives are promising. They also inspire others to care about seeing their proposals put into action and to actively support their ideas. The hallmarks of a talented marketing communicator? Consider this opinion from Spencer Stuart executive search consultant Jerry Noonan:

> A good marketer creates a well-understood story about the marketplace . . . [The story] has to be factual, and logical, and structured, but [also] engaging and interesting enough so that people can instinctively embrace it. And sometimes marketers get very complicated with graphs, and charts, and data, and the story is gone. All the facts may be right, but the story is gone. And then, likewise, if

[the story is] overly simplified and trite, it's not going to be credible. Good marketers have that ability to find a way to tell the story where everyone can believe it. You want the marketers initially, and ultimately the organization, to have the market in their head, heart, and gut. They understand the facts and the relevant, specific information they need to know. They believe in their heart and their gut such that every decision they make is naturally filtered through the market and all the relevant variables.[1]

What Noonan is describing here is the blending of the science and art of persuasion in your internal communications about marketing. The science part of the equation comes from your use of information and analysis to achieve credibility. The art derives from the ability to evoke emotion in order to engage your audience in your message. By using science, you appeal to your audience's head; through art, you appeal to their heart. When you appeal to both head and heart in your internal communications, your constituents want to *hear* your story (your idea or proposal for an initiative), they want to *tell* that story to others, and they want to *play a role* in the story.

Remember: The root of the verb *to communicate* means *to make common* or *to bring together.* Thus, the aim of your internal communication is to unify people throughout your organization behind your marketing initiatives, strategies, and tactics. With this as the goal for your internal communications, how might you best blend information and emotion to present potent, persuasive proposals to your internal constituents? The following guidelines can help.

Just the Facts, Ma'am

In the realm of business, *facts* usually consist of numbers representing data, analyses, trends, the potential or actual value of a business opportunity or investment, and performance.

---

1. From a telephone interview on September 29, 2003. Jerry Noonan worked for over 20 years in marketing management for such companies as

Executives make decisions based on their assessment of these numbers. And the contributions of marketing and other professionals are valued according to numerical assessments. Raw data can help set the stage for your persuasion campaign by painting a picture of an intriguing opportunity or a dire threat that must be addressed. To paint that picture, think about all the numbers you might present to top management and peers to convince them of the value of your idea. Then decide which numbers will most motivate your audience to embrace your idea.

For example, a brand manager at Mars who advocated the introduction of a bite-sized version of the Snickers candy bar effectively used one number to clearly and repeatedly answer the question "Why go bite-sized?" Her goal? To convince the manufacturing staff of the idea's value.[2] Every time she visited the plant to define processes for developing machinery that could cut the candy into small pieces, she reminded production managers of the ultimate reward of supporting her idea: "Did I tell you that this will be a one hundred twenty-five million dollar business?" In her view, no other facts or numbers mattered. The "one hundred twenty-five million dollar business" was *the* number that communicated clearly to everyone in the organization *why* marketing and manufacturing were working so hard to solve the technical problem raised by the notion of creating a bite-sized version of the product.

To be sure, the company researched hundreds of other numbers to answer questions regarding *who, what, how,* and *when.* But those numbers involved logistics. They helped the company make the practical decisions needed to carry out the initiative successfully. They didn't motivate the brand manager's internal constituents nearly as much as the $125 million dollar figure did.

Let's consider another example of how to select the right

Nabisco, PepsiCo, and Polaroid and now specializes in executive search assignments in marketing in the Boston office of Spencer Stuart.

2. "The Big Fat Silver Lining: Blockbuster Lessons for Challenging Times," Marketing Conference, The Conference Board, October 1–2, 2003.

numbers with which to make your case. This example is hypothetical. Suppose John, a marketer in the breakfast-cereal unit at BestFoods, advocates development of a low-carbohydrate cereal. He presents his case to top management, showing them the following numbers:

- 25 million Americans — over 10 percent of all adults — are on the Atkins Diet.[3] This figure is up from 10 million just five years ago.
- Beef and egg consumption are up this year over last year by 20 percent and 25 percent, respectively. This is the biggest annual increase for both foods since the early 1970s.
- Books on the Atkins Diet and the South Beach Diet (which also advocates low-carb intake) are topping the *New York Times* bestseller list in the advice category.
- A new low-carb pasta product has just been launched by our biggest competitor in California. Sales have hit $5 million, with distribution in just two grocery chains.
- Our cereals are the highest in carbohydrates of all the leading brands. They have 39 grams of carbs per serving, compared to an average of 24 grams per serving in other products.
- Excessive intake of carbohydrates causes obesity, a worsening problem in the United States. It also causes diabetes. Indeed, the American Diabetes Association is mounting a big campaign to warn overweight adults of the threat.

These facts and figures paint an intriguing picture of a potential jump in American consumers' demand for low-carb products — a major opportunity for BestFoods. But raw data isn't enough to present a compelling message to John's audiences within the organization. To persuade and inspire them to support his ideas, he must *interpret* data in ways that answer his audiences' core question: "Why should we devote time, en-

3. "Atkins Diet Fuels Surging Demand for U.S. Beef," *Forbes.com,* November 14, 2003.

ergy, and money to implement your idea?" In addition, many seasoned executives have an understandable skepticism regarding numbers. They've seen people distort data to support dubious conclusions and present information in misleading ways in order to obscure the truth behind the numbers. As strategy consultant Watts Wacker said, "I've never met a database I couldn't make say whatever I wanted . . . I am very suspicious of how the 'science' side [of marketing] gets manipulated."[4]

To overcome executives' healthy suspicion regarding manipulation of numerical data, John obviously will need to present numerical information in accurate, honest ways. But to answer that all-important question, "Why?" he must also weave in the second part of the persuasion equation: emotion.

Stir Up Those Passions

You know that generating sales requires evoking particular emotions within consumers regarding your company's products and services. After all, the facts, figures, and features associated with a product only go so far: They appeal primarily to a potential customer's reason. For example, a customer looking over sport utility vehicle (SUV) models in a showroom might say: "Hmmm . . . Those new fold-down seats and gear bags in this SUV will help me organize my belongings better when I'm packing for a camping trip." But it's the feelings that a product stirs in a customer's heart that most determines whether he or she will buy. For instance, this shopper may be coolly assessing the prospect of being more organized while packing for camping trip. Yet he'll feel his pulse quicken when he envisions taking off in the SUV for a week of uninterrupted communion with nature, during which he has all the equipment and supplies he needs to survive in the wilderness. It's that vision of self-contained independence that stirs his passions.

In a similar vein, you can blend emotion with information

4. Telephone interview with authors, August 20, 2003.

in your internal communications to inspire top management, colleagues, and staff to embrace your ideas. Consider these techniques:

• **Share *your* passion.** Founder and CEO of Starbucks Howard Schultz instructs readers of his book to "pour your heart into it" if you want to build your business.[5] Recognizing the power of emotion to motivate, Schultz opens his book with a quotation from Antoine de Saint-Exupery in *The Little Prince*: "It is only with the heart that one can see rightly." Schultz has long inspired audiences with his love for the "mystery and romance" of the "coffee experience."

Likewise, you can arouse your internal constituents' enthusiasm for your ideas by communicating your own passion. For example, John at BestFoods, who's arguing for development of a low-carb breakfast cereal, could augment his intriguing facts and figures with an impassioned and sincere story about his own fervent commitment to healthy living. "Ever since my health scare last year," he might say, "I've made a disciplined effort to eat healthier and exercise regularly. By cutting down on carbs, I've lost twenty pounds, and my doctor told me last month that I'm healthier than ever — even with a family history of heart disease. I credit these diet changes with actually extending my life."

• **Inspire with stories of victory.** Winning teams — and organizations — often experience an emotion that amounts to ecstasy. You can evoke this feeling, and thereby win listeners' commitment to your idea, by relating stories of victories that your company has achieved. For instance, John might remind top managers of the time when BestFoods took a chance and introduced an innovative new product that scored a major hit in the marketplace. After relating this story, he could then link that victory to the current opportunity for success that he believes his idea for a low-carb cereal could generate — if the executive team supported it.

5. Howard Schultz, *Pour Your Heart Into It: How Starbucks Built a Company One Cup at a Time*, Hyperion Press, 1999.

- **Build suspense.** Few among us fail to experience tension while watching a thriller on TV or at the movies. The best film directors know how to build suspense through music, actors' facial expressions, clever camera angles, and other tactics. After creating tension through such means, they resolve the tension by showing how the plot plays out: The murderer lurking around the corner suddenly reveals his face — and we realize with triumphant satisfaction that it's the creepy neighbor after all, just as we had suspected. The bad guy is finally caught by the authorities, and we breathe a sigh of relief. The lead character realizes, after much agonized waiting, that she in fact does not have a terminal illness. Her family gathers around her to celebrate, and we weep with joy along with them.

As the preceding examples suggest, when tension in a story is resolved, audiences experience an intense release of emotion. This experience, in turn, causes them to feel a deep and meaningful connection to the story and its characters. Savvy marketers can evoke a similar feeling of connection to themselves and their story (their proposal) by building suspense in the minds of their audience. How might our fellow marketer John create tension for top management in presenting his case for development of a low-carbohydrate cereal? Perhaps he could emphasize disturbing details about competing companies' success with launching similarly cutting-edge products. He might also use stark graphics to show how these firms have been slowly stealing customers and market share from his company. He could then resolve the tension — and stimulate emotional release — by demonstrating (through compelling numbers) how his company could regain these losses by launching a blockbuster product. If he uses this technique skillfully, his listeners will feel a series of emotions: nervousness about falling behind the competition, relief that there's a way out of their predicament, and, finally, excitement about putting John's proposed solution into practice.

- **Draw analogies.** An *analogy* — a comparison between two unrelated ideas or things — can also evoke powerful emotions in the hearts of your listeners. For example, while testifying in Microsoft's antitrust case, CEO Bill Gates argued that telling his company to remove its web browser from its operating system would be like telling automotive manufacturers to remove radios from their cars to prevent radio companies from going out of business. Even if the analogy was flawed (General Motors and other automakers don't manufacture the radios in their cars), it had the desired effect. At the time, observers said that Gates's analogy hit a home run in the company's defense.[6]

Appealing to your audience's head and heart gains you the support you need to implement the good ideas that will generate cash for your company. Thus, persuasion can help you deliver on marketing's brand promise in the firm. But a persuasive bent isn't enough. You also need to establish transparent, repeatable processes. In Chapter 2, we maintained that standardized processes help you settle on and consistently use often-ambiguous marketing terms. In the following, we argue that by establishing consistent processes, you demonstrate your ability to deliver reliably on marketing's brand. Let's examine this aspect of Managing South more closely.

ESTABLISH TRANSPARENT, REPEATABLE PROCESSES

As we've seen, marketing entails a world of processes — including segmenting markets, creating advertising campaigns, conducting customer research, designing web sites, and so forth. And experts in the field can debate endlessly about how best to carry out these processes. It's impossible to say what the best way of segmenting markets may be at a particular company, for example. However, if you hope to win the credibility you need to earn your superiors' and peers' support for your good ideas, you must apply marketing processes consistently and in ways that others view as reliable. Just as finance professionals achieve stature by using transparent, repeatable processes to interpret numbers and report corporate performance, marketing professionals can — and must — do the same.

6. Steve Lohr, "In Senate Testimony, Gates Champions Microsoft," *New York Times*, March 4, 1998.

To show you what we mean, let's examine one particularly important marketing process: segmenting markets.

Segmenting Markets

If you're like most marketers, you probably spend a significant amount of time identifying the best target markets for your organization's products and services. Though experts readily agree that establishing a target market for an offering is essential to success, they disagree on how best to segment a market. For example, should you group consumers into categories based primarily on demographics (such as older consumers or large families)? Behavior (for example, people who smoke)? Personality characteristics (for instance, individuals who value autonomy)? Lifestyle (such as people who are physically active)? The benefits that an offering provides (for instance, preventing tooth decay)? A combination of some or all of these characteristics?

Whether your company sells to consumers or other businesses — and whether market segmentation occurs during product design, product launch, or product lifecycle transitions — you need to develop a consistent, defensible method for dividing your market into distinct groups of buyers, or segments. As you know, segmenting enables you to identify a target group and position your offerings to attract members of that group. And as you might guess, when you make a convincing case for the segmentation process you've chosen, you further build credibility for the marketing function.

For example, suppose you believe that it's best to segment the market according to the principle benefit that different groups of consumers want from a particular product or product category. You decide to use the toothpaste market to illustrate your case, and you present Table 10.1 to top management.[7]

7. Allen Weiss, "How to Segment Markets," MarketingProfs.com, March 1, 2005; drawing from Russell Haley, "Benefit Segmentation: A Decision-Oriented Research Tool," *Journal of Marketing*, July 1968.

Table 10.1
Segmenting the Toothpaste Market

Segment Descriptor	Segment Name			
	Sensory	Sociable	Worrier	Independent
Principle benefit sought	Fruity or minty flavor, product appearance	White, bright teeth	Decay prevention, plaque and gum disease avoidance	Price
Demographic	Children	Young people	Families, older consumers	Men, large families
Behavioral pattern	Seekers of appealing taste, texture, etc.	Smokers	Heavy users of dental supplements	Heavy users of toothpaste
Personality	High self-involvement	High sociability	Hypochondriac	High autonomy
Lifestyle	Hedonistic	Active	Conservative	Value-oriented

To argue your case for segmenting by "principle benefit sought," you point out to your audience that the demographic, behavioral, personality, and lifestyle descriptors *may or may not* correlate directly with principle benefits sought. For example, perhaps many smokers would care just as much about avoiding gum disease or paying low prices as they would about having whiter teeth. And maybe people who are hypochondriacs prefer mint-flavored toothpastes because they perceive them as healthier and cleaner than the more sugary-tasting products.

You then explain why you believe it's best to segment by benefit sought rather than the other descriptors. "This is the only way we can be sure we're sending a clear message to the market about what our products provide," you say. "And it's the only we can know for certain that we're delivering what the customer wants." To back up your argument, you introduce the simple example shown in Table 10.2, which depicts product names in bold for each segment.

Table 10.2
Segmenting the Cereal Market by Benefit

Segment Descriptor	Segment Name	
	Health conscious	**Sweet tooth**
Benefits sought	Healthy/nutritious food	Sweet/sugary flavor
Young	**Rough Riders**	**Honey Bears**
Old	**Bran Flakes**	**Sugar Blend**

You note that by segmenting the cereal market according to benefits sought, you can clearly communicate the benefits of each product to its corresponding segment. Now you show your audience Table 10.3, which segments the cereal market not by benefits but by age group. You note that, if you had segmented the cereal market by age group rather than benefits, you wouldn't be able to craft a clear message about the advantages of each product for the intended segment.

Table 10.3
Segmenting the Cereal Market by Age Group

Segment Descriptor	Segment Name	
	Old	**Young**
Benefits sought	Unknown	Unknown
	Sugar Blend	**Honey Bears**
	Bran Flakes	**Rough Riders**

The executives nod in agreement, but one of them says, "Okay, I understand what you're saying. But how exactly do you determine which benefit segments to identify?" You explain that you use the following guiding principles:

• **Usage:** Light users and heavy users of a product often care about different benefits. For instance, people who drink a lot of coffee throughout the day may want a coffeemaker that can generate small amounts of fresh, tasty brew at frequent intervals during a day. By contrast, people who only occasionally drink coffee to jump-start their day after a late night may care less about taste and freshness and more about price.

• **Application:** Customers who use products that are mission-critical — that is, if the product fails, the customer's business fails — care about different benefits than those who use non-mission-critical products. For example, a brokerage firm that has installed a sophisticated computer network system — which enables it to track detailed information in real time — would likely go out of business if the system crashed for more than a few hours. That firm will care most about benefits such as system reliability, data recoverability, and so forth.

• **Experience with product category:** Consumers who have a lot of experience with a product category will want different benefits than novice users. To illustrate, a seasoned computer geek may care more about a laptop's sophistication, while a beginner computer user will probably care most about the quality of the company's help desk.

In addition to outlining these guiding principles for segmenting a market by benefits sought, you explain the importance of testing your assumptions about these segments. For example, you conduct market research to determine whether the different benefits-based segments in fact prefer the different benefits you've theorized. If you find that they don't, you reconfigure the segments and repeat the research process. "How do you know when you've got it right?" one of your listeners asks. You reply: "We've hit it right when we see that the segments we've defined are *measurable* — we can identify the segment's size — and when they're *reachable* through specific media."

Intrigued by your presentation, your listeners give you the go-ahead to segment the market by benefits sought for a new product line your company is developing. And when the line is finally launched, it scores a smashing success in the marketplace.

In addition to leveraging the power of persuasion and establishing transparent, repeatable processes, two additional steps can enable you to deliver on the brand promise that you've made: forging productive working relationships with agencies and making the right marketing decisions. We examine each of these in the following sections.

FORGE PRODUCTIVE WORKING RELATIONSHIPS WITH AGENCIES

As a marketing practitioner, you work extensively with ad agencies and other vendors. By forging productive working relationships with these collaborators, you increase the chances of delivering on marketing's brand promise. But establishing these relationships isn't easy. "It's like a marriage. It takes time. You can't give up," notes Cathy Constable, who has worked on both sides of the desk — as a brand manager for 18 years at Saatchi & Saatchi and as vice president of marketing communications and brand management at AT&T.[8] "There isn't always an answer to every problem," Constable adds. "But if we work it together, and know we're on the same page together with open dialogue and communications built on trust, we will be successful."

Building productive relationships with agencies starts with understanding the typical points of friction that arise in these collaborations. For example, marketers often blame

8. "Reach Out and Trust Someone," *Reveries Magazine,* January 2004.

their agency partners for missing opportunities, failing to be proactive, staffing the account with mediocre talent, and — the ultimate crime — subpar work. Agencies, for their part, frequently accuse their clients of not taking full advantage of the agencies' best ideas, of putting agencies in a defensive position, and of tying agencies' hands with limited budgets and other constraints.

How do you guard against these problems? Consider these guidelines:

- **Clarify expectations during the pitch.** While reviewing pitches from agencies you're considering working with, clarify your assumptions about how each agency will service your account and meet your needs. Get answers to the following questions: "Who will handle our project, and what are their qualifications? How much of their time will they devote to our account?" "How will we deal with changes in the project or conflicts that arise?" "Who will make which decisions?" "What will the costs be and how will they be allocated?" "What will the financial variables be, for example, staffing, performance incentives, and liability of media contracts?"
- **Address staffing and financial concerns.** Once you begin working with an agency, questions and problems may arise between your staff and the agency's staff regarding who has authority over what and who is responsible for what. To minimize such problems, establish clear lines of authority and responsibility, and ensure that all participants feel comfortable sounding the alarm if problems arise in the working relationship. Hold constructive gripe sessions characterized by respectful but honest exchanges rather than venting and finger-pointing. And regularly review costs and staff changes to ensure that the project remains on track and continues to meet both parties' expectations.
- **Clarify work processes.** Determine how you and the agency will handle any staff shortages and turnover, how you will measure the agency's performance, what the ad campaign's key objectives are, and how digital assets created by

the agency will be managed (for example, who will store them, and how might they be reused?).

By applying these guidelines, you sweeten the odds of a more successful collaboration with the vendors and agencies you work with — and of creating the results your company wants.

MAKE SMART MARKETING DECISIONS

You make decisions every day, as an individual and as a participant in teams and departments. And as you've probably realized, making smart decisions is one of the most daunting challenges of business. Yet to deliver on marketing's brand promise, it's essential that you master this challenge. Through well-informed, thoughtful decisions, you produce the results that matter to your firm.

There are many resources out there offering ideas for how to make smart decisions. But here's one approach that you may find helpful.

1. **Frame the decision.** Framing a decision means asking a question that guides your decision process. That question can set you on a productive path — or a destructive one. For example, when John Sculley was vice president of marketing at Pepsi and trying to decide how best to beat archrival Coca-Cola, he framed the decision with the question: "How can we design our bottles better?" He and other Pepsi executives had assumed that Coke's classic bottle was the company's most powerful competitive advantage. As a result of framing the decision in this way, Pepsi executives spent millions of dollars researching new bottle designs before realizing that they had asked the wrong question. The company, Sculley realized, didn't know enough about what consumers wanted to merit such investment in bottle designs.[9] Sculley shifted gears and began studying how people actually consumed Pepsi and

9. John Sculley, *Odyssey: Pepsi to Apple*, Harper & Row, 1987.

other soft drinks in their homes. He decided to design packaging that made it easier for people to get more soft drinks into their homes. The larger and more varied packaging choices Pepsi developed pushed the company from a distant second to a strong competitor for first in the category—and made the classic Coke bottle virtually extinct.

2. Gather intelligence. Once you've framed your decision properly, the question you've posed will guide you to gather the right information to further inform your decision — as the Pepsi example demonstrates.

3. Reach relevant conclusions. In evaluating the intelligence you've gathered, make sure you're drawing informed conclusions from what you're seeing in the data. Evaluate all the information with an objective eye — resisting the common tendency to consider only data that confirms your current theories. Practice basic principles of good research — such as ensuring you've obtained a sufficiently large sample of data to draw solid conclusions and checking your interpretations of the data with others to see if they have additional valuable viewpoints on what the information is telling you.

4. Take appropriate action. Based on the conclusions you've drawn from the data, identify the actions you'll take. Sculley took appropriate action when he decided to design Pepsi packaging in ways that bore no resemblance to the classic Coke bottle and that served the consumer needs he had identified.

5. Learn from experience. Whenever you make a decision, evaluate the outcome. If your decision didn't generate the results you wanted or it caused unintended consequences — such as lower-than-expected sales or problems with quality — learn from the experience. Track your decisions over time to see where your decision-making weaknesses lie. For example, do you tend to underestimate the amount of time a project will require? Do you often fail to gather information that disconfirms your assumptions? Look for patterns, and adjust your decision-making process to strengthen any weak areas.

By exercising your powers of persuasion; establishing transparent, repeatable processes for key marketing activities; forging productive working relationships with agencies; and making smart marketing decisions, you position yourself to deliver on your marketing brand's promise: generating cash flow for your company. And you lay the groundwork for the next part of this book: Managing West. In the following chapters, you'll shift focus to identifying and leveraging the tantalizing opportunities that change presents — for your organization *and* your career.

Your Brand-Delivery SWOT Analysis

1. How persuasive an internal communicator are you? Evaluate yourself on the following criteria: use of information while advocating an idea to top management or peers, ability to share your passion for your ideas, use of victory stories, ability to build suspense, and use of compelling analogies. Do you tend to appeal more to your audience's head or heart? How do your attempts at persuasion typically turn out — do your listeners often embrace your ideas? Or do they more often reject them?

2. What steps might you take to improve your persuasive powers? For example, could you join a club that helps members sharpen their presentation skills? Could you take a course or read a book on the subject? Might you practice presentations with a trusted friend or colleague to hone your skill?

3. How consistently do you and your staff use marketing terminology? Which words and phrases have meanings on which everyone in your organization can agree? Which tend to have ambiguous or multiple meanings?

4. How might you create shared meaning of important marketing terminology? For instance, could you conduct meetings at which your staff and others in your organization review ambiguous terms and decide on specific meanings for them?

5. How transparent and repeatable are the processes you use to carry out important marketing activities, such as segmenting markets, building brands, and designing web sites? What additional processes would benefit most from more transparency and consistency?

6. What steps might you take to make important marketing processes more transparent and repeatable? To illustrate, could you research several suggested ways of carrying out a process and select the one that seems most effective to you? Could you establish checklists for important processes and use them to ensure that you execute these processes the same way each time?

7. How productive are your working relationships with agencies? How might you forge better relationships with these partners?

8. How do your most important marketing decisions usually turn out? What steps could you take to build a better decision-making track record?

PART FIVE

Manage West

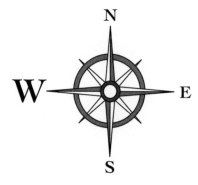

11

Leverage Fresh Opportunities on the Business Frontier

You've mastered the art of Managing South — using the resources under your control to define a brand for your marketing function that says cash flow in no uncertain terms and identifying ways to deliver on that brand promise. Now it's time to Manage West — to size up the many alluring opportunities out there on the frontier that can help you further enhance perceptions of marketing's value in your organization. In American history, the notion of gazing West has always evoked images of new possibilities, novel challenges, and one-of-a-kind risks. These images of opportunity apply just as much in the realm of marketing.

But new possibilities come in many different forms — including intriguing marketing technologies; radical practices applied by leading-edge organizations; and new services and products offered by marketing agencies, vendors, and other suppliers. And each of these opportunities brings both promise and peril. Confronted with such complexity, how do you determine which opportunities will help you exert the *most* impact on your firm's cash flow? Which tools and services will enable you to assess more accurately how your marketing activities are affecting cash flow? How do you figure out whether a claim that an IT vendor or ad agency rep is making is hype — or truth? How can you be sure you've adequately analyzed the risks that a new technology, service, or practice brings?

This chapter presents a road map for navigating through the rocky terrain of opportunity. As you use this road map to go West, you'll find guidelines for evaluating new possibilities for your marketing department or team. You'll also discover strategies for seizing what may be the most shining opportunity of all: reclaiming marketing's proud heritage and esteemed reputation in organizational life. As you'll see, the marketing profession hasn't always occupied secondary or even tertiary status in the corporate world. You *can* help revive the golden age of marketing — indeed, you must if marketing is to maximize its value for organizations.

But knowing how to evaluate opportunities isn't enough to make you a marketing champion. You also need to act on your assessments of those opportunities. To that end, we conclude the chapter with an analysis of common barriers to action and ideas for surmounting those barriers. Armed with the guidelines in this section, you'll be well prepared to climb into that covered wagon, crack the whip, and head for that ever-beckoning realm of opportunity: the West.

EVALUATING NEW OPPORTUNITIES

We're living in a time of massive and rapid change — in technology, work processes, competitive strategies, and consumer preferences. And these shifts bring intriguing new opportunities. Yet the pace and magnitude of the changes we're experiencing make it more difficult than ever to evaluate these opportunities with a clear eye. All too many businesspeople, lured by the flash and dazzle of a new technology or by glowing case studies of how a new practice has revolutionized companies everywhere, jump on the bandwagon. Beguiled by new possibilities, they neglect to carefully assess the novel opportunity's promise — or gauge its potential costs and risks.

Take CRM software. When this technology first became available, purveyors touted it as *the* tool for cultivating close, long-term relationships with customers and generating rich knowledge about consumers' buying behavior. Excited by images of enduring customer loyalty, soaring profits, and shrinking customer-service costs, many companies invested heavily in the software — only to discover a painful truth: Technology

itself doesn't create cash-generating, profitable customer relationships if a company doesn't first clarify its customer strategy and then tailor all of its processes, including its use of IT,
to support that strategy. Blinded by CRM's alluring promises,
many organizations even misused the technology — badger-
ing customers with telemarketing and direct-mail campaigns
that drove them away. Result? Hapless firms watched as their
CRM investments disappeared into a black hole while customers defected — and profits dried up.

But CRM is just one of many marketing technologies that
present both promise and peril, depending on how carefully a
business evaluates the opportunity. Marketing operations
management (MOM) software is another example. Intended
to give companies greater control over their marketing operations and to improve those operations' efficiency, MOM
promises to equip firms with a major competitive advantage.
By using MOM to streamline activities such as project management, budgeting, planning, reporting, and brand and vendor management, companies have set out to reduce time to
market, measure the results of their marketing activities more
accurately, and improve communication of marketing strategies.

Yet like CRM, MOM has farther-reaching ramifications — including stiff resistance from numerous quarters
within an organization — than many business leaders initially
assume. As Gartner vice president John Radcliff warns, "Trying to automate marketing processes is probably not going
to be very well received in a lot of cases. People need to be
handled very carefully. It should not be seen as, 'Here's some
technology. Implement it, and off we go.' It's key to realize
that it's very much about *business process change*, with real consequences for people who are not in IT."[1] Firms that adopt and
implement MOM without first thinking through the potential
impact on people and processes throughout the organization
risk introducing chaos and triggering resistance. This is
hardly the picture of efficiency and competitive prowess danc-

1. Telephone interview with authors, January 10, 2004.

ing in executives' heads when they first envisioned adopting
the technology.

The lesson? There are many alluring new tools, resources,
and ideas out there. And it's become increasingly difficult to
determine which of them will prove to be merely passing fads
and which will, in fact, offer your company valuable advantages. We don't mean to imply that all new opportunities are
suspect and should be avoided. Rather, when executives fail
to both carefully assess an opportunity's potential and use it
properly, even the best-intended tool can prove costly and
downright dangerous for your firm. As a marketing champion, you have a clearly defined task: to separate hype from
real help — and to follow up on opportunities that enhance
marketing's power to generate cash flow. But how do you fulfill this task? The following guidelines can help.

Resist Innovation for Innovation's Sake

In evaluating an intriguing new technology, process, or practice, it's easy to get caught up in the mob psychology that can
sweep through the business world. Many executives fall victim to the all-too-common trap of innovating for innovation's
sake. That is, they conclude that, to remain competitive, they
must use the same tools or apply the same practices that everyone else is using or that best-in-class companies have adopted.
And they don't consider how well an innovation addresses
real and important changes — such as shifts in consumer
needs or changes in competitive strategies — that are unfolding in the business arena.

To avoid this peril, ask yourself what's happening in the
larger world around you whenever you find yourself intrigued
by a new opportunity. Which of these changes will a particular innovation help you manage better — with the end result
being greater cash flow for your firm? For example, how
might a new advertising practice enable your firm to take advantage of and profit from the fragmentation of media that
you see happening around you? How will a new process help
the company avoid the price wars that have erupted as con-

sumers have gained increasing access to comparative information about product pricing and quality through the Internet? How might a novel technology offered by a vendor empower your organization to distinguish important patterns in customer buying behaviors across different regions in which your firm operates?

Again, no matter how impressive an opportunity may look, it has no value to your firm unless it addresses an actual need based on real changes. And in the case of your marketing function, that need can take several forms — each related to cash flow. Specifically, you must *respond to real-world changes in ways that enhance cash flow.* For example, you may decide to adopt a new technology that helps you identify customers who are willing to pay premium prices for your firm's offerings, thereby generating more cash for your firm. You also need to *constantly assess your activities' impact on cash flow.* For instance, to fill this requirement, you may elect to hire a vendor who can help you more accurately estimate the long-term revenues that a new marketing strategy may generate.

Change Your Conversation with Vendors

Oftentimes, opportunity comes knocking in the form of agencies, suppliers, consultancies, and vendors who seek to dazzle you with their innovative products and services. To avoid getting hooked by offerings that have little relevance to your ability to generate cash flow, you must change the way you converse with these purveyors.

This means developing a healthy skepticism for the best-practice case studies and "here's how our customer benefited" vignettes that many vendors insist on presenting while hawking their wares. Case studies may contain some interesting and even useful information. However, too many executives swallow them whole without considering how representative the cases are of their own company's situation. For instance, a software application that helped one rival company triple its revenues may be useless to your firm if your company uses a markedly different business model or competitive strategy.

Under these circumstances, a case study extolling the virtues of the application will reveal little or nothing of the tool's potential for your firm.

Rather than inviting vendors to show you case studies, ask them to demonstrate how their product or service generated measurable value for a client company facing challenges similar to your firm's and operating under similar assumptions. Demand quantifiable evidence of gains that the vendor helped the client achieve. Relentlessly link the discussion to cash, by asking questions such as, "How will your product help me identify new, future sources of cash flow for my firm?" "How will your service enable me to harvest more cash?" or "In what ways will your offering let me measure my department's impact on cash more accurately?" If you get an evasive or confused response, move on: That supplier or agency either doesn't have your company's best interests at heart, or they don't understand or appreciate marketing's link to cash flow. In either case, you won't likely establish a productive working relationship with them.

Of course, as with any vendor you're considering using, conduct a disciplined evaluation process that includes a request for proposal, interviews with references, and clarification of expectations and deliverables. Obviously, the greater the investment required to adopt a new product or service, the more care you'll want to take during this evaluation process.

Take Stock of the Risks

In evaluating any opportunity, it's just as vital to assess the risks as it is to total up and admire the potential rewards. But assessing risk takes some mental discipline. Why? By our very nature, we're wired to see only what we want to see. And we tend to open ourselves only to information that confirms what we already believe — or want to believe. Seeking disconfirming evidence — for instance, data suggesting that an intriguing new marketing practice created disastrous results at one company — is difficult, if not downright painful.

To combat mental biases against getting a comprehensive

picture of an opportunity's rewards and risks, establish checks and balances and use them. The following tips can help:

- Every time you collect a story or anecdote suggesting the benefits of a new tool or resource, actively search for another example indicating the opportunity's dangers.
- While evaluating a potential new technology, practice, or idea, ask yourself, "If I persuade my company to adopt this, what's the worst thing that could go wrong? And are we in a position to deal effectively with that possible outcome?"
- Discuss your thoughts about a new opportunity with colleagues and acquaintances inside and outside of your company. Ask them to play devil's advocate by arguing against adoption of a new idea or practice. Compare their arguments to your own business case for seizing the new opportunity. Which is stronger?
- If you know of a company that has adopted a new marketing tool or service, see whether you can meet with your counterpart there to get his or her insights into the opportunity's risks. Ask questions such as, "What hidden costs did you discover in the process of using this tool?" "What went wrong during the implementation, and how did you deal with each problem?" "In what ways did this new opportunity fail to meet your expectations or serve your needs?" "If you were to adopt another new idea along these lines in the future, what would you do differently during the implementation?"

By applying these and other guidelines, you greatly reduce the chances of missing an important — and potentially costly — risk presented by an otherwise attractive opportunity.

Be a Silo Spanner

As we've seen, many marketing practitioners fail to consider a novel idea's or tool's potential impact on other functions and departments within their company. For instance, a new software application designed to improve marketing process efficiency or customer relationships may require managers in sales, IT, logistics, and other units to alter the way they operate or to establish entirely new processes. These managers may be unwilling to make those changes because doing so would require them to take time out of already jammed schedules. Or they may simply lack the resources — personnel, equipment, funding — for effecting such changes.

In some cases, the application you're advocating may even conflict with technology already in use in other departments or with policies established by the enterprise. To illustrate, suppose you feel certain that visitors to your company's web site would buy more products if the ordering process were streamlined. But when you present this idea to the IT group, you learn that the changes you're advocating simply aren't possible, given the firewall security protocols that have been established for the firm's computer system. Or perhaps you want to launch a web-only promotion to attract a new customer segment and gather important information about that segment's demographics. You present your idea to sales — only to encounter widespread concern that the promotion will cannibalize sales of existing offerings.

For all these reasons, you need to think and behave like a silo spanner whenever you're weighing a new opportunity's potential pros and cons. (To refresh your knowledge of silos and ways to span them, revisit the Managing East chapters.) The most talented silo spanners take pains to master at least some of the technical language and concepts regularly used by their colleagues in other departments. Of course, you can't be expected to know everything about IT, R&D, supply chain management, and other disciplines throughout your firm. However, you *can* identify which groups' support you'll need most to leverage major opportunities to generate cash for your company.

To illustrate, suppose you believe that your company could greatly bolster cash flow by overhauling how its web site looks and functions or by rethinking how it gathers and analyzes customer data. If many of the new opportunities you're seeing lie in the realm of IT, you would definitely want to become as fluent as possible in the lingo and inner workings of IT. Acquire a basic understanding of how your firm's web site and customer database operate, what these systems' limitations are, and how the experts discuss the system's functionality. By knowing how to talk the talk, you enhance your credibility when presenting ideas to your peers in IT. You also more quickly anticipate the wider technical ramifications of implementing a new process or practice.

RECLAIMING MARKETING'S LOST HERITAGE

Of all the opportunities beckoning your marketing department or team, perhaps the most promising one is this: to reclaim marketing's lost heritage as a crucial business discipline. Think about it: Traditionally, many CEOs at U.S. businesses came up through marketing or sales on their way to the C suite. Nowadays, fewer of them do so. Most newly minted CEOs have backgrounds and expertise in decidedly nonmarketing-related disciplines, including finance and operations.

Why the shift? Some experts maintain that when an industry is growing fast, markets expand correspondingly. And during these boom times, businesses place a higher value on executives who have extensive experience in and deep knowledge of marketing. By contrast, when an industry is running on mostly mature markets (as has been the case for many industries in the United States during recent decades), business leaders have a less-clear sense of what marketing can contribute to a firm's success. In American enterprises, marketing may have lost its glow in part for this reason. To increase profits, top managements had to turn to the pursuit of cost efficiencies — using such disciplines as Total Quality Management and Six Sigma — so those with financial and operational backgrounds were chosen as leaders. Likewise, growing interest in CEOs with a finance background may stem from the increasing complexities of financial markets and significance of Wall Street. And interest in an operations background may stem from the accelerating globalization of enterprise.

Though such changes can powerfully mold perceptions of marketing's value, those perceptions may have little or no relation to marketing's *actual* value — its ability to uncover new sources of cash (through upstream activities) and to harvest that cash (through downstream activities). The fact remains that your marketing department or team possesses the *most* extensive body of knowledge and set of skills needed to generate cash for your company. For example, you and your team:

- Know how to segment markets in ways that support your company's business model and generate the most profits.
- Understand how to articulate a compelling brand promise for your company and its offerings, so customers are willing to pay a premium for your products and services.
- Maintain a repository of information about the market overall, rather than snippets of data describing specific accounts — so you can spot major changes and respond with offerings that expand market share or stake out entirely new territory in the competitive arena.
- Know how to frame marketing messages in terms of benefits that consumers value, rather than product or service features, so consumers can quickly see why they should buy.
- Have experience in conducting market research to assess the short- and long-term revenue-generating potential of offerings your company is thinking about developing.

How many of your peers can do all this and more? Not many. But don't assume that your colleagues and members of the executive team will concur. To change their perceptions of marketing's value to match your function's actual contribution, you must continually demonstrate marketing's ability to carry out these crucial cash-generating activities. Only then will you help reclaim the proud legacy that marketing has enjoyed in the past.

The key? Constantly seek opportunities to highlight your group's unique abilities and to show how important marketing skills can enhance cash flow in varied parts of your company. Let's once again use your firm's web site as an example. Many non-IT professionals — including marketing practitioners — view the web as a mysterious, high-tech phenomenon that has little to do with them and their role in the company. But your firm's web site is actually just one of the many communication vehicles and tools you can use to build a brand for your organization and its offerings. As with a printed brochure, radio spot, TV commercial, magazine ad, or broadcast e-mail, the content and functionality of your firm's web site enable you to convey your brand promise to consumers — and thus appeal to target markets. Table 11.1 shows just a few examples.

Web strategies like those shown in Table 11.1, among many others, fall squarely in your purview. Of course, many of them entail varying degrees of technical complexity — ranging from simple text changes to the installation of complicated functions. As we've discussed, to make a credible business case for your proposals, you need a working familiarity with how your firm's web site operates. You also must think through how your ideas, if implemented, will affect the IT staff and other groups throughout your organization. Even seemingly simple changes often require more time and resources than everyone involved initially assumes — or may be willing or able to implement. Using your company's web site to generate more cash makes supreme sense in your effort to reclaim marketing's heritage. But this and other similar efforts will fly only if you educate yourself on their practical ramifications.

ACT ON YOUR ASSESSMENTS
OF OPPORTUNITIES

Knowing how to evaluate new opportunities with an eye toward cash flow and toward reviving marketing's legacy isn't enough to make you a marketing champion. You must also act on your assessments of these fresh possibilities and the rec-

Table 11.1
Conveying Your Brand Promise Through Your Web Site

If you want to tell the market that . . .	Consider . . .	For example . . .
Your company is on the leading edge of technology	Pushing for high-tech functionality in your firm's web site.	A real-estate company alters its web site so visitors can get 360-degree views of each room in properties featured on the site.
Your firm is driven by its core values	Adding values-related content to your web site	An apparel retailer that touts its respect for the environment places a prominent message on on its home page announcing the decision to cut back on catalog mailing. It also posts its its catalog on the web site, providing visitors with an alternative way to view products.
Your organization cares deeply about simplifying life for consumers	Ensuring that your web site is easy to use	A company sets up its shopping-cart function so buyers are prompted to fill out new-customer infor-mation only once. The firm also presents web-site text as short paragraphs and provides links so visitors don't have to keep scrolling to read each page.

(continued)

ommendations you make to others based on your evaluations. Without action, you can't turn marketing activities into the hard, cold cash your firm needs to remain competitive.

Yet taking action can be unnerving — which is why many professionals (marketers included) hesitate to do so. Why the reluctance? Barriers to action are legion, as you'll discover in the following.

Table 11.1 (*continued*)

If you want to tell the market that . . .	Consider . . .	For example . . .
Your organization has the highest standards	Ensuring that the site is free of errors	An enterprise hires a professional editor to correct spelling, grammar, punctuation, and style errors in the web-site content.
Your company has a treasure trove of valuable information to offer consumers	Providing site visitors with free samples of information	A global economics research firm that sells analytical reports to client companies creates a set of public pages on its web site from which visitors can download free sample reports.
Your firm offers products for the most discerning consumers	Selling high-end product lines only on your web site	A sporting-goods retailer, after learning that most visitors to the company's store want low-end sports equipment, offers technically sophisticated equipment only on its web site.

Understanding Barriers to Action

Anyone seeking to put an idea into action can expect to encounter numerous obstacles. For example, when you recommend a course of action or initiate action yourself, you take a risk: Your decision may turn out to be unwise, or you may get results you didn't intend. Fear of making a mistake and suffering painful consequences causes many people to avoid taking action. Distrust is another culprit: If you don't believe that the people on your team or in other departments have the willingness and skills to help implement your ideas, you won't likely push your proposals.

People who take action also risk triggering resistance from others whose contributions are essential to executing the good idea. Resistance takes numerous forms — everything from a "We don't do things that way around here" mentality to concerns that an idea, once implemented, would render certain roles less important. Fear of activating resistance can in itself be a powerful obstacle to running with an idea.

As we've seen, business illiteracy can also prevent marketing professionals from moving forward with their ideas. If you don't know how to use the language of business or master the jargon of specific disciplines within your organization, you can't communicate effectively about your ideas and collaboratively develop plans for implementing them. Yet language can be a double-edged sword: Many people use talk as a substitute for action because they've learned that talk — especially when it's critical or negative — can give the impression of intelligence and business savvy.

Likewise, a lack of people skills — in particular, knowing how to navigate through your company's political terrain — can keep even brilliant marketers from winning the support they need to get their great ideas off the ground. Corporate politics are often driven by internal competition for limited resources. And rewards are typically doled out based on individual performance rather than collective performance. Thus, results gained through collaboration with others may go unrecognized and unappreciated. Moreover, many companies reward short-term results more than long-term outcomes and focus on past performance far more than potential future gains. Meanwhile, people in highly politicized organizations tend to hoard best practices rather than sharing them with others across the organization — seeking to grab credit for themselves rather than doing what's best for the company. All of these tendencies spell difficulty for any marketing professional advocating a course of action designed to generate longer-term results gained through cross-functional collaboration. And these often represent the most valuable opportunities for marketing.

Like many professionals in a variety of other disciplines, you may also feel paralyzed at times by the amount of work on your plate. Faced with a wide array of tasks, you might be tempted to deal with the easy, short-term, urgent-but-not-important activities. Result? The more complex and vastly more crucial courses of action needed to generate cash for your company get left by the wayside.

Facing so many obstacles to acting on valuable new opportunities, how might you move past those barriers? You'll need discipline, patience, and practice. The following guidelines can help.

Surmounting Barriers to Action

The most effective marketers apply several practices to side-step the obstacles to action that we all encounter when aiming to get great ideas off the ground. Consider these particularly potent strategies:

- **Set priorities.** Identify the tasks and activities that must be carried out in order to seize advantage of the most valuable opportunities you've identified. For instance, suppose you believe that overhauling your company's web site will generate the greatest increase in short- and long-term cash among many other opportunities you've evaluated. In this case, you'd want to focus your limited time and energy on mastering the language of IT so that you can talk about your ideas intelligently with the people who will have to effect your desired changes. You'd probably also want to reserve time in your busy schedule to cultivating mutually beneficial relationships with the IT managers. By forging these positive bonds, you'll build up the political capital you'll need to draw on when your project rolls into action and encounters the inevitable snags. As another example of a high-priority task, you'd likely want to study other companies' web sites to document the types of functionality and content that you consider the most strategically relevant for your own firm.
- **Combat destructive internal competition.** Even if you don't occupy a high-level position in your company, you can still take steps to mitigate damaging internal competition. For example, if you have direct reports, you can plant the seeds for

a collaborative culture by hiring people based on their ability and willingness to work with and cooperate with others. Technical skills, such as knowing how to create a compelling brochure or produce a powerful TV commercial, are important in any new hire. But people skills are even more crucial in getting cross-functional managers and employees to collectively implement valuable action plans. Once you've hired these collaboration-savvy folks, reward them for their ability to make things happen by working with others.

As another tactic for reducing destructive internal competitiveness, identify an external threat around which you can rally the troops — such as a new competitor, an innovative technology that will soon render your company's offerings obsolete, or a possible imminent regulatory change that will constrain your firm's ability to compete. As many talented political leaders have discovered, nothing pulls people together faster and more powerfully than the presence of an outside enemy. To that end, do whatever it takes to ensure that executives and colleagues throughout your company are aware of the outside threat you've identified. And point out how your proposed course of action will help the firm combat that threat.

• **Learn by doing.** Often, we acquire the most valuable knowledge by putting an idea into action despite all our fears and other obstacles that may arise. Sure, formal seminars and training programs can provide us with helpful information. But it's all too easy to become a permanent student so as to avoid stepping of the cliff and taking the plunge. As the old adage says, experience is the best teacher.

To benefit from experience, establish disciplined processes that enable you to learn from every course of action you undertake. For example, every time you implement a decision, review the results with cold-eyed objectivity. Ask yourself, "How well did my actual results reflect my desired outcomes?" "What could I have done differently to generate a better outcome?" "What worked well, and how can I apply those practices to subsequent courses of action?" "What didn't work so well, and why?" If possible, ask a trusted colleague to explore these questions with you. Often, an unbiased observer can provide additional insights into how to take action more effectively the next time around.

• **Use action-oriented language.** In communicating about your ideas with executives and colleagues, strive to use action-oriented language rather than talking in theoretical or abstract terms about your proposed plan. Let's use your proposed overhaul of the company web site to illustrate this point as well. You'll be far more compelling if you use phrases like, "trump the competition," "slash the excess verbiage on the site," "point site visitors in the right direction," and "hook new customers with our web offers" than if you used language such as "the time has come for change," "it's interesting what other companies are doing with their web sites," and "this is an important effort."

By applying these and other practices, you knock over the typical barriers that prevent so many marketing professionals from acting on the juicy opportunities they've identified for their firms. But identifying, evaluating, and implementing new possibilities is just one part of Managing West. The other part entails leveraging a different kind of opportunity: securing a satisfying future for yourself in the marketing profession. We'll explore that terrain in the next chapter.

Your New Opportunities SWOT Analysis

1. How do you typically evaluate new opportunities for your marketing department? What criteria must an opportunity meet in order for you to deem it valuable?

2. To what extent do you emphasize cash-flow potential when evaluating an opportunity? How might you take cash flow into account more consistently in your evaluation approach?

3. When considering a new technology, practice, idea, or service presented to you by a vendor, agency, or consultancy,

what information do you rely on to arrive at an assessment of the opportunity? What new types of information would help you evaluate the opportunity through a cash-flow lens?

4. What percentage of high-level executives in your firm has a background in marketing? If the percentage is low, how might you improve the picture? Are there particular skills and types of knowledge that you could showcase to reposition marketing as a valued discipline in your organization? Consider your department's or team's unique abilities to segment markets, build brands, research market changes, and so forth.

5. Which barriers to action most often prevent you from implementing your good ideas or gaining others' support for your proposed courses of action? How might you remove those barriers? Consider enhancing your ability to prioritize your activities, using action-oriented language, hiring and rewarding collaborative behavior in your team, and learning by doing.

6. Of all the new opportunities you've encountered recently, which one or two strike you as *most* promising for your marketing department and your company? Why? What are the key activities and tasks that must be accomplished in order to seize advantage of those opportunities? What steps will you take to accomplish those activities and tasks? And when will you take those steps?

12

Lead the Way in the Cash-Flow Frontier

Throughout the earlier chapters in this book, we've explored the many ways in which marketing creates value for organizations — particularly by identifying new sources of cash flow for the future and harvesting cash in the short term. We've examined strategies that can help you not only generate cash flow for your company but also maximize it. And we've presented tactics for correcting inaccurate and stereotypical perceptions of marketing in the minds of the executive team and your colleagues in other functions such as R&D and sales.

However, your journey to becoming a marketing champion isn't complete until you yourself are viewed as a cash-flow leader by others throughout your firm. Ultimately, the marketing function in your company won't be able to exert influence and create a positive impact unless individual marketing executives, managers, and practitioners are recognized as uniquely valuable. Without this perception of individual value, you stand little chance of building a satisfying career that lets you make a measurable contribution to your organization.

To that end, we focus this Managing West chapter on a different type of opportunity: identifying ways to make your own unique and indisputable mark in your company as a cash-flow leader. Regardless of your position in your firm — executive, manager, team leader, individual contributor — the practical suggestions we offer in the following can help you highlight your special value to the organization and further enhance marketing's image.

MARKET YOURSELF

Just as you use your marketing knowledge and skills to identify and reap profitable opportunities for your company, you
can apply those same assets to market yourself in your firm.
By marketing yourself, we mean convincing others that you
offer unique value that your company can't get from anyone
else. Indeed, just as an effective marketing campaign communicates the special value a product offers to consumers, a
savvy personal marketing campaign sends the same message
about you as an individual.

To market yourself, you can call on many of the same skills
you use to build awareness and appreciation for your company's products and services among consumers. And you may
apply many of the same processes. Take market segmentation.
The advantage to segmenting consumer markets is that you
identify groups of consumers that offer the most promising
opportunities to generate cash flow for your firm. And you
weed out consumers who are least likely to be interested in
your company's offerings.

You can segment your internal customers — your CEO,
CFO, and colleagues in functions such as R&D and sales — in
similar fashion. How? Ask yourself, "Who among these constituencies am I most likely to form a productive partnership
with?" "Whom do I *need* to partner with in order to maximize
cash flow?" "Which of these individuals do I stand little or no
chance of partnering with — given my company's culture and
structure, or given personality differences?" "Which of these
powerful people need or like me?"

The fact is, your company — like any other — probably
contains some people who simply aren't ever going to view
marketing as important or appreciate the value that you bring
to the table through your individual abilities. Marketing yourself in part means distinguishing between these lost causes
and the real opportunities to establish productive partnerships — and focusing your energies on the latter. For example,
if you determine that R&D is inherently incapable of cooper-
ating with marketing, concentrate instead on helping to build

a first-rate sales organization in your firm, as discussed in Chapter 7.

This process of identifying opportunities also entails stepping back and asking yourself whether your entire company is willing and able to appreciate marketing. Let's face it: Some organizations, by their very nature, are marked by a combative culture or one that's obsessed with technology, finance, or some other nonmarketing function. In such an environment, marketing professionals may never achieve much standing, no matter how hard they try. If this describes your situation, the best response may be to move on — to find a company in which your skills and the profession of marketing will be welcomed. As that esteemed prayer goes, "God grant me the *serenity* to accept the things I cannot change, the *courage* to change the things I can, and the *wisdom* to know the difference."

Yes, leaving a company may be painful, and may make you feel that you've failed somehow. But remember: It's very difficult to transform an entire company's culture; even the most powerful CEOs can't do it. Also, remind yourself that you don't try to market a product to all consumers — just to those who will most likely value the benefits that your offering provides. Likewise, you won't be right for every organizational setting. Nor will every company be right for you.

GET A REPUTATION

As people from many different fields of endeavor have discovered, more professional opportunities come your way when you gain a reputation for having certain valued personal traits. For instance, when you're known for having strong people skills, others become more interested in working with you as well as considering and supporting your ideas. After all, who can resist someone who gets along well with others? People skills abound, but the basics include the following:

- Inviting others' opinions and ideas
- Respecting and valuing differences in opinion, work styles, and priorities

- Showing interest in others' lives
- Understanding and speaking others' professional language
- Appreciating the unique challenges each of your colleagues faces in his or her role
- Resolving differences productively rather than letting them sour professional relationships
- Showing appreciation for the value and skills that others bring to the table

These may look simple on the surface, but for some people, developing these traits takes practice and effort. We've offered ideas for strengthening several of these skills — such as mastering the language of business and job shadowing to familiarize yourself with colleagues' work — in earlier chapters in this book. In particular, we've emphasized the importance of serving as a silo spanner. As we explained in the Managing East chapters especially, silo spanners collaborate with their cross-functional colleagues so as to remove the interdepartmental competition and tensions that can stymie a company's efforts to do what's best for customers. Examples of silo-busting strategies include demonstrating the importance of focusing on the customer, leveraging technology to transfer customer data among departments, explicating shared goals, and forming and participating in cross-functional teams.

To enhance some of the other people skills mentioned in the preceding, including conflict resolution, you can use additional resources such as books, training seminars, and professional coaches. Still other abilities — such as showing interest in others' lives — stem from inherent qualities. That is, you'll find it much easier to demonstrate interest in a colleague's life if you actually *feel* interested.

This point brings up another personal trait that you'll want to develop or strengthen: natural curiosity. The best marketers have an innate interest in finding out all manner of things — how people perceive their needs and make purchasing decisions, why consumers' preferences change, why one product is so much more successful than another, what competing companies are doing to capture more market share, and so forth. Such professionals also have a burning curiosity about aspects of life outside of marketing. For instance, they're fascinated by other industries, other professions, and other skill sets. In fact, research has shown that the broader the pool of knowledge and experience a person has, the greater his or her ability to see new connections and generate fresh ideas. By acquiring a variety of experience, you develop skills that may seem extraneous at the time but that may benefit you later in life in surprising ways. See the box titled "Steve Jobs: Connecting the Dots" for an example.

◆◆◆◆◆

Steve Jobs: Connecting the Dots

Steve Jobs—CEO of Apple Computer and of Pixar Animation—acquired diverse, seemingly unimportant experiences in his early life that later proved valuable. For instance, after he dropped out of Reed College to save his working-class parents money, his curiosity led him to audit courses that he found interesting. Intrigued by examples of beautiful calligraphy that he found on posters and drawer labels around the campus, he decided to take a calligraphy course offered by Reed. There, he learned about typography—including typefaces, letter spacing, and letter combinations.

At the time, Jobs never envisioned putting his interest in calligraphy to practical use. But 10 years later, when he and his business partners were designing the first Macintosh computer, he found himself calling on this long-buried skill. "[The Mac] was the first computer with beautiful typography," Jobs said during his June 2005 commencement address at Stanford University. "If I had never dropped in on that single course in college, the Mac would have never had multiple typefaces or proportionally spaced fonts. And since Windows just copied the Mac, it's likely that no personal computer would have them... Of course, it was impossible to connect [these] dots looking forward when I was in college. But it was very, very clear looking backwards ten years later."

The lesson? Be curious about everything life has to offer—and let your curiosity guide you to explore new interests and talents. As Jobs points out, "You can't connect the dots looking forward ... So you have to trust that the dots will somehow connect in your future. You have to trust in something—your gut, destiny, life, karma, whatever. This approach has never let me down, and it has made all the difference in my life."

Source: "'You've Got to Find What You Love,' Jobs Says." *Stanford Report*, June 14, 2005.

◆◆◆◆◆

Like people skills and natural curiosity, knowing how to build on your strengths and work around your weaknesses is another trait that generates new opportunities to provide visible value to your firm. In today's business world, marketers are expected to possess a superhuman set of abilities. Consider skills required for jobs in Apple Computer's marketing division, listed on the company's web site. These skills include developer relations, event organizing, graphic design, and marketing communications. Additional required talents include product marketing, public relations, research and analysis, and worldwide marketing.[1]

Can one person really be expected to do all of this — and do it well? Of course not. Moreover, as we've seen, marketing can encompass so many different activities and responsibilities that each organization may require a unique set of skills from its marketing practitioners. The marketing talents needed at a company like Intel, for instance, are probably decidedly different from those required at P&G or a services firm such as banking giant Wells Fargo.

Because you can't possibly possess all the skills that will be required in every company, you need to know how to leverage your strong points and compensate for your not-so-strong points. One way to do this is to draw on resources under your control. For example, suppose you lack the top-notch market research skills needed to present a compelling, scientifically rigorous proposal to the R&D team. Or you have those skills but have never gotten along with the head of R&D. In this

1. www.apple.com/jobs/marketing/index.html. Accessed February 7, 2006.

case, consider calling on a direct report who does possess the requisite abilities or interpersonal chemistry. If you don't directly supervise employees, draw on other talents. For instance, assemble a small team of people with complementary technical and interpersonal skills who can guide a marketing project that requires the cooperation of the IT and R&D groups. Again, the right fit between personnel and project will differ depending on the individuals involved and the corporate culture.

Another way to deal with the complexities of strengths and weaknesses is to ask yourself, "Which of my skills best enable me to identify and leverage opportunities to maximize cash flow for my organization?" "What skills do my fellow team members or direct reports have that enable them to enhance cash flow?" "How well do these skills complement one another?" "Are we suffering from any skills gaps? If so, how can we fill those gaps?" Once more, your answers to these questions will vary depending on whether you're a manager, team leader, or individual contributor.

Finally, develop a reputation for taking initiative — for knowing how to make things happen and get things done. As we mentioned in Chapter 11, speaking the language of business can earn you credibility because it reveals that you know what you're talking about. And in many organizations, people who sound smart receive a lot more opportunities than those who don't. But talk alone isn't enough to secure you a solid future in marketing as a cash-flow leader. You also need to prove that you can make the tough decisions and get concrete results. This means being able to tolerate the risk that comes with committing to a course of action. With every decision you make, you have only so much information to work with. Therefore, your choices may prove wise or unwise. As difficult as it may be to face this kind of uncertainty, you need to look beyond the discomfort, take the risks, and strive to build the best possible track record of success in your role.

When you develop the preceding personal traits, you increase your ability to influence others in ways that benefit your company and lead to positive collaborations with colleagues. See the box titled "A Marketing Champion at Bristol-Myers Squibb" for an apt example.

A Marketing Champion at Bristol-Myers Squibb

Wendy Dixon, CMO at Bristol-Myers Squibb (BMS), embodies the personal traits and experience essential to delivering unique value to her organization. Her PhD in biochemistry from Cambridge University in England, her 20 years in pharmaceutical marketing, and her passion for working with scientists to develop new, much-needed medicines have all earned her immense credibility in her organization. In particular, Dixon enjoys the respect and appreciation of the company's R&D team—no easy feat in many firms.

Drawing on her individual influence, Dixon leads her marketing team's work with the company's scientists to ensure that new products are developed with an understanding of the marketplace and of customers' needs. Listen as she explains how this works at BMS:

> I've heard from many industries that the scientists and marketers don't talk with each other. But actually, I think this is one of the things that's gone particularly well at BMS. Our scientists as a whole are sophisticated enough and open enough—particularly when they have the opportunity to work with strong, knowledgeable marketers—to recognize that they will be able to do their jobs better if they work with the marketers, understand customers' needs, and integrate those needs into their development programs for products. And I've been very impressed by the partnership which has a commitment from both sides of the organization. It boils down to the individuals involved. This transformation to marketing excellence has been something that everybody in the company wanted. It's a lot of work, but people have been very receptive to it and to learning new skills.

Dixon also emphasizes the importance of shared objectives and incentive plans to successful collaboration among functions in BMS. In addition, brand leadership teams "live together, virtually, with the brand. . . Openness and understanding of the scientific needs and issues, and similarly, receptivity to market research and ways of integrating it into the design of clinical trials" are all key ingredients to BMS's success. Clearly, the personal qualities that Dixon brings to the job have played a major part in her ability to facilitate valuable collaboration within her company.

Source: MarketingProfs.com, December 6, 2003. Reprinted by permission from MarketingProfs.com.

◆◆◆◆◆

CONQUER THE TIME CRUNCH

These days, marketers are pulled in more directions than any other professionals. Think about it: In your company, managers in virtually every function call on you to provide information about the market and the company's customers, deliver judgments on proposed courses of action, and make tough, high-stakes decisions that can ultimately exert a major impact on your firm. Harris, a marketing executive we know, reported that he spends two-thirds of his time in meetings during a typical day. Though meetings often fulfill important needs, you can't make things happen as long as you're sitting with a group of other people in a conference room. Harris's meetings left him with only one-third of every day to work on actual marketing activities.

In many organizations, the pressure is immense — the expectations, outrageous. If you're not careful, you can get sucked into the vortex and lose sight of what's *really* important in your job: carrying out the activities linked to planting seeds for future sources of cash and harvesting that cash.

With limited time and energy, you need a disciplined approach to setting priorities. That means determining which activities you will handle, and which would best be handled by someone else or not handled at all. For example, if you have direct reports, you may have experienced the proverbial monkey problem, in which subordinates bring their problems to the boss for solving. Of course, you want to be a supportive manager, and solving other people's problems can make you feel like a hero. But if letting other people's monkeys cling to

your back is preventing you from fulfilling your *real* job responsibilities — such as identifying new markets or cultivating
relationships with customers — you're not delivering much
unique value to your company. So the next time an employee
comes to you with "I can't get this report to print out right" or
"Joe didn't get me those numbers that I needed," firmly but
respectfully return the monkey to its proper owner. Encourage your direct report to generate his or her own ideas for
solving the problem or to deal directly with the person responsible for the monkey in the first place.

One disciplined way of managing your time better is to define the few key goals that, if you achieve them, will enable
you to harvest cash or lay the groundwork for future cash for
your firm. The list of goals you develop will differ depending
on your organization's competitive strategy and its business
model. For instance, if your company is seeking to expand
market share through offering low-priced, mass-market products, your goals as a marketer will differ from objectives you
might set if you worked for a B-to-B firm that was developing
one-of-a-kind, very expensive, and complex solutions for big
companies.

Once you've made your list of objectives, use it as a refer-
ence point in deciding how to spend your time and energy. If
someone suggests that you take on a project or engage in an
activity that doesn't relate to any of your goals, learn to say no.
This can be difficult: Harris, when asked why he kept going to
all those meetings, explained, "It's the culture of the company;
you can't change it." You certainly can't change a culture, but
you *can* change your own behavior. And when you do, you
initiate small shifts that may ultimately exert a big impact.
For instance, by devoting just a bit more time each day to
cash-generating activities and projects, Harris improves his
chances of achieving far more important objectives.

In deciding which projects and activities to say yes to, resist the temptation to agree to requests simply because you
and the requestor get along well. Though it's enjoyable to collaborate with people you like, the question of whether the effort will enable you to achieve your vital objectives should

take precedence. To illustrate, suppose that analyzing recent customer purchase behavior with the sales manager would help you identify factors that prompt customer defections. And addressing those factors so as to increase customer loyalty is a major objective on your list. But you don't get along well at all with the sales manager. Indeed, your relationship with this person is downright nasty. Interpersonal tensions aside, you'd better find a way to work with him or her on this project — because the effort constitutes a valuable use of your time and energy.

Of course, deciding which projects deserve the lion's share of your time and energy is one thing. *Managing* those projects is quite another. With complex initiatives involving many different people and numerous activities unfolding in parallel, keeping your marketing projects on track takes immense care and discipline. Project-management software can help you maintain order, keep everyone involved updated on the initiative's status, and document who's responsible for doing what and when. If you're iffy about your project-management abilities, also consider taking a workshop or reading a book on the subject. Most managers count project management among the more challenging and frustrating aspects of their work. Thus experts have developed many resources on this topic that can prove helpful to you.

See the box titled "Setting Priorities at SAS" for an example of one marketing executive who applies these principles — with excellent results.

◆◆◆◆◆

Setting Priorities at SAS

When Jim Davis became director of product strategy at software giant SAS in 1999, his responsibilities included talking to industry analysts, the press, and strategic customers to find out what technology developments would advance SAS's position in the marketplace. According to CEO Jim Goodnight, Davis was a great fit in the CMO position, because "understanding the technology and how it can be applied to real-world issues is essential in software marketing."

To that end, Davis focuses his energy and time on activities that link directly to his priorities. For example, he engages in *pragmatic marketing*—gathering information about customer requirements to inform the product development process, rather than encouraging creation of whiz-bang technologies and then finding ways to sell them. As Goodnight explains, "Before Jim took over, marketing was a mess. . . . The bottom line [now] is making sure [we sustain] the partnership between [the people doing] the requirements gathering on the outside and those who are actually developing the solution." With his ability to set and focus on priorities, Davis contributes an essential ingredient to SAS's success.

Source: Christopher Caggiano, "Mr. Do-It-All," *CMO Magazine*, February 2005.

◆◆◆◆◆

FIND A MENTOR

No matter where you are in the organizational hierarchy, you can further differentiate the value you provide by drawing on the insights and support of a good mentor. How do you select a mentor? In keeping with our theme regarding breadth of knowledge and experience, try to find someone who works in another part of the company, for example, in sales, R&D, IT, or some other function. Through your mentoring relationship with this person, you can gain a valuable perspective on how his or her function operates, what its challenges and capabilities are, and what language its practitioners speak. Your view of the organization will broaden, improving your ability to link marketing activities to cross-functional strategic goals and thereby producing valuable results for the company.

In selecting a mentor, you'll also want to look for individuals whom you regard as particularly effective in what they do. Are they well connected? Do they have large circles of influence? Do they enjoy the respect and admiration of numerous people in the organization? The more you can answer yes to these questions, the more valuable your mentoring relationship will prove.

In establishing a mentoring relationship, you don't necessarily need to approach the process in a formal way. Depending on the person you're considering, the process could be as simple as regularly inviting the person to grab some lunch and getting his or her opinions and thoughts about ideas you're exploring. For example, suppose you believe that your company could benefit from adopting a new customer-data analytics software application. In this case, you could ask your mentor, "Who do you think needs to weigh in on this? Where would you say the real resistance to this idea will come from in the company? Any thoughts about how to evaluate applications and select a vendor?"

In addition to gaining your mentor's thoughts and insights on possible initiatives, you can use your mentoring relationship to clarify career goals and plans. For instance, your mentor may have valuable insights into what direction the company may be heading in terms of its competitive strategy and what opportunities a change in direction may present for marketing professionals in the organization.

Wondering why anyone would want to mentor you — that is, what's in it for them? The answer is simple. Mentors like to mentor because they enjoy helping others develop their professional and personal skills. Oftentimes, they also receive something valuable in return — such as the knowledge that a talented person in your department is available to participate in a cross-functional task force that the mentor is leading or that a consultant your group used did a great job and may be useful for a project that the mentor's unit is implementing. For these reasons, ensure that your encounters with your mentor are a two-way street: Be willing to share information you have that may be of value to your mentor as well as asking questions to draw on your mentor's expertise.

Winning a reputation as a cash-flow leader isn't easy. But the payoff is well worth it: You establish a virtuous cycle in which you gain others' appreciation and therefore win their support for your good ideas. And your good ideas in turn generate valuable cash for your company — further enhancing your reputation and winning you even more collaboration from others. Become a marketing champion, and your company wins, your colleagues win, and *you* win.

YOUR LEADERSHIP FUTURE SWOT ANALYSIS

1. How do you think you're perceived as a leader in your organization? Do executives and your colleagues view you as providing unique value that they and the company can't get from anyone else? What evidence would you draw on to answer these questions?

2. In what respects do you market yourself in your organization? How effective are these efforts? What steps might you take to improve their effectiveness?

3. What aspects of your company do you believe you have the power to change in order to provide more visible value to the firm? What aspects do you believe you cannot change? How might you better focus on changing the things that lie within your control?

4. Of all the personality traits discussed in this chapter that are important for effective marketers, which do you possess naturally? Which do you need to acquire or strengthen? How might you work on developing the traits you need more of?

5. How effectively do you manage your time and energy in your role as a marketer? What percentage of your time do you spend on activities related to your most important objectives? How might you free up time and energy to invest in projects and activities related to your key objectives?

6. Once you've identified projects that merit your time because they relate to your core objectives, how successfully do you manage those projects? What might you do to become a more effective project manager?

7. Do you have a mentor in your organization? If so, what value does your mentor provide you? And what value do you provide him or her? If you don't have a mentor, how might you go about establishing a relationship with one? Which individuals in your organization strike you as promising mentors? Why?

Index